BIG BUSINESS

BIG BUSINESS

The European Experience in the Twentieth Century

YOUSSEF CASSIS

OXFORD

UNIVERSITY PRESS

OXFORD

UNIVERSITY PRESS

Great Clarendon Street, Oxford OX2 6DP

Oxford University Press is a department of the University of Oxford.
It furthers the University's objective of excellence in research, scholarship,
and education by publishing worldwide in

Oxford New York

Athens Auckland Bangkok Bogotá Buenos Aires Calcutta
Cape Town Chennai Dar es Salaam Delhi Florence Hong Kong Istanbul
Karachi Kuala Lumpur Madrid Melbourne Mexico City Mumbai
Nairobi Paris São Paulo Shanghai Singapore Taipei Tokyo Toronto Warsaw

and associated companies in Berlin Ibadan

Oxford is a registered trade mark of Oxford University Press
in the UK and in certain other countries

Published in the United States
by Oxford University Press Inc., New York

ISBN 0-19-828965-0 (Hbk.)
ISBN 0-19-829606-1 (Pbk.)

Printed in Great Britain
on acid-free paper by
Bookcraft (Bath) Short Run Books
Midsomer Norton

100 2184554

For Charlotte

PREFACE

THIS book was originally intended to be a comparative study of business élites in Britain, France, and Germany from the late nineteenth to the mid-twentieth century. This was a key social and occupational group, which had clearly emerged as the dominant force at the top of European societies. I was interested in the specific type of relationships between economic power, social prestige, and political influence prevailing in each of the three countries, and how this had affected their historical development. However, I soon felt uncomfortable with the traditional portrayal of British businessmen, especially when compared to their German counterparts. From a socio-political point of view, the images of endemic weakness and repeated failures were fundamentally at odds with the general course of British and European history. After all, Britain until the 1960s was a larger economy than either France or Germany, with a significantly higher per capita income; she controlled a far larger empire; and she had emerged victorious in two world wars against Germany without having to experience, as in the case of France, the trauma of defeat and occupation. British businessmen were thus part of the élites of a far more successful country. Could there be such a discrepancy between business history and general history?

This led me to investigate more closely the foundations of businessmen's economic power, in other words the large companies, especially their size, sectoral distribution, and performance. The findings confirmed my original suspicion: by and large, British business did far better than is usually credited. In the process, however, what was originally conceived as a short introductory chapter has grown into five chapters making up half the book (Parts I and II) and reassessing the position and performance of big business in Britain, France, and Germany; while the second half (Parts III and IV) re-examines in this light some of the determinants of business performance. The chronological span has also been extended and recent developments briefly considered, as the discrepancy between business and general history no longer applied from the 1960s onwards. The result is an attempt at a global analysis of big business in twentieth-century Europe, encompassing its economic, social, and political dimensions. The fact that no such book has been written before, leaving an important gap to be filled, has been a further incentive.

Such an analysis can only be comparative, and this book is conceived as an essay in comparative history. Risks of imbalance or bias are inherent in any wide-ranging comparison. They can be limited by combining the use of the existing literature with empirical research based on

compatible sources for the three countries—in this case a detailed analysis of an original sample of companies and businessmen. Big business has
been defined in terms of a miminum level of company size (see introduction to Part I) and its development and sectoral distribution have been
compared using this criterion. For the analysis of performance, a sample
of companies representing big business in all economic sectors has been
established for the years 1907, 1929, 1953, 1972, and 1989; while the chairmen and managing directors of these companies provide an adequate
sample for the analysis of business leadership. The basic information concerning the companies and their leaders has been extracted from the usual
commercial and biographical yearbooks, almanacs, directories, and so on.
The huge secondary literature is used to complement this basic information. Given that some 250 companies and more than 1,000 businessmen
have been included in the study, the use of archival material is only
sparing.

Comparisons will be most effective when dealing with countries pre-
senting on the one hand a relative homogeneity—in size, level of economic development, historical experience, and so on—but on the other
enough differences to help identify national specificities. Britain, France,
and Germany are particularly well suited for such a purpose: though of
similar size as well as geographical and cultural proximity, their respective periods of stronger and weaker economic performance have not
always synchronized. Moreover, each country has at different times been
seen as embodying a type of capitalism—personal as opposed to managerial for the early century, market-dominated, bank-dominated, and
state-dominated for the more recent decades—which could be found elsewhere in Europe or indeed in the world. Of course, comparisons with the
global leader are not only tempting, but valuable in order to measure the
gap separating the followers from assumed best practices. There is no lack
of comparative studies between each of the three countries and the United
States, the world's dominant economy since 1914. However, business
development was on an altogether different scale in an economy already
two and a half times larger than the British (the largest in Europe until
the 1960s) in 1913, almost four times larger in 1929, and almost five times
larger in 1960. The same applies, though to a lesser extent and only for
the last quarter of the century, to Japan. As for comparisons with smaller
European countries, they pose an inverse problem: truly large companies
emerged only recently in smaller European countries such as Belgium,
Holland, Sweden, and Switzerland, and they still remain far less numerous than in their larger neighbours; while the differences resulting from
their status as small countries pose major problems in a global analysis
integrating the social, political, and international dimensions.

A comparative analysis needs a starting-point, and Britain has been
placed at the centre of this three-country comparison. This is explained

partly by the author's now long-standing association with, and interest in, Britain. More importantly, big business is closely conected to Britain's central historiographical debate, which remains the country's relative decline since the late nineteenth century. Big business and business élites can be (and have been) seen as carrying a decisive responsibility in this decline: any controversy concerning their role will thus be an integral part of the country's soul-searching. The major concern about the legacy of the past is more dramatic in Germany, as it still revolves around the origins, nature, and consequences of the Third Reich. Controversies have surrounded the responsibility of big business both in the short term (through its relationship with Nazism) and in the long term (through the belated and timid self-assertion of the bourgeoisie); but in no sense have these been the central issues of German history. France is in between. The old concern about economic backwardness has been pushed to the sidelines in the wake of the country's sustained economic growth during the *Trente Glorieuses*, though the French are recurrently worried about their economic and business performance. The most passionate discussions remain centred around the war years: the 1940 defeat, the Vichy regime, occupation, and collaboration. The role of big business is relevant to both debates, in terms reminiscent of Britain in the former, of Germany in the latter. Many of the myths surrounding big business and the rise of Hitler, or the German *Sonderweg*, or the 'Malthusianism' of the French *patronat*, have now been destroyed, often by resorting to the comparative method. The myth of Britain's 'entrepreneurial failure' remains well entrenched, though there are increasing signs that its turn is coming soon. Contributing to the final push was another reason to put Britain at the centre of the comparison.

The comparative method is at once extremely rewarding and desperately frustrating. It is rewarding because, as Marc Bloch reminds us, it can lead historians towards true explanations; more modestly—and more realistically—it can prevent them from addressing the wrong questions.[1] But it is also, and mostly, frustrating because of the immensity of the task and thus the necessity of dealing with a limited number of issues; the difficulty of fully understanding the complexities of several countries; the feeling of never knowing as much as the national specialist and of laying oneself open to criticism from every quarter.

I have therefore been especially appreciative of the help I have received. The project has been based in Britain, where I have enjoyed the privilege of a long-standing visiting fellowship at the Business History Unit at the London School of Economics, undoubtedly the best place in Europe to undertake comparative research in business history; my thanks go to its director, Terry Gourvish, for his unfailing support, to Sonia Copeland,

[1] M. Bloch, 'Pour une histoire comparée des sociétés européennes', *Revue de synthèse historique* (Dec. 1928), repr. in *Mélanges historiques*, 2 vols. (Paris, 1923), i. 24.

administrative assistant, and to the many scholars met there over the years with whom I have discussed aspects of this work. The original idea for this book germinated when I took part in an international research group on the German bourgeoisie in the nineteenth century at the Center for Interdisciplinary Research at the University of Bielefeld, and then when I gave a series of lectures on European entrepreneurs at the École des Hautes Études en Sciences Sociales in Paris. I am extremely grateful to Jürgen Kocka and Louis Bergeron for giving me these two unique opportunities of working in a most stimulating environment. Two prolonged stays at the Free University in Berlin were also possible thanks to the hospitality of Jürgen Kocka, Hartmut Kaelble, and Hannes Siegrist. The Leverhulme Trust and the Nuffield Foundation have enabled me to benefit for a year from the help of a research assistant. I am grateful to Fabienne Debrunner for her valued contribution in collecting data on companies and businessmen in the three countries. Financial assistance from the Fonds National Suisse de la Recherche Scientifique has been essential for prolonged leaves of absence from my teaching at the University of Geneva and extensive travels across Europe.

Comments on papers presented at seminars in London, Oxford, Edinburgh, Glasgow, Reading, Paris, Lyons, Berlin, Bielefeld, and Geneva have helped shape my ideas. Several people have given me material or made suggestions: Dolores Augustine, François Caron, Emmanuel Chadeau, Christophe Charle, Philip Cottrell, Wilfried Feldenkirchen, João Gonçalves, Hervé Joly, Geoffrey Jones, Karin Kaudelka-Hanisch, Arthur Knight, Maurice Lévy-Leboyer, Jacques Marseille, Martin Müller, Chris Napier, Roger Nougaret, Toni Pierenkemper, Alain Plessis, Christine Shaw, and Nick Tiratsoo. Patrick Fridenson, Leslie Hannah, Geoffrey Owen, Harm Schröter, and Peter Wardley have read parts or all of the manuscript and made valuable and helpful comments. The responsibility for any error is of course only mine.

My special thanks go to David Kynaston for his friendship, constant encouragement, and especially for his skilful polishing of my English during the final stage of writing this book. I owe a great debt to Frances, for whom the experience of European big business has not always been a happy one. The book is dedicated to my daughter Charlotte.

                                                                    Y. C.

CONTENTS

LIST OF TABLES

PART I

BIG BUSINESS

What is big business? The question might seem superfluous more than sixty years after the publication of *The Modern Corporation and Private Property* by Berle and Means, more than fifty years after James Burnham's *The Managerial Revolution*, and a full generation after Chandler's *Strategy and Structure* and Galbraith's *The New Industrial State*.[1] All the major questions related to big business have been raised, if not always answered, long ago—from the power of the large corporations and the emergence of the professional manager to the advantages of internalizing contractual transactions and the effects on economic growth. Following Alfred Chandler's enormous influence in the last thirty years,[2] the major debates in business history have centred around the emergence, development, and role of the 'modern business enterprise', the definition of which has been perfected by considering not only size, but other factors such as integration, diversification, market share, and managerial capabilities. Familiarity with big business has increased in recent years with annual publications since the 1960s of lists of the largest companies. The layman would not have to be hard pressed to give a dozen famous names such as General Motors, Ford, IBM, General Electric, Standard Oil, Shell, BP, ICI, Krupp, Siemens, Hoechst, Renault, Michelin, Fiat, Nestlé, Philips, Sony, Toyota, and so on.

However, when it comes to big business in Europe, in particular before the 1960s, there remains a good deal of confusion and a priori judgements: confusion about the frontiers of big business and the firms making up its population, a priori judgements about the countries where big business has been flourishing in the twentieth century. It is no coincidence that the four seminal books referred to above all concern the United States of America, where big business reached from an early stage a far higher level of development. Big business in Europe has consisted of a diversity of national experiences, hence the difficulty of subjecting it to historical analysis. The question is thus: what is big business *in Europe*, and how far does the definition extend beyond the dozen or so 'big names'? Answers so far have been unsatisfactory, because large firms are usually identified on the basis of national rankings rather than actual size. Whatever the country or period studied, big business is automatically equated with the largest industrial companies. Lists

[1] A. A. Berle and G. C. Means, *The Modern Corporation and Private Property* (New York, 1932); J. Burnham, *The Managerial Revolution: What is Happening in the World* (New York, 1941); A. Chandler, *Strategy and Structure* (Cambridge, Mass., 1962); J. K. Galbraith, *The New Industrial State* (London, 1967). A good introduction to the subject, with a selection of the most relevant publications on the subject, is B. Supple (ed.), *The Rise of Big Business* (Aldershot, 1993).

[2] As is well known, *Strategy and Structure* was followed by two other classics, *The Visible Hand* (Cambridge, Mass., 1977) and *Scale and Scope* (Cambridge, Mass., 1990).

of the 50, 100, or 200 largest companies have been established for most industrialized countries,[3] and have proved extremely useful as a tool for historical analysis;[4] the present study is no exception to the rule.

One question, however, is rarely asked: should the *largest* companies of a given country be all considered as *large* companies? For economies of the size of Britain, France, or Germany, there can be little doubt about the top 50, though Maurice Lévy-Leboyer was wise enough not to include more than 40 companies for the year 1912 in his study of the French *grand patronat*.[5] Before the 1960s, companies at the lower end of the top 100 were not necessarily large, and those ranked between 100 and 200 almost certainly not. In *The Visible Hand*, Alfred Chandler lists all American industrial enterprises with assets of $20 million or more in 1917 (280 in total), which could be considered as a reasonable lower limit. In Germany, only 24 companies had reached this size (80 million marks) in 1913, and this was the country usually considered as coming closest to the American model of big business development. The assets of the company ranked 200th in Germany in 1913 were hardly higher than $3 million, those of the company ranked 101st (Daimler-Motoren) did not reach $6 million, with just over 3,000 workers: a *Mittelstand* company in every respect. The same was true in 1930: for example the firm ranked 151st, the mechanical engineering company Buckau R. Wolf AG, did not employ more than 1,950 people. Such a gap betwen American and European companies is not really surprising.

[3] For Britain, see P. Payne, 'The Emergence of Large-Scale Companies in Great Britain, 1870–1914', *Economic History Review*, 20/3 (1967); L. Hannah, *The Rise of the Corporate Economy* (2nd edn. London, 1983); D. Jeremy, 'The Hundred Largest Employers in the United Kingdom, in Manufacturing and Non-manufacturing Industries, in 1907, 1935, and 1955', *Business History*, 33/1 (1991); P. Wardley, 'The Anatomy of Big Business: Aspects of Corporate Development in the Twentieth Century', *Business History*, 33/2 (1991); for Germany see J. Kocka and H. Siegrist, 'Die 100 grössten deutschen Industrieunternehmen im späten 19. und frühen 20. Jahrhundert: Expansion, Diversifikation und Integration im internationalen Vergleich', in N. Horn and J. Kocka (eds.), *Recht und Entwicklung der Grossunternehmen im 19. und frühen 20. Jahrhundert* (Göttingen, 1979) and H. Siegrist, 'Deutsche Grossunternehmen vom späten 19. Jahrhundert bis zur Weimarer Republik', *Geschichte und Gesellschaft*, 6 (1980); see also for Germany W. Feldenkirchen 'Concentration in German Industry 1870–1939', in H. Pohl (ed.), *The Concentration Process in the Entrepreneurial Economy since the Late 19th Century* (Stuttgart, 1988); for France, see J. Houssiaux, *Le Pouvoir de monopole* (Paris, 1958). Finally, A. Chandler established lists of the 200 largest American, British, and German industrial companies for his magisterial study *Scale and Scope*.

[4] For example, the lists established by Kocka and Siegrist, 'Industrieunternehmen', and by Siegrist 'Deutsche Grossunternehmen', have been used in socio-political studies of German big business such as W. Mosse, *Jews in the German Economy: The German-Jewish Economic Elite 1820–1935* (Oxford, 1987); H. A. Turner, *German Big Business and the Rise of Hitler* (Oxford, 1985).

[5] M. Lévy-Leboyer, 'Le Patronat français, 1912–1973', in M. Lévy-Leboyer (ed.), *Le Patronat de la seconde industrialisation* (Paris, 1979), 137–88.

However, even within Europe, there is no guarantee that by simply juxtaposing national lists, one is comparing like with like. In 1930, for example, the British steel company Stewarts & Lloyds, with £5,514,000 capital, did not rank among the country's top 60 (taking together industry, finance, and services), but it would have ranked 17th in Germany and 1st in France!

Another problem is that big business is too often reduced to manufacturing industry.[6] Chandler's 'modern business enterprise' is an industrial firm, even though its forerunners were the railway companies. The importance of manufacturing industry in modern economic growth does not need to be emphasized, and the fascination it has exerted on generations of economic and business historians is understandable. Big business, however, is a wider concept. Excessive attention to the structure of the firm has led to losing sight of a basic fact: that big business is a matter of large-scale operations, of money and power, whatever the type of activity or the forms of organization. In the course of the twentieth century, big business in Europe has included firms involved in banking and finance, in insurance, and in wholesale and retail trade; in transport, railways at first and later shipping, tramways, and airways; in mining extraction, especially coal, but also gold and diamonds; in oil, gas, and electrical distribution; as well as in a number of services such as publishing, advertising, cinema, and telecommunications. Such activities, which have attracted a great deal of interest on the part of historians, are rarely included in comparative appraisals of big business in Europe.[7]

For the history of big business in Europe is by essence comparative. And comparative history too often means hierarchy, with implicit or explicit reference to the superiority of a model of development. There is, for example, a persistent belief that large firms emerged later in Britain and France than in Germany, and this has been seen as reflecting one aspect of Germany's 'economic superiority'. Such a belief, however, is at odds with the reality of big business development in the three countries—especially, as we shall see, in Britain. This discrepancy would not matter very much if it had not led a number of scholars, especially Americans, to conclude that Britain's loss of economic predominance should be attributed to her entrepreneurs' attachment to family capitalism and their reluctance to embrace the managerial form of business organization character-

[6] For example Chandler, *The Visible Hand* and *Scale and Scope*, or recent surveys such as C. Schmitz, *The Growth of Big Business in the United States and Western Europe, 1850–1939*, (Basingstoke, 1993).

[7] See for example Wardley, 'Anatomy of Big Business', who attempted to highlight the role of large companies in the service sector in Britain and their previous neglect by economic historians.

istic of the large corporation.[8] In a similar vein, the now discarded thesis of French economic 'backwardness', which enjoyed an undoubted vogue among American scholars in the 1950s and 1960s, contended that French entrepreneurs were reluctant to extend the size of their firms in order to preserve their family interests.[9]

Defining and identifying big business in Europe is thus an essential preliminary task. In a comparative perspective, this task requires a yardstick with which to measure big business development in both space and time. Many measures of a company's size are available: turnover, paid-up capital, market value of capital, total assets, workforce. None is perfect. Turnover gives the value of a company's total sales and provides homogeneous data for international comparisons. Most international rankings published since the 1960s by the financial press are based on this criterion. Unfortunately it is not easily applicable for the first half of the twentieth century, the very period for which we lack international comparisons. Market capitalization provides a dynamic insight, as it reflects the investor's perception of a business; it might not, however, be best suited for international comparisons, especially in the earlier part of the century, given the unequal development of the stock market in the three countries.[10]

A convenient measure for this period is provided by workforce. It can be assumed that companies of a similar size in the same sector roughly employed the same number of workers, both manual and clerical, in Britain, France, and Germany, despite possible differences in productivity levels. Workforce's main advantage as a yardstick lies in its independence from a series of factors likely to bias international comparisons, in particular a company's legal form (private or limited), accounting practices, or fluctuations in the exchange rates and currency depreciations. Big business, however, is not entirely made up of large employers. Some sectors, in particular the heavy industries, have traditionally relied on a massive labour input, while others, primarily though not exclusively banking and finance, have been more dependent on capital. Workforce must thus be complemented by one or several other criteria. Despite its imper-

[8] See in particular Chandler, *Scale and Scope*, W. Lazonick, *Business Organization and the Myth of the Market Economy* (Cambridge, 1991); but this view impregnates most analyses of British business history.

[9] For a discussion of this question in a comparative perspective, see Y. Cassis, 'Divergence and Convergence in British and French Business in the 19th and 20th Centuries', in Y. Cassis, F. Crouzet, and T. Gourvish (eds.), *Management and Business in Britain and France: The Age of the Corporate Economy* (Oxford, 1995).

[10] This is a problem encountered by Christopher Schmitz in his recent attempt to rank the world's 100 largest companies in 1912. He adopted the somewhat unsatisfactory solution of using market capitalization for 63 companies and total assets for 37. 'The World's Largest Companies of 1912', *Business History*, 37/4 (1995).

fections, paid-up capital constitutes a convenient and adequate corrective. Workforce and paid-up capital thus correct each other, and can be used in conjunction in order to identify the world of big business in twentieth-century Europe.

The more difficult question concerns the size which should be considered as the minimum required for a company to qualify for 'big business' status. The notion of big business has of course varied over time. What would have been considered a large firm a century ago is unlikely to be more than a medium-sized one today. Thus 1,000 employees has been proposed as a possible benchmark for the pre-1914 years.[11] Such a size was no doubt respectable at the time, but enterprises of this dimension were already fairly widespread and certainly too numerous to be all part of the world of big business. The 100 largest British employers in 1907 all had a workforce exceeding 4,000.[12] In France, where big business was less developed, 23 firms in the iron and steel industries and 44 in textiles employed more than 1,000 people in 1906.[13] As far as workforce is concerned, I suggest 10,000 employees for the entire period. It is a high threshold for the early part of the century, when 5,000 is probably a more realistic figure; it can, however, be used as a landmark to perceive the main phases of development of the large firm in the course of the century, and to base on common ground comparisons between countries and sectors. The figure concerning paid-up capital requires periodical adjustments to take account of endemic currency depreciations. A figure of £2 million before 1914, £3 million for the period of monetary stability in the mid- to late 1920s, and £5 million for the early to mid-1950s provides a good corrective to the use of workforce as an indicator of big business status.[14]

The first part of this book is conceived as a journey across the world of big business in Britain, France, and Germany in the twentieth century, using as a flexible guide the criteria defined above. The objective is to identify which were the *large* firms in each of the three countries, and the changes which have taken place in the course of

[11] J. Kocka and N. Horn, 'Introduction', in Horn and Kocka (eds.), *Recht und Entwicklung*, 12.
[12] Jeremy, 'The Hundred Largest Employers'.
[13] F. Caron, in *Histoire économique et sociale de la France* (Paris, 1981).
[14] The figures for 1929 and 1953 are slightly lower than the 1907 figure (£2 million, 50 million francs, 40 million marks) at constant price. This is justified by the fact that firms often held on to their historical capital, preferring to increase reserves or issue loan capital. Adjusting the figure for 1907 for each of the three countries, and then converting it into pounds sterling, also results in some discrepancies which are not entirely ironed out by movements in the exchange rate. As analytical tools rather than definite measures, the round figures chosen for paid-up capital are entirely adequate. However, account has been taken of these differences in interpreting global results.

the century. This will enable us to compare the *size* and *composition* of the world of big business in Britain, France, and Germany: how many firms were included in this group, and how they were distributed between sectors and branches. In the process, we will come across a vast number of names, and the enumeration might at times appear fastidious. But the business world is made up of actual firms with which it is essential to become familiar, as many of them will be encountered time and again as the book moves on to discuss other themes.

1

The World of Big Business Before 1914

Big business is a twentieth-century phenomenon. Large firms, even very large firms, had of course existed earlier. The combined capital of the Rothschilds (London, Paris, Frankfurt, and Vienna) has been estimated at over £20 million in 1863,[1] which even fifty years later would make it one of the largest companies in Europe. Railway companies were the first real giant firms of the industrial age: in 1850 in Britain, nineteen railway companies had a capital in excess of £3 million, at a time when only a handful of industrial companies had a capital of more than £500,000.[2] Nevertheless, the vast increase in the number of large companies and the new dimension taken by the size of the largest firms broadly coincided, in Europe and in America, with the turn of the century. Technical innovations, expanding markets, improved communications, intense competition, new investment facilities, government regulation, and entrepreneurial motivation—all contributed, in varying degrees, to offer formidable opportunities for business expansion in the closing decades of the nineteenth century.[3] In Germany only three industrial companies employed more than 10,000 workers in 1887: Krupp, already the largest firm in the country with 20,000 employees, and two other metallurgical firms.[4] Twenty years later, their number had risen to twenty-three, five of them employing more than 30,000 people.[5] In Britain a wave of mergers from which emerged some of the most important companies in the country took place between 1888 and 1914 and reached its peak in 1899.[6]

[1] B. Gille, *Histoire de la maison Rothschild*, vol. ii (Paris, 1967).
[2] T. Gourvish, *Railways and the British Economy 1830–1914* (London, 1980), 10.
[3] See Chandler, *The Visible Hand* and *Scale and Scope*; A. Chandler and H. Daems (eds.), *Managerial Hierarchies: Comparative Perspectives on the Rise of the Modern Industrial Enterprise* (Cambridge, Mass., 1980); N. Lamoreaux, *The Great Merger Movement in American Business, 1895–1904* (Cambridge, 1985); L. Hannah, *The Rise of the Corporate Economy* (2nd edn. London, 1983); J. Kocka, 'Entrepreneurs and Managers in German Industrialization', in P. Mathias and M. M. Postan (eds.), *The Cambridge Economic History of Europe*, vol. vii, part 1 (Cambridge, 1978); C. Schmitz, *The Growth of Big Business in the United States and Western Europe, 1850–1939* (Basingstoke, 1993); B. Supple (ed.), *The Rise of Big Business* (Aldershot, 1993).
[4] J. Kocka and H. Siegrist, 'Die 100 grössten deutschen Industrieunternehmen im späten 19. und frühen 20. Jahrhundert', in N. Horn and J. Kocka (eds.), *Recht und Entwicklung der Grossunternehmen im 19. und frühen 20. Jakrhundert* (Göttingen, 1979). The two other firms were the Manfeld'sche Kupferschifferbauende and the Vereinigte Königs- und Laurahütte, with respectively 16,334 and 10,681 employees.
[5] Ibid. The rise of less gigantic firms is equally spectacular: more than fifty companies employed 5,000 people or more in 1907 as against only eight twenty years earlier.
[6] Hannah, *Rise of the Corporate Economy*.

Table 1.1. Estimated number of large companies in Britain, France, and Germany, 1907–1912

	Britain	France[a]	Germany
Nominal capital (£2 m. or more)	93	21	45
Workforce (10,000 or more)	17	10	23

[a] France: 1912.

Sources: Stock Exchange Yearbook; Annuaire Desfossé; Handbuch der deutschen Aktiengesellschaften; D. J. Jeremy, 'The Hundred Largest Employers in the United Kingdom, in Manufacturing and Non-manufacturing Industries, in 1907, 1935 and 1955', *Business History,* 33/1 (1991); J. Kocka and H. Siegrist, 'Die 100 grössten deutschen Industrieunternehmen im späten 19. und frühen 20. Jahrhundert', in N. Horn and J. Kocka (eds.), *Recht und Entwicklung der Grossunternehmen im 19. und frühen 20. Jahrhundert* (Göttingen, 1979); various yearbooks and directories; company monographs.

By the early twentieth century, Britain was the European country where big business had reached its highest development, well ahead of Germany and France (Table 1.1). In 1907, about 100 British companies worked with a capital of at least £2 million, which was more than twice as many as in Germany, and more than four times as many as in France (Table 1.1).[7] As far as *industrial* companies were concerned, however, the advent of giant firms in the early twentieth century was more pronounced in Germany, where the number of firms employing 10,000 people was higher than in the other two countries: 23 firms as against 17 in Britain and 11 in France. This was a result of the huge development of German heavy industry in the late nineteenth century. Interestingly, if the benchmark is lowered to 5,000 employees, a more appropriate figure for the pre-1914 years, then Britain had a higher number of large industrial companies than Germany: 59 as against 49 in 1907. Figures are necessarily less reliable at this level of size and should be considered with caution; they suggest, however, a wider spread of large industrial companies in Britain below the level of the giant firm.

Big business was also much more diversified in Britain. In the early twentieth century, big business was almost synonymous with banking and heavy industry in Germany and France, whereas it included a broader range of activities in Britain (Table 1.2). In Germany in 1907 there

[7] Railway companies are not included in these figures. They were the largest companies in Britain and France, but as the Prussian network had been nationalized by Bismarck in 1879, their inclusion would have widened the gap with Germany. In addition, even in Britain and France, they became increasingly regulated and assimilated to public services; as a result they drifted to the fringes of the world of big business, mostly providing successful businessmen with prestigious directorships. Central banks have also been left out of this study.

Table 1.2. Sectoral distribution of companies with capital of £2 million or more, 1907–1912

	Great Britain	France	Germany
Industry	41	2	16
Heavy industries	10	0	12
Textiles	8	0	0
Food, drink, tobacco	11	0	0
Electrical engineering	1	1	4
Chemicals	4	1	0
Others	7	0	0
Finance	21	13	20
Banking	6	13	20
Other finance	15	0	0
Services	23	6	7
Trade	2	0	0
Transport	11	4	5
Communications	5	0	0
Utilities	5	2	2
Foreign and colonial	8	0	2
Total	93	21	45

Sources: *Stock Exchange Yearbook*; *Annuaire Desfossé*; *Handbuch der deutschen Aktiengesellschaften*.

were twenty banks and twelve firms from the coal, iron, and steel industries among the 45 companies with a paid-up capital of £2 million or more. And, not surprisingly, out of the 24 firms employing 10,000 people or more, 19 belonged to the heavy industries. By 1911 in France, 13 companies out of the 21 with a capital £2 million or more were banks, while 8 out of 11 firms with 10,000 employees or more were coal, iron, and steel companies. Contrast these figures with the distribution of the 93 British firms working with a capital of £2 million or more in 1907, where only 21 were financial institutions (including a mere 6 banks), and only 10 coal-mining or metal-manufacturing enterprises. Companies from the heavy industries obviously made up a fair proportion of the country's largest employers, though not an overwhelming one as in Germany and France: 9 of the 17 firms with 10,000 employees or more belonged to this sector.

BANKING AND FINANCE

Such a low proportion of financial institutions among the largest British companies might appear surprising given the major role played by financial services in the British economy. However, relying on paid-up capital as a measure of size would in this case be misleading. English commercial banks, unlike their Continental counterparts, confined their activities to deposit banking operations—that is, on the assets side, mostly short-term loans, discounts, and investments in highly marketable securities. They thus worked with a much smaller capital, but with larger deposits, than the French and German banks. In 1907 the then largest British bank, Lloyds Bank, had a capital of £3.85 million, as against £10 million for the Deutsche Bank and for the Crédit Lyonnais. Measured by total assets, however, the leading British banks were among the largest in the world in the early twentieth century, though not (as one might have expected) the largest. On the eve of the First World War, five European commercial banks were roughly of equal size, with total assets exceeding £100 million. Three were British: Lloyds Bank, Midland Bank (then called the London City and Midland Bank), and Westminster Bank (then called the London County and Westminster Bank). One was French, the Crédit Lyonnais, and one German, the Deutsche Bank. Six other banks stood a little behind, with total assets between £40 million and £60 million: two British banks, Barclays Bank and the National Provincial Bank; two French banks, the Société Générale and the Comptoir National d'Escompte de Paris; and two German banks, the Dresdner Bank and the Disconto-Gesellschaft.

British banks reached a giant size through a long process of amalgamations which started in the mid-nineteenth century and reached its peak between 1890 and 1918. During these crucial years, Lloyds and Midland, until then medium-sized provincial institutions based in Birmingham, were transformed into City-based colossi with a network of branches covering the entire country; the modern Barclays Bank was formed in 1896 by the merger of twenty private banks; and two old-established London banks, the London and Westminster and the London and County, had to merge in 1909 to keep their position at the top of the British banking hierarchy.[8] German and French banks followed a different route, mostly based on internal growth. French commercial banks built a national network of branches without taking over local banks. The Crédit Lyonnais took over a single bank before 1914, and the Comptoir d'Escompte only eight. The expansion of the big German banks took yet another form. They hardly opened any branches outside Berlin, nor did they launch into a large-scale amalgamation policy. They rather established 'community of interests', based on cross-shareholding and pooled profits, with a number of provincial banks. The Deutsche Bank had such links with fourteen banks, includ-

---

[8] See J. Sykes, *The Amalgamation Movement in English Banking 1825–1924* (London, 1926); F. Capie and G. Rodrik-Bali, 'Concentration in British Banking, 1870–1920', *Business History*, 29/3 (1982); Y. Cassis, *City Bankers, 1890–1914* (Cambridge, 1994); A. R. Holmes and E. Green, *Midland: 150 Years of Business Banking* (London, 1986).

ing large provincial banks such as the Bergisch-Märkische Bank, the capital of which stood at £3 million.[9]

Before 1914, especially in France and Germany, big business in banking extended far beyond the small group of leading financial institutions based in the capital. In Germany no less than fifteen provincial banks had more than £2 million capital, including the Schaafhausenscher Bankverein in Cologne, the Commerz- und Diskonto Bank in Hamburg, and the Essener Creditanstalt in Essen. French banking was more international. In addition to a few large provincial banks (such as the Crédit du Nord based in Lille, the Société Nancéenne de Crédit based in Nancy, or the Société Marseillaise de Crédit in Marseille), French large banks included the leading *banques d'affaires* (investment banks), in the first place the Banque de Paris et des Pays-Bas (Paribas), and a number of foreign and colonial banks such as the Banque de l'Indochine, or the Crédit Foncier d'Algérie et de Tunisie.[10] In Britain the overseas banks also worked with a comparatively small capital, none of which reached £2 million before 1914. On the basis of their total assets, however, such banks as the Hongkong and Shanghai Banking Corporation, the Chartered Bank of India, Australia and China, the London and River Plate Bank, or the Bank of Australasia were undoubtedly large companies.[11]

As a result of their comparatively low capital, British banks do not appear at the top of the lists of the country's largest companies measured by share capital; with less than £4 million, Lloyds Bank was only in fourteenth position in 1907. In Germany, on the contrary, the largest company in 1907 was the Deutsche Bank, with £10 million capital, ahead of Krupp and the Dresdner Bank, with £9 million each, while another three banks were among the top six.[12] The gap between banks and industrial companies was even wider in France. The Crédit Lyonnais was the largest company with a share capital as high as that of the Deutsche Bank. But the capital of the largest industrial company (excluding public utilities), Saint-Gobain, was only £2.4 million. The prominent position of finance within British business, which was far greater than in France or Germany, did not depend on the size of a few large banks, but on the role of the City of London, which acted as financial centre of the world in the half-century preceding the First World War. The bulk of world trade was then financed through the medium of bills of exchange drawn on London. With

---

[9] M. Pohl, *Entstehung und Entwicklung der Universalbankensystem: Konzentration und Krise als wichtige Faktoren* (Frankfurt am Main, 1986); 62–7; J. Riesser, *Zur Entwicklungsgeschichte der deutsche Grossbanken mit besonderer Rücksicht auf die Konzentrationsbestrebungen* (Jena, 1906), 210–15.

[10] See E. Bussière, *Paribas: Europe and the World, 1872–1992* (Antwerp, 1992); M. Meuleau, *Des pionniers en Extrême-Orient* (Paris, 1990).

[11] On these banks, see G. Jones, *British Multinational Banking, 1830–1990* (Oxford, 1993).

[12] 'Die 100 grössten Unternehmen im Deutschen Reich 1907, geordnet nach der Höhe des voll einbezahlten Grundkapitals', unpublished list kindly given to me by Jürgen Kocka.

40 per cent of the world's total export of capital in 1913 raised on its financial markets, London was the leading centre for the issue of foreign loans
and equity. The nominal value of the securities quoted on the London
Stock Exchange was larger than that of the New York and Paris Stock
Exchanges combined. The City was the world leader in shipping and
insurance (in particular with Lloyd's of London) as well as in actual
trading activities.[13]

All this was big business indeed, and gave rise to a number of large,
non-banking finance and investment companies, with more than £2
million capital, which did not exist in any other European financial centre:
mortgage companies such as the Australian Mortgage, Land and Finance
Company, with £3 million capital in 1907, investment trusts such as the
Debenture Corporation with £2 million, or South African mining investment companies such as the Central Mining and Investment Corporation
with £6 million. Moreover, some of the City's most glamorous financial
operations, such as the issue of foreign loans, were not handled by firms
of huge proportions. This was a peculiarity of the financial sector. The
capital of the City merchant banks rarely exceeded £1 million.[14] Yet in
terms of economic power and influence, they fully belonged to the world
of big business, as did their counterparts of the Parisian *haute banque*.[15]

HEAVY INDUSTRY

For well over half the twentieth century, big business was epitomized by
heavy industry: coal, iron, steel, and in their wake shipbuilding, heavy
machinery, and the armaments industry. Not only, as we have seen, were
the largest companies massively concentrated in this sector. The blast-
furnaces, the harshness of labour conditions for armies of proletarians,
the perpetuating dynasties of ironmasters, the crucial role of iron and
steel in warfare have all contributed to shape the symbolic perception of
this industry. Moreover, because of its strategic importance, a strong
heavy industry was long seen in political circles as a mark of economic
virility.

In the three countries, heavy industry formed a major part of big business before 1914, but nowhere was its position so strong as in Germany.
It was a truly dominating position, resulting from the formidable growth
of the German iron and steel industry in the 1880s and 1890s which led

---

[13] See Y. Cassis, *La City de Londres, 1870–1914* (Paris, 1987); R. Michie, *The City of London:
Continuity and Change, 1850–1990* (Basingstoke, 1992); D. Kynaston, *The City of London*, ii.
Golden Years 1890–1914 (London, 1995).

[14] See S. Chapman, *The Rise of Merchant Banking* (London, 1984).

[15] See Cassis, *City Bankers, 1890–1914*, and 'Small and Medium-Sized Companies in the
Financial Sector in Europe', in M. Müller (ed.), *Strategy and Structure of the Small and Medium-
Sized Enterprises since the Industrial Revolution* (Stuttgart, 1994).

to her overtaking Britain by the turn of the century. Although the importance of areas such as Upper Silesia or Saarland should not be overlooked,
it was the Ruhr which stood at the very heart of Germany's economic and
military power, making up 65.5 per cent of the country's coal extraction,
and respectively 42.5 per cent and 53.6 per cent of its pig iron and crude
steel production in 1913. Moreover, and unlike Britain and France, iron
and steel was Germany's leading exporting industry, with 13 per cent of
the country's total on the eve of the First World War. But the dominating
position of the German heavy industry was also a matter of number and
size. Germany had many more large companies in the sector than Britain
and France, and these companies were on the whole substantially larger.
This did not only derive from the fact that Germany produced more iron
and steel than Britain and France—though she extracted less coal than
Britain—thus giving firms greater opportunities for internal growth. It
also derived from the degree of integration, both vertical and horizontal,
of the industry. Backwards integration in coal extraction, in particular,
had become a common feature of the industry. It had been encouraged
by the successful cartelization of the coal industry through the powerful
Rhenish-Westphalian Coal Syndicate: by merging with iron and steel
producers, collieries could avoid both the quotas and the prices imposed
by the cartel, which did not apply if used in their own iron and steel
works.

By the early 1910s, five 'mixed' companies had emerged at the top of
German heavy industry.[16] The oldest and largest was the legendary
Krupp, founded as early as 1812 by Friedrich Krupp, which had grown
not only as a fully integrated coal, iron, and steel concern, but also as one
of Europe's leading armaments manufacturers with a commanding position in Germany and a privileged relationship with the Kaiser.[17] In second
place was Gelsenkirchener Bergwerks Aktiengesellschaft (GBAG), originally only a coal-mining company, though one of the largest in the country
with more than 6 million tons extracted in 1905, and led by one of Imperial Germany's most famous salaried managers, Emil Kirdorf; it diversified in iron and steel-making through the acquisition in 1904 of two
major producers, the Schalker Gruben und Hütten-Verein and the Aach-
ener Hütten-Verein. Deutsch-Luxemburg, led since 1906 by Hugo Stinnes,
moved from relatively small beginnings in 1901 to third position through
a series of mergers, the most significant of which was the takeover in 1910
of Dortmunder Union. By contrast, the phenomenal rise of Deutscher
Kaiser, the group founded by August Thyssen in 1883, was almost entirely

---

[16] See W. Feldenkirchen, *Die Eisen- und Stahlindustrie des Ruhrgebiets 1879–1914: Wachstum,
Finanzierung und Struktur ihrer Grossunternehmen* (Wiesbaden, 1982).

[17] There is an abundant literature on Krupp, though there is still no entirely satisfactory
academic study. See in particular W. Manchester, *The Arms of Krupp 1587–1968* (London,
1969); G. von Klass, *Krupps: The Story of an Industrial Empire* (London, 1954).

attributable to internal growth.[18] The fifth major group was Phoenix, another acquisitive company, which ended a decade of merger activity by taking over the Hörder Verein in 1906. Behind the 'big five' were another good dozen large companies, each employing more than 10,000 workers, including the Gutehoffnungshütte, the group controlled by the Haniel family and one of the oldest in the Ruhr; Harpener Bergbau, one of the few remaining independent collieries (with more than 6 million tons extracted in 1907 and a workforce of 26,000); and, among the largest firms in Upper Silesia, Hohenlohe Werke, Oberschlesische Eisenbahnbedarf, and Kattowitzer. Despite their huge size, the big five did not control more than about a third of Germany's iron and steel production, and less than a fifth of her coal extraction.[19]

The position of French heavy industry was hardly less dominating. Its share of big business was about the same as in Germany. The sector's two leading firms, Schneider and de Wendel, were almost as legendary names as Krupp and Thyssen. The Comité des Forges was the most powerful business pressure group in France, as was its German counterpart, the Central Verband Deutscher Industrieller. Nevertheless, heavy industry did not, so to speak, weigh as heavily in France as in Germany. Textiles rather than metallurgical products were the main exports of French industry. More importantly, despite its impressive growth in the decade preceding the First World War, France's overall production (5,207,000 tons of pig iron and 4,687,000 tons of crude steel in 1913) remained far below that of Germany (respectively 16,761,000 and 17,609,000 tons).[20] Another notable difference was the lesser degree of integration of the French firms. Ironically, despite the permanent problems posed to the French iron and steel manufacturers by the country's shortage of coal resources, half of the French large heavy industry companies (measured by workforce) were collieries. The two largest companies were the Mines d'Anzin and the Mines de Lens, in the department of Nord-Pas-de-Calais, which each employed more than 16,000 workers and produced around 3.5 million tons of coal in 1908–12. Such a size was reached through an impressive level of horizontal concentration: the two firms ensured a third of the region's production in 1908–12, while the nine largest collieries in the Nord-Pas-de-Calais were responsible for more than half of the country's output of coal.[21]

Schneider and de Wendel, the two leaders in the French heavy indus-

[18] See W. Treue, *Die Feuer verlöschen nie: August Thyssen-Hütte 1890–1926* (Düsseldorf, 1966).

[19] Feldenkirchen, *Eisen- und Stahlindustrie*, 268. In terms of total assets the actual percentages were 16.1 for coal, 31.2 for pig iron, and 30.5 for steel. The percentages were very close in terms of production (respectively 21, 34.8, and 30.7), though the five largest producers were not necessarily the same firms.

[20] B. R. Mitchell, *Abstracts of European Historical Statistics* (2nd rev. edn. London, 1980).

[21] M. Gillet, *Les Charbonnages du Nord de la France au XIXe siècle* (Paris, 1973), 122–4.

try, were firms of unquestionable European proportions. De Wendel, *maîtres de forges* since the eighteenth century and the dominant force in Lorraine, were already employing more than 3,000 workers in 1825. Their workforce had increased almost tenfold by 1913; they then allegedly produced 1.25 million tons of pig iron and 1.2 million tons of steel.[22] Since 1871, however, the firm and the family had been divided between France and Germany, the bulk of their productive facilities being in 'Lorraine occupée'. De Wendel's arch-rivals, Schneider, started as ironmasters in Le Creusot in 1836 and had become by the early twentieth century a fully integrated and diversified group, especially in heavy engineering and armaments, where they were Krupp's and Vickers's chief competitors in the global markets.[23] Two other firms employed more than 10,000 workers before the war: Marine-Homécourt and Châtillon-Commentry & Neuves-Maisons, both the product of a turn-of-the-century merger between a larger firm from the Centre (Forges et Aciéries de la Marine et des Chemins de Fer, Châtillon Commentry) and a smaller firm from Lorraine (Homécourt, Neuves-Maisons). Factor costs had become increasingly disadvantageous for the Centre's iron and steel industry since the 1870s, and firms responded on the one hand by reorienting their production towards high-quality steels and heavy engineering, and on the other by investing in expanding areas, especially in Lorraine, as well as in Russia.[24] Otherwise, no significant merger took place in French heavy industry. In the country's two principal regions of iron and steel production (the Lorraine, where rich iron ores were discovered in the early 1880s, and the Nord, which was endowed with coalfields), major firms such as Longwy or Pont-à-Mousson in Lorraine, and Denain-Anzin or Nord-Est in the Nord, did not employ more than 5,000 to 7,000 people before the First World War. Nevertheless, French ironmasters' business position was solidly entrenched in the Parisian business community. Many companies had their head office in the capital, even though their plants might be far away in the regions.[25]

Big business in the British heavy industries differed from both its German and French counterparts. There was a number of very large firms, but most of them had diversified their production into shipbuilding and armaments. This was especially the case with the sector's three leading firms: Vickers, placed by some commentators ahead of Krupp in 1914;[26] their old rivals Armstrong Whitworth; and John Brown. They all employed more than 20,000 workers; but the shipbuilding industry

[22] P. Fritsch, *Les Wendel, rois de l'acier français* (Paris, 1976), 68, 147.

[23] See J. A. Roy, *Histoire de la famille Schneider et du Creusot* (Paris, 1962).

[24] M. Rust, 'Business and Politics in the Third Republic: The Comité des Forges and the French Steel Industry, 1896–1914', unpub. Ph.D. thesis (Princeton University, 1973), 23–4.

[25] See J. M. Moine, *Les Barons du fer* (Nancy, 1989).

[26] C. Trebilcock, *The Vickers Brothers: Armaments and Enterprise, 1854–1914* (London, 1977), 31.

included several other large companies such as Harland & Wolff, Cammel-Laird, Workman Clark, or Beardmore.[27] In terms of overall output, the British iron and steel industry stood somewhat between France and Germany, with 10,425,000 tons of pig iron and 7,787,000 tons of crude steel in 1913. Yet British metal manufacturing companies were much closer to their French than to their German counterparts both in terms of size and of degree of integration. The two largest firms, however, Guest, Keen & Nettlefolds and Bolckow Vaughan, which employed respectively 21,700 and 18,000 employees, were also among the country's major coal producers. As in France, only two other iron and steel manufacturers employed more than 10,000 people before 1914, Stewarts & Lloyds and Dorman Long. Stewarts & Lloyds was the result of the 1902 merger between the largest tube-maker of Scotland and the largest tube-maker in England, while Dorman Long merged in the same year with Bell Brothers. No real giant firm emerged in the British coal industry, by then 'one of the economic wonders of the world', accounting for 25 per cent of global coal production in 1909–13.[28] Even though the industry was more than seven times as large as its French counterpart, it was much less concentrated, the top ten producers accounting for only about 10 per cent of output.[29] Large firms were of comparable size and number in the two countries.

A long historiographical tradition has judged and condemned the British steel industry and its leaders for entrepreneurial failure, although they were rehabilitated in the 1970s by the then 'new' economic history to which their decisions appeared entirely rational. This debate cannot be reopened here.[30] Whatever its performance, the iron and steel industry was an essential component of British big business in Edwardian England. Yet there is little doubt that it was less in the forefront than its Continental counterpart. There are two reasons for this. The first reason is that British iron and steel industrialists did not set up companies of the size reached by their German competitors. Why this should have been the case has aroused much discussion, though demand conditions seem to have been the major factor. Briefly stated, Britain was a mature, slowly expand-

[27] See S. Pollard and P. Robertson, *The British Shipbuilding Industry, 1870–1914* (Cambridge, Mass., 1979).

[28] M. Dintenfass, *Managing Industrial Decline: The British Coal Industry between the Wars* (Columbus, Oh., 1992), 3.

[29] R. Church, *The History of the British Coal Industry*, iii. *1830–1913: Victorian Pre-eminence* (Oxford, 1986), 399.

[30] On this question, see especially D. Burn, *The Economic History of Steelmaking, 1867–1939* (Cambridge, 1940); T. H. Burnham and G. O. Hoskins, *Iron and Steel in Britain* (London, 1943); P. Temin, 'The Relative Decline of the British Steel Industry', in H. Rosovsky (ed.), *Industrialization in Two Systems* (New York, 1966); D. McCloskey, *Economic Maturity and Entrepreneurial Decline: British Iron and Steel Industry, 1870–1913* (Cambridge, Mass., 1973); B. Elbaum, 'The Steel Industry to 1914', in B. Elbaum and W. Lazonick (eds.), *The Decline of the British Economy* (Oxford, 1986).

ing market, while the faster-growing markets of Germany and America were closed to her producers by protective tariffs. Free trade at home reinforced this situation, the more so as Britain tended to specialize in higher-quality open hearth steel, more suitable for shipbuilding, which absorbed as much as 30 per cent of British steel output by 1910–13. And in these conditions, the import of foreign steel for re-rolling was often more advantageous than investment into integrated plants. The second reason is that big business was already much more diversified in Britain than in Germany and France; heavy industry was one among a number of other important sectors.

THE DIVERSITY OF BRITISH BIG BUSINESS

It is widely assumed that the large firm emerged in capital goods in Germany, and in consumer goods in Britain. At first sight this seems obvious. One only has to glance at the list of the fifty largest industrial companies in Britain in 1905, ranked by capital,[31] to be struck by the number of breweries. There were no less than fifteen, including Watney, Combe, Reid with a share capital of more than £6 million, Guinness with £4.5 million, Bass with £2.7 million, Whitbread with £2.3 million. Most of them—Guinness was the exception—had to raise vast amounts of capital in the 'scramble for property' of the late 1880s and 1890s, when brewers paid increasingly inflated prices to purchase public houses.[32] Property owners they might have been, but the top breweries were none the less large companies, though they were smaller if measured by workforce: even the largest among them did not employ more than 3,500 to 4,000 people. In the food component of the branded consumer goods industry, firms such as Cadbury, Fry, and Rowntree employed a similar number of people, but worked with a much smaller capital.[33]

The largest British company in 1907 was Imperial Tobacco, with £15.5 million share capital, appreciably more than Krupp, whose capital was a mere £9 million. The company was established in 1901 through the merger of thirteen tobacco manufacturers in order to resist the American offensive on the British market. The overwhelmingly dominant force in the combination was the firm W. D. & H. O. Wills, of Bristol, which controlled

[31] See the list established by P. Payne in 'The Emergence of Large-Scale Companies in Great Britain, 1870–1914', *Economic History Review*, 20/3 (1967), and Hannah in *Rise of the Corporate Economy*.

[32] See T. R. Gourvish and R. G. Wilson, *The British Brewing Industry 1830–1980* (Cambridge, 1994), 267–313.

[33] R. Fitzgerald, *Rowntree and the Marketing Revolution 1862–1969* (Cambridge, 1995), 223, 616. The capital of Rowntree was £400,000 in 1907; that of Fry was £1,000,000. The biscuit manufacturer Huntley & Palmers was the only firm in the industry to reach larger dimensions, with £2,400,000 capital and 6,500 employees in 1907. See T. A. B. Corley, *Quaker Enterprise in Biscuits: Huntley and Palmers of Reading, 1822–1972* (London, 1972).

nearly 60 per cent of the company's capital at its foundation. Wills's prodi-
gious rise in the late nineteenth century dated from the purchase in 1883
of the exclusive patent of the Bonsack cigarette-making machine, soon to
secure them a 55 per cent market share.[34] Big business was also strongly
represented in the British textile industry. The wave of horizontal mergers
of the last years of the nineteenth century gave birth to a number of huge
companies, whether measured by capital or workforce. The largest British
employer in 1907 was the Fine Cotton Spinners & Doublers' Association,
with 30,000 workers and £4.5 million share capital; the company was
founded in 1898 through the merger of thirty-one cotton-spinning firms,
some more than 100 years old, and introduced from the start a centralized control and co-ordination between the constituent firms. The Calico
Printers' Association employed more than 20,000 workers with £5 million
share capital; it was founded in 1899, but took a few years before being
able to rationalize what was at first a mere federation of family partnerships. The Bleachers' Association, founded in 1900, had a capital of more
than £4.5 million and more than 11,000 employees. The immensely successful firm of J. & P. Coats, thread manufacturers, was the country's third
largest company with £10 million share capital; it employed nearly 13,000
people.[35]

Emphasizing the strength of the consumer goods industry is, however,
only part of the story. The main characteristic of British big business in
the early twentieth century was its diversity. In the United Kingdom, big
business had by then penetrated *all* industrial sectors, including the 'new'
industries, even though the latter were not as strong as in Germany. We
have already noted the presence of large firms in the heavy industries. In
chemicals, the largest European company in 1907 was not German, but
British. This was United Alkali, created in 1905 by the merger of all the
British producers of soda using the Leblanc process, who were threatened
by the users of the more economic Solvay process. However, despite its
£5 million share capital and 12,000 employees, United Alkali is one of the
best examples of a corporate giant with feet of clay: the firm was soon to
decline, a victim of its dependence on an obsolete technology. But other
major firms quickly appeared, in the first place United Alkali's main competitor, Brunner Mond & Co., which had secured in 1883 the rights to use
the Solvay process in Britain; and the Nobel Dynamite Trust Company,
the main subsidiary of the international dynamite trust created by Alfred

---

[34] See B.W. E. Alford, *W. D. & H. O. Wills and the Development of the UK Tobacco Industry,
1786–1965* (London, 1973).
[35] H. W. Macrosty, *The Trust Movement in British Industry* (London, 1907), 117–54; A. C.
Howe, 'Dixon, Sir Alfred Herbert (1857–1920), Cotton Manufacturer', in D. Jeremy (ed.), *Dictionary of Business Biography*, 5 vols. (London, 1984–86), vol. ii, and 'Lee, Lennox Bertram
(1864–1949), Calico Printer', in Jeremy (ed.), *Dictionary of Business Biography*, vol. iii.

Nobel, their share capital approaching £3 million in 1907.[36] Lever Brothers was growing even more rapidly in another field of the chemical industry, the manufacture of soap. The capital of the firm founded in 1885 by William Lever, and registered as a limited company in 1894, had risen to almost £5 million in 1907 and over £10 million in 1913.[37] These successes, however, should not conceal the weaknesses of the British chemical industry, which had enjoyed world dominance in the nineteenth century: not only was it threatened in its traditional stronghold, heavy chemicals, but it hardly made any inroads in its most dynamic field, organic chemistry and its application to dyestuffs.

The situation looked even more alarming in electrical engineering, where there was no company even remotely approaching the size of the German giants. And yet the General Electric Company (GEC) and British Westinghouse, a subsidiary of the American Westinghouse Electric and Manufacturing Co., had reached a respectable size before 1914. British Westinghouse was conceived on a gigantic scale in 1899 by George Westinghouse, the founder of the American parent company, and after the reductions implemented a few years later it employed 5,000 people by 1907. The General Electric Company was founded much more modestly in 1887 by two Bavarian immigrants, Hugo Hirst and Gustav Byng, and grew steadily to employ 6,000 people twenty years later.[38] In mechanical engineering, Britain's competitive advantage lay in textile machinery; the workforce of the major firms was around 4,000 to 5,000, though the undisputed leader in the field, Platt Brothers, which enjoyed world supremacy, employed 12,000 people in 1907.[39] In railway equipment, the Metropolitan Amalgamated Railway Carriage & Wagon Company, created by Dudley Docker in 1902 through the successful combination of five manufacturers of rolling of stock, employed nearly 14,000 people.[40] In the oil industry, the Royal Dutch Shell group, formed by the amalgamation in 1906 of Royal Dutch and the Shell Transport & Trading Company, was the world's second most powerful group behind Standard Oil. And even though Shell only controlled 40 per cent of the group, the latter worked under the British flag and had its headquarters in London. Finally, though

[36] W. J. Reader, *Imperial Chemical Industries: A History*, i. *The Forerunners, 1870–1926* (Oxford, 1970).

[37] See C. Wilson, *The History of Unilever*, 2 vols. (London, 1954), vol. i; W. J. Reader, 'Lever, William Hesketh, 1st Viscount Leverhulme of the Western Isles (1851–1925), Soap and Food Manufacturer', in Jeremy (ed.), *Dictionary of Business Biography*, vol. iii.

[38] See R. Jones and O. Marriott, *Anatomy of a Merger: A History of GEC, AEI and English Electric* (London, 1970); R. P. T. Davenport-Hines, 'Hirst, Hugo, Lord Hirst (1863–1943), Electrical Engineering Entrepreneur', in Jeremy (ed.), *Dictionary of Business Biography*, vol. iii.

[39] See D. A. Farnie, 'The Textile Machine-Making Industry and the World Market, 1870–1960', *Business History*, 32/4 (1990).

[40] See R. P. T. Davenport-Hines, *Dudley Docker: The Life and Times of a Trade Warrior* (Cambridge, 1984).

public utility companies were often municipally owned and rarely reached big business proportions before 1914, the venerable Gas, Light & Coke Company, founded in 1812, which supplied gas to the London area, was the largest of its kind in Europe and one of Britain's largest companies with £21.6 million capital.[41]

More, and earlier, than elsewhere in Europe, big business penetrated the service industries in Britain. The most conspicuous instance was, not surprisingly, shipping. Britain still owned some 40 per cent of the world's steam tonnage in 1914, and vessels under British flag carried some 50 per cent of all international trade by volume in 1912. In 1900 ten shipping companies had a tonnage exceeding 100,000 tons, as against three in France and Germany.[42] The consolidation which took place in the first decade of the twentieth century saw the emergence of the so-called 'big five': Cunard, Furness Withy, Ellerman Lines, Royal Mail Steam Packet, and Peninsular & Oriental Steam Navigation Company (P. & O.).[43] Dock companies also reached giant sizes: the capital of the London and India Docks (formed in 1901 by the merger of the London and St Katharine Docks and the East and West India Docks) reached £11 million. Mostly unknown—and unsuspectedly large—firms also emerged in the world of international trade and commerce. Merchant houses were traditionally medium-sized family partnerships. However, a number of them turned themselves into investment groups, controlling a variety of overseas subsidiaries in trading, manufacturing, mining, or financial enterprises. The capital of groups controlled by merchant houses such as E. D. Sassoon & Co., Finlay & Co., Ralli Brothers, or Butterfly & Swire in the Far East, Balfour Williamson & Co. in South America, or Knoop in Russia has been estimated at above £4 million, far in excess of the partners' capital in the controlling London firm.[44]

Retail trade also reached big business proportions in Britain in the late nineteenth century, with not only large department stores such as Whiteleys and Harrods, which employed some 6,000 people in 1907, but also chain stores, which only emerged in continental Europe after the Second World War. Before 1914, Thomas Lipton and Home & Colonial Stores were already fully fledged retailing chains, the former with 242 shops in Britain, 38 branches abroad, and £2.5 million capital in 1898, when it was con-

[41] See P. Chantler, *The British Gas Industry: An Economic Study* (Manchester, 1938); T. I. Williams, *A History of the British Gas Industry* (Oxford, 1981).

[42] Michael Smith, 'The Unlikely Success of Chargeurs Réunis', *Entreprises et histoire*, 6 (1994), 23.

[43] G. Boyce, *Information, Mediation and Institutional Development: The Rise of Large-Scale Enterprise in British Shipping, 1870–1919* (Manchester, 1995). This was the situation following the merger in 1914 between P. & O. and the British India Steam Navigation Company, one of the country's largest companies.

[44] S. D. Chapman, 'British Based Investment Groups before 1914', *Economic History Review*, 38/2 (1985), 230–51. These groups have not been included in the estimates of the number of large companies in Britain given in Table 1.1.

verted into a limited company.[45] W. H. Smith experienced a similar growth in newspaper distribution, its workforce increasing from 4,156 in 1887 to 8,285 in 1905 and 10,358 in 1911.[46] The two decades before the First World War saw the emergence of the cheap press, which in turn marked the entry of newspaper publishing into the world of big business. The *Daily Mail*, launched by Alfred Harmsworth (later Lord Northcliffe) in 1896, was the first newspaper whose circulation reached 1 million copies by the turn of the century, at the time of the Boer War. Other papers were founded or acquired by the same proprietor, including the *Daily Mirror*, launched in 1903, whose circulation reached 1.2 million by 1914. The *Observer* was acquired in 1905, and *The Times* in 1908. Harmsworth's company, Associated Newspapers, was incorporated in 1906 with £1.6 million capital.[47]

Finally, both the extent and nature of big business in Britain were affected by the country's dominant position in the world economy, and the possession of an immense colonial empire. As we have seen, the City of London was the seat of many financial companies, which channelled a large portion of British capital into a variety of foreign investments before 1914.[48] Large companies operating abroad were most prominent in mining. The Rio Tinto Company, founded in 1873 to exploit copper mines in Spain, soon became one of the world's leading suppliers of sulphur and copper and by 1913 had extended its productive facilities to Britain, Algeria, and the United States.[49] The South African gold and diamond mining companies attracted a large amount of foreign direct investment in the 1880s and 1890s. The diamond conglomerate De Beers Consolidated Mines, established in 1888 by Alfred Beit, Cecil Rhodes, and Julius Wernher (and registered in Kimberley), had a capital of £4.5 million, the Consolidated Gold Fields of South Africa £3.25 million. Telegraph companies were a legacy from an earlier age. The Anglo-American Telegraph Company, with £7 million capital, had been founded in 1866 to lay the first Atlantic cable between Britain and the United States; while the Eastern Telegraph Company, with £6 million, was created by the same group in 1872 to link Britain with the Far East.[50]

[45] See D. Oddy, 'Lipton, Sir Thomas Johnstone (1850–1931), Grocer', in Jeremy (ed.), *Dictionary of Business Bigraphy*, vol. iii; P. Mathias, *Retailing Revolution* (London, 1967).

[46] C. Wilson, *First with the News: The History of W. H. Smith 1792–1972* (London, 1985), 448.

[47] See C. Shaw, 'Harmsworth, Alfred Charles William, Viscount Northcliffe (1865–1922), Newspaper and Periodicals Proprietor', in Jeremy (ed.), *Dictionary of Business Biography*, vol. iii.

[48] See P. L. Cottrell, *British Overseas Investment in the Nineteenth Century* (London, 1975); M. Edelstein, *Overseas Investment in the Age of High Imperialism: The United Kingdom, 1850–1914* (London, 1982); L. Davis and R. Huttenback, *Mammon and the Pursuit of Empire: The Political Economy of British Imperialism, 1860–1912* (Cambridge, 1987).

[49] See C. Harvey, *The Rio Tinto Company: An Economic History of a Leading International Mining Concern 1873–1954* (Penzance, 1981).

[50] See H. Barty-King, *Girdle round the Earth: The Story of Cable and Wireless and its Predecessors to Mark the Group's Jubilee 1929–1979* (London, 1979).

THE NEW INDUSTRIES IN GERMANY

The fascination provoked by the rise of the German electrical and chemical industries in the late nineteenth century has had few parallels since the beginnings of industrialization. The combination of bold entrepreneurship, application of science to industry, a high level of business organization, and availability of long-term financial facilities has been seen as the optimum conditions for the breakthrough of the second industrial revolution. The German electrical and chemical industries have thus received a great deal of attention—deservedly so, given the importance of these industries in the modern industrial world—but at the risk of over-emphasizing their weight in the world of German big business before 1914. Alfred Chandler in *Scale and Scope* devotes more pages to chemicals and to electrical machinery than to metals before 1914. Although this is understandable from his perspective, the creation of industrial capabilities, the fact remains that the companies listed under 'primary metal industries' accounted for 37 per cent of the total assets of the German 200 largest industrial companies in 1913, as against 14 per cent for 'electric and electronic equipment' and 13 per cent for 'chemicals'.[51]

The largest companies were in electrical engineering. Two giants dominated the industry: Siemens and the Allgemeine Elektricitäts-Gesellschaft (AEG). The oldest company was Siemens & Halske, founded in 1847 by Werner Siemens. The firm prospered in the following decades by producing and installing cables, telegraphs, signals, and other measuring devices. However, the boom in the German electrical industry did not occur until the 1880s with the development of new products, especially lamps and telephones as well as heavy material such as generators, accumulators, transformers, and other equipment for power stations, factories, tramways, and railways. The AEG was founded in 1883 by Emil Rathenau as the Deutsche Edison Gesellschaft to take advantage of these new opportunities, changing its name to AEG four years later. Growth was breathtaking: its capital rose from 5 million marks (£250,000) in 1887 to 100 million twenty years later; its workforce from 2,000 to 30,000. By 1890 AEG had overtaken Siemens as the largest German electrical company. Competition forced Siemens & Halske to react. Following Werner von Siemens's retirement in 1890, it turned itself into a limited company in 1897, introduced a new centralized organization, and took over one of its competitors, Schuckert & Co., in 1903. Siemens henceforth comprised two separate companies, though partly managed by the same men: Siemens Schuckertwerke became the high-voltage division of the group, Siemens & Halske its low-voltage division as well as the group's holding company.

---

[51] Calculated from Chandler, *Scale and Scope*, 696–704.

Siemens's workforce rose from 3,000 in 1890 to 57,000 in 1913; its turnover from 16.5 to 415 million marks.[52]

The industry was strongly oligopolistic, Siemens and AEG controlling about 70 per cent of the market. Following a series of mergers and acquisitions, only four large companies remained in existence in 1905: these were, besides Siemens and AEG, Bergmann Elektrizitäts-Werke and Felten & Guilleaume-Lahmeyer. Siemens and especially AEG also had stakes in electricity generating companies. The Berliner Elektrizitäts-Werke, one of the main power-stations in Berlin, and the only truly large company in electricity supply with £3,200,000 capital, was a subsidiary of AEG. The electrical industry and its leaders enjoyed enormous prestige in Imperial Germany, and with two companies among the country's top ten formed a highly visible yet, compared to banks and iron and steel companies, only a small part of the world of big business in Germany.

The situation was rather similar in the chemical industry. The 'big three' in the early twentieth century were already Badische Anilin und Soda Fabrik (BASF), Bayer, and Meister, Lucius & Brüning (Hoechst), all founded between 1863 and 1865. They embodied Germany's overwhelming superiority in organic chemistry, especially in dye products, with 75 to 80 per cent of world production in 1913, the 'big three' alone accounting for some 60 per cent. The major companies also diversified their production, in heavy chemistry (sulphuric acid, chlorine), partly as backward integration to fulfil their own requirements, but also in pharmaceutical products and celluloid films.[53] Firms, however, were not as large as their counterparts in electricals. The 'big three' were of roughly the same size. Yet, whether measured by capital or by workforce, they did not count among the largest corporations of the day. In 1907 none of them employed more than 9,000 people. Hoechst had the highest share capital with £1,280,000, which put it only in 73rd position in an overall ranking of German companies (and in 27th position among industrial companies only). But they were growing rapidly: in 1913 Bayer and BASF were respectively the 13th and 14th largest German industrial enterprises according to total assets[54] and both employed more than 10,000 people.

[52] See J. Kocka, 'Family and Bureaucracy in German Industrial Management, 1850–1914: Siemens in Comparative Perspective', *Business History Review*, 45/2 (1971), and *Unternehmensverwaltung und Angestelltenschaft am Beispiel Siemens, 1847–1914* (Stuttgart, 1969); G. von Siemens, *History of the House of Siemens*, 2 vols. (Freiburg, 1957); *50 Jahre AEG* (Berlin, 1959); Chandler, *Scale and Scope*.

[53] J. Beer, *The Emergence of the German Dye Industry* (Urbana, Ill., 1959); F. Haber, *The Chemical Industry during the Nineteenth Century* (Oxford, 1958), and *The Chemical Industry 1900–1930: International Growth and Technical Change* (Oxford, 1971); Chandler, *Scale and Scope*.

[54] W. Feldenkirchen, 'Concentration in German Industry, 1870–1939', in H. Pohl (ed.), *The Concentration Process in the Entrepreneurial Economy since the Late 19th Century* (Stuttgart, 1988), 144.

In other industrial sectors, large companies were the exception. In textiles, the Norddeutsche Wollkammerei- und Kammgarnspinnerei (Nordwolle) employed 8,000 people in 1907. Other firms of some significance in textiles, such as the woolcomber Stöhr & Co., or in food and drinks, such as the brewer Schultheiss or the chocolate-maker Stollwerck, hardly employed more than 2,000 to 3,000 people. Firms were of a similar size in mechanical engineering (Demag, Deutz, Humboldt) with the exception of the Bavarian company MAN (Maschinenfabrik Augsburg Nüremberg), employing nearly 12,000 workers in 1907. Another company, the manufacturer of railway equipment Orenstein & Koppel, enjoyed rapid growth in the few years preceding the war, its workforce increasing from 3,700 to 15,000 and its capital from £550,000 to £2,225,000 between 1907 and 1913. Public utilities in water, gas, and electricity supply were often municipally owned, and those in the private sector did not develop into truly large companies before the First World War.[55] In the nascent oil industry, the initiative was taken by the big banks. The Deutsche Bank founded Deutsche Petroleum while the Disconto-Gesellschaft took control of Deutsche Erdöl, founded by Rudolf Nöllenburg.[56] Their capital had reached £2 million by 1913, but they did not experience the rise of their English competitors and their growth was to be halted by the war.

Unlike Britain, big business made few inroads in the German service industries. One major exception was shipping. The two leading companies Hamburg-Amerika Packetfahrt AG (HAPAG) of Hamburg and Norddeutscher Lloyd of Bremen were among the country's largest companies, each with £6,250,000 capital, and although the industry as a whole was smaller than its British counterpart, the HAPAG, under Albert Ballin's leadership, became the world's largest shipping company by the eve of the war. Less is known about merchant houses, but they are unlikely to have remotely approached the size of the leading British investment groups, many of which had in fact been founded by German immigrants keen to take advantage of the opportunities offered by Britain's position in the world economy.[57] Hamburg's merchants, for example, were small, or at best medium-sized, family firms.[58] Attempts at creating large firms in retail trade remained embryonic. On the other hand, the diffusion of the cheap press did lead to the rise of a few newspaper magnates, such as Rudolf Mosse, Leopold Ullstein, and August Scherl, all based in Berlin.

[55] The Rheinischwestfälisches Elektrizitätswerk (RWE) had a capital of £1.3 million in 1907, the Wasserwerke für das Nördliche Westfälische Kohlenrevier £1.1 million, and the Deutsche Continental Gas Gesellschaft £1.05 million.

[56] J. Riesser, *Die deutsche Grossbanken und ihre Konzentration* (Jena, 1912), 342; F. Pinner, *Deutsche Wirtschaftsführer* (Berlin, 1924), 232–5.

[57] S. D. Chapman, 'The International Houses: The Continental Contribution to British Commerce, 1800–1860', *Journal of European Economic History*, 6 (1977).

[58] N. Ferguson, *Paper and Iron: Hamburg Business and German Politics in the Era of Inflation, 1897–1927* (Cambridge, 1995), 36–7.

No German newspaper, however, had a circulation comparable to what was then attained in Britain or France. That of the *Berliner Tagblatt*, launched by Rudolf Mosse in 1872, was 230,000 on the eve of the war. Newspaper companies, however, were reaching a significant size: August Scherl GmbH was floated in 1911 with 20 million marks (£1 million) capital.[59] Nevertheless, all this only amounted to a handful of companies and did not really broaden the scope of German big business in the early twentieth century.

BIG BUSINESS IN FRANCE

Big business was more restricted in France. Before 1914 it displayed neither the characteristic German strength in the new industries, nor the diversity of opportunities existing in the British economy. Nevertheless, outside banking and the heavy industries, at least one large company had emerged in every area of business activity. Perhaps surprisingly the two largest French industrial companies, measured by capital, were in chemicals (Saint-Gobain) and electrical engineering (Thomson-Houston), each with £2.4 million. Saint-Gobain had been founded by Colbert in 1665 and was by far the oldest large European company still in existence in the early, or indeed the late, twentieth century. Its activities were in fact divided between chemicals and glass-making. The former accounted for 62 per cent of the company's profits between 1890 and 1913, mainly through the production of sulphuric acid and superphosphates, which made up respectively 41 and 47 per cent of French total production.[60] With the exception of the Solvay group, strongly established in France as well as in Germany, the other French chemical companies remained small or medium-sized firms. Kuhlmann, which was to become one of the country's leading companies, did not employ more than 2,000 to 2,500 people before the war.

In electrical engineering, the market leader Thomson-Houston mostly relied on the use of foreign technology. The Compagnie Française pour l'Exploitation des Procédés Thomson-Houston, known as Thomson-Houston Française (THF), had been established in 1893 by an agreement between the General Electric Company of America and a group of French industrialists, mostly connected with the gas industry (through the Compagnie pour la Fabrication des Compteurs et du Matériel des Usines à Gaz). The new company was granted the exclusive right to manufacture and sell material from the American parent company in France and her colonial empire, as well as in Spain, Portugal, and Italy. Although General

[59] K. Koszyk, *Deutsche Presse im 19. Jahrhundert* (Berlin, 1966), 280–95.
[60] J. P. Daviet, *Un destin international: La Compagnie de Saint-Gobain de 1830 à 1939* (Paris, 1988).

Electric held some 40 per cent of THF's capital at its foundation, its share
diminished rapidly with successive capital increases and the company
passed almost entirely into French hands. THF's domination of the French
electrical industry was overwhelming before 1914, especially as a supplier
of equipment to tramway and electricity supply companies (with as much
as a 60 per cent market share) and as a holding company with a controlling stake in a wide network of electricity companies.[61] The Compagnie
Générale d'Électricité, a future giant of the industry, was founded in 1898
by Pierre Azaria, a Cairo-born Armenian, through the merger of three
small to medium-sized companies. In the next fifteen years it solidly
established itself in all fields of the electrical industry, though two-thirds
of its turnover still derived from its metallurgical activities.[62] However,
with hardly more than 2,500 employees in 1906[63] it was not yet a large
company. Mechanical engineering had traditionally been weak in France.
Nevertheless, the Société Alsacienne de Constructions Mécaniques, with
more than 10,000 employees, was as large as any other company in this
sector in Europe. Founded in 1826, it manufactured locomotives, steam
engines, and textile machinery;[64] most of its works, however, were then
on German territory.

As in Germany, big business did not emerge in the French food and
drink industries, while tobacco was a state monopoly. The only arguable
exception was the sugar refinery Say which, with £1.52 million capital,
was one of the largest French industrial companies before 1914.[65] The
textile industry has long been the favoured example of those defending
the thesis of the Malthusianism of the French *patronat*, its reluctance to
create large firms through business concentration in order to preserve
family interests. In fact, French textile companies, a large number of which
employed between 2,000 and 3,000 workers, were not smaller than their
German counterparts. It was the size of the British firms which was the
exception. There were no large firms in the oil industry either; and though
the Rothschilds had been a major international force since 1886 through
their interests in the Caspian and Black Sea Petroleum Company, known
as Bnito by its Russian initials, they sold them to Royal Dutch in 1912. Oil
imports and distribution were undertaken by a dozen private firms; three
of them, Fenaille et Despaux, Desmarais Frères, and Les Fils de A. Deutsch,
controlled 60 per cent of the market.[66] Public utilities, on the other hand,

[61] See P. Lanthier, 'Les Constructions électriques en France: Financement et stratégies de
six groupes industriels internationaux, 1880–1940', thèse de doctorat (University of Paris-X
(Nanterre), 1988).
[62] See *Alcatel Alsthom: Histoire de la Compagnie Générale d'Électricité* (Paris, 1992).
[63] Archives Nationales, F12 8500/LH8h.d.31.
[64] See B. Dézert, *La Croissance industrielle et urbaine de la porte d'Alsace* (Paris, 1969).
[65] See J. Fiérain, *Les Raffineries de sucre des ports en France (XIXe–début XXe siècles)* (Paris,
1976).
[66] E. Faure, *La Politique française du pétrole* (Paris, 1938).

did give rise to a number of large companies, not only (unlike in Britain and Germany) in the water industry, with the Compagnie Générale des Eaux, but also in electricity supply, with the Compagnie Parisienne de Distribution d'Électricité, capitalized at £4 million.

French big business was stronger in the service industries. As in Britain and Germany, the major shipping companies—the Compagnie des Messageries Maritimes, founded in 1851 to provide subsidized postal service, and the Compagnie Générale Transatlantique, founded by the Péreire brothers in 1861—were among the country's largest companies. They were comparable in size (if measured by tonnage rather than capital) to their foreign competitors, even though the French position in world shipping fell from third to sixth between 1860 and 1910.[67] Little is known about French firms engaged in international trade; however, they are likely to have been closer in size to their German than to their British counterparts. But in retail trade France with Britain was a pioneer of the department store, that 'monument to bourgeois culture',[68] in particular with the Bon Marché, one of the oldest (founded 1869) and largest (4,500 employees in 1906) in the world, as well as other large Parisian stores such as the Louvre, Samaritaine, Printemps, and Galeries Lafayette. Chain stores, on the other hand, remained non-existent, with the exception of Hachette, W. H. Smith's counterpart, in newspaper distribution.[69] As in Britain, and more than in Germany, newspaper publishing was becoming big business in France. The popular press appeared even earlier than in Britain, with the *Petit Journal*'s circulation reaching 600,000 in 1880 and a million in 1890. It was, however, to decline, mainly because of competition from the *Petit Parisien*, whose circulation reached a million in 1902 and 1.45 million in 1913. Both the Société du 'Petit Journal' and the Société du 'Petit Parisien', Dupuy et Cie were newspaper groups, which published several other papers, mainly weekly magazines. They were thus sizeable companies, even though this was not necessarily reflected in their capital; this was especially the case with the Société du Petit Parisien, which never increased its original capital of 3 million francs (£120,000).[70] Finally, if French colonial companies were exceptionally profitable during this period,[71] such companies as the Phosphates et Chemins de Fer de Gafsa or Mokta-El-Hadid, with respectively £720,000 and £800,000, can only be

[67] Smith, 'Chargeurs Réunis'.

[68] B. Miller, *The Bon Marché: Bourgeois Culture and the Department Store, 1869–1928* (London, 1981), 3.

[69] See J. Mistler, *La Librairie Hachette de 1826 à nos jours* (Paris, 1964).

[70] C. Bellanger *et al.* (eds.), *Histoire générale de la presse française*, iii. *De 1871 à 1940* (Paris, 1972); F. Amaury, *Histoire du plus grand quotidien de la IIIe République: Le Petit Parisien, 1876–1914* (Paris, 1972).

[71] J. Marseille, *Empire colonial et capitalisme français: Histoire d'un divorce* (Paris, 1984), 110–13, who records rates of profit on capital of up to 123.4% for the Compagnie des Mines d'Ouasta and 84.6% for the Charbonnages du Tonkin.

considered as large companies within the context of the low capitalization of French business. The alleged weakness of French big business should thus be put in context. Consisting of a combination of groups of interests and large companies, the 'grandes affaires' were a prominent feature of French economy and society during the *belle époque*.

2

From the 1920s to the 1950s

The turmoils of the period described by Eric Hobsbawm as the 'Age of Catastrophe'[1] could hardly have left big business untouched, although the effects should not be over-emphasized. Two world wars and the most severe depression of the twentieth century did alter the international balance of economic and political power. Germany's ascendancy was momentarily shattered. France grew stronger until halted by the slump of the 1930s, followed by defeat and occupation. Britain, which had enjoyed the status of premier world power, had to cede world leadership to the United States. Within the European context, however, the general trend of the period was Britain's clear pre-eminence over her two main Continental rivals. At the same time, changes were taking place within the world of big business, as a result of three main factors: the growing importance of the new industries; higher levels of business concentration and attempts at industrial rationalization; and the growth of state intervention.

The impact of the new industries was felt most strongly in Britain and France, partly because of their relative backwardness in some of them, and partly because of their greater dynamism in others. The demands of the First World War led to a strong development of the chemical and electrical industries. They did not entirely catch up with their competitors in Germany, but certainly reached full 'big business' status in their own country. The more recent motor car industry had an even faster rise, with France taking an early lead before being overtaken by Britain in the 1930s.

The idea of economic rationalization enjoyed a vogue in big business circles in the 1920s. The basic principle was to produce more efficiently, and to achieve greater profits, which could be partly redistributed to the workforce in order to improve industrial relations. Rationalization thus implied plant modernization, best achieved through mergers. Merging two or more companies was the best way to limit the extent of overlap, to close the most outdated factories, and also to increase financial capacity so as to be able to meet the requirements of a vast modernization programme. Mergers were frequent in the 1920s, some on a spectacular scale, though in all three countries the objectives of rationalization were rarely successfully met. They came to an almost complete standstill in the

[1] E. Hobsbawm, *Age of Extremes: The Short Twentieth Century, 1914–1991* (London, 1994).

following decades—marked by economic depression, war, and reconstruction—and did not resume on a large scale until the 1960s.

State intervention in the economy reached hitherto unknown levels as a result of the constraints of the war economy and was to transform profoundly relationships between government and business in the twentieth century. The most fundamental measure was the direct control taken by the state, through nationalization, over key sectors of the economy. The Popular Front in France made a first step in this direction in 1936, by nationalizing railways and war-related industries and by reforming the constitution of the Bank of France. But it was in the aftermath of the Second World War that the movement swept Europe. Major nationalizations, about which there was an undoubted consensus, took place in Britain and France. Germany, however, stood aside from the movement: partly because of US opposition, but also as a result of the Christian Democrats and their neo-liberal project's victory in the 1949 elections, the first to be held in the new Federal Republic.[2] However, part of German manufacturing industry, besides public utilities, transport, and communication, was already in state hands. Its share extended to as much as 50 per cent of the automobile industry (through Volkswagen's direct ownership) and to 20 per cent of coal, iron, and steel, as well as substantial interests in shipbuilding and chemicals (in this case indirectly, through holding companies such as VEBA or VIAG).[3]

Did nationalized enterprises still belong to the world of big business? Yes and no. No, because big business means, at least to a certain extent, large private profits or the expectation of such profits, including through stock market operations; nationalized companies are obviously excluded from this capitalist logic. Yes, because nationalized companies often enjoyed a large degree of managerial autonomy and tended to operate according to the same principles as privately owned companies. This particularly applied to those belonging to the competitive sector of the economy, such as the French car-maker Renault nationalized in 1945, or the British steel industry nationalized somewhat unwillingly by Labour in 1949 before being de-nationalized—one did not yet talk of privatization—by the Conservatives in 1953. Railways and utilities, which formed the bulk of the post-war nationalizations, or even the coal industry, nationalized in both Britain and France, were in a different situation: the former were heavily regulated and partly publicly owned, the latter was a loss-making industry. In addition, with the rise of salaried managers, differences between the leaders of private and public compa-

---

[2] Good comparative analyses in A. Prost (ed.), 'Les Nationalisations d'après guerre en Europe occidentale', *Le Mouvement social*, 134 (1986).

[3] VEBA (Vereinigte Elektrizitäts- und Bergwerks AG), formed in 1927 by the state of Prussia, had interests in mining and electricity, VIAG (Vereinigte Industrie-Unternehmungen AG) in the metallurgical and chemical industries.

Table 2.1. Estimated number of large firms in Britain, France, and Germany, measured by paid-up capital, 1929 and 1953

	Britain	France	Germany
1929 (£3 m. or more)	186	2	55
1953 (£5 m. or more)	150	12	67

Sources: Stock Exchange Yearbook; Annuaire Desfossé; Handbuch der deutschen Aktiengesellschaften.

nies became, as we shall see, less marked, although far from totally non-existent.

From a big business perspective, the striking, often overlooked feature of the period is the widening of the gap separating Britain from the rest of Europe. This may surprise, granted that real GDP grew at the same rate of 1.3 per cent in Britain and Germany between 1913 and 1950, compared with a slower 1.1 per cent in France.[4] However, mainly as a result of territorial changes following two world wars, the overall size of the British economy became substantially larger than that of Germany. In 1913 Britain's GDP was 5 per cent higher than that of Germany; in 1950 the difference was 70 per cent. The gap with France remained more or less unchanged, with a slight decrease from 69 to 64 per cent.[5] The gap in GDP per head also remained significant, growing from a 54 to a 69 per cent difference between Britain and Germany during the same years, and again slightly decreasing from 47 to 36 per cent between Britain and France.[6]

Given these differences at the macro-economic level, one would expect Britain to have maintained the higher level of business development which she had already enjoyed in the early twentieth century. In fact she increased the gap with Germany and France by a wide margin, and in all sectors. The number of large companies in Britain rose significantly in the inter-war years, and again in the aftermath of the Second World War. In 1929 the number of companies working with a capital of £3 million or more was three times as high as in Germany (Table 2.1). Even measured by workforce, British firms then outdistanced their German competitors, with nearly 40 of them employing 10,000 people or more in 1929, as

[4] A. Maddison, *Dynamic Forces in Capitalist Development* (Oxford, 1991), 50.

[5] In 1985 US relative prices, the figures were, in $ million: 176,986 for Britain, 174,539 for Germany, and 108,738 for France in 1913; and 284,594 for Britain, 166,888 for Germany, and 173,569 for France in 1950; ibid. 199.

[6] The figures were, in dollars at 1985 US prices, 4,024 for Britain, 2,606 for Germany, and 2,734 for France in 1913; and 5,651 for Britain, 3,339 for Germany, and 4,149 for France in 1950; ibid. 6–7.

Table 2.2. Estimated number of large companies in Britain, France, and Germany, measured by workforce (10,000 employees or more), 1929 and 1953

	Britain	France	Germany
1929	39	22	27
1953	65	20	26

Sources: D. J. Jeremy, 'The Hundred Largest Employers in the United Kingdom, in Manufacturing and Non-manufacturing Industries, in 1907, 1935 and 1955', *Business History*, 33/1 (1991); H. Siegrist, 'Deutsche Grossunternehmen vom späten 19. Jahrhundert bis zur Weimarer Republik', *Geschichte und Gesellschaft*, 6 (1980); various yearbooks and directories; company monographs.

against 27 in Germany (Table 2.2). The growth of big business in Britain continued in the following decades. In 1955, 65 British firms employed 10,000 people or more; the workforce of 38 of them equalled or exceeded 20,000, as against 11 only in Germany. In financial terms, 38 British companies had a capital of £10 million or more, as against 15 in Germany and 3 only in France.

These differences tend to be obscured by the emergence in the 1920s of a few truly giant firms, on a scale hitherto unknown. There was, admittedly, no British or French firm approaching the size of the Vereinigte Stahlwerke in iron and steel, Siemens in electrical engineering, and IG Farben in chemicals, which each employed more than 100,000 people. The workforce of the two largest British employers in the mid-1930s, Unilever and ICI, stood respectively at 60,000 and 56,000. Nevertheless, taken as a whole, big business weighed much more heavily in Britain than in Germany, where the number of large firms remained remarkably stable: 27 industrial enterprises employed 10,000 people or more in 1929, and 26 in 1953 (there were already 23 in 1907). And following the dismantling of IG Farben and the Vereinigte Stahlwerke, Siemens was the only German company employing more than 100,000 people in the early 1950s. In France the *number* of large companies drew much nearer that of Germany in the inter-war years: 22 French firms employed more than 10,000 people in the late 1920s. As in Britain there were no equivalents to the German giants. The largest French employer in 1929 was the steel-maker de Wendel, with some 33,000 workers. However, big business was henceforth more evenly spread on either side of the Rhine, even though in terms of capital the devaluation of the franc widened the gap separating French companies from their largest European competitors. The number of large French companies slightly decreased after the Second World War following the nationalization of the collieries, amongst the largest firms in the country. The order of magnitude, however, remained the same as in Germany.

THE RISE OF BIG BUSINESS IN BRITAIN

Even more than early in the century, the new dimensions achieved by large firms were the result of far-reaching mergers. It is often forgotten that the first big wave of mergers which followed the First World War in Europe did not take place in the German chemical industry, but in British banking, shortly before the war ended. In 1918, five mergers took place, involving the ten largest banks in the country, and resulted in the formation of five huge banks which immediately came to be known as the 'big five': Barclays Bank, Lloyds Bank, the London Joint City and Midland Bank (which shortened its name to Midland Bank in 1923), the London County Westminster and Parr's Bank (from 1923 the Westminster Bank), and the National Provincial and Union Bank of London (from 1923 the National Provincial Bank).[7]

One of the consequences of this vast amalgamation movement was that the British banks became considerably larger than their German and French rivals, whether compared in terms of capital, deposits, or total assets. In 1928 the paid-up capital and total assets of the *smallest* of the 'big five', the National Provincial Bank, were respectively £9.48 million and £288 million. For the *largest* German bank, the Deutsche Bank, the figures were respectively £7.5 million and £146 million, and for the largest French bank, the Société Générale, £4 million and £86.5 million. In that year, the total assets of the Midland Bank, the largest British bank and indeed then the largest bank in the world, reached £408 million.[8] These differences, however, were also due to the difficulties encountered by the German and French banks, which will be discussed in a moment. At the very time when the City's world financial leadership was being challenged by New York, the gap separating London from the major Continental centres was actually widening. However, despite their new gigantic size, the clearing banks remained only one of the wheels, though an essential one, of the mechanism of the City. Rather than taking entrepreneurial initiatives, whether in the City or the British economy as a

---

[7] J. Sykes, *The Amalgamation Movement in English Banking, 1825–1924* (London, 1926); A. R. Holmes and E. Green, *Midland* (London, 1986).

[8] *Banking Almanac* (1928).

whole, they were content for decades to operate a price cartel and remain strictly within the frontiers of deposit banking, while from the 1930s their assets were dominated by government debt. Their working margin diminished after the war, as they became the main target of the financial authorities in their policy of credit control.[9] The leading merchant banks, despite being much smaller in size (Schroder's capital, for example, was £3.2 million in 1929[10]), were thus able to remain highly influential not only in the worlds of big business and high finance but also through their close relationship with the political sphere.

British big business was already fairly diversified before 1914, and in that respect more modern than its German and French counterparts. This continued during the inter-war years. What changed, however, was the balance between sectors, in particular between the so-called 'old' and 'new' industries. The 'new' industries might not have replaced the old ones, in terms of either share of industrial output or employment,[11] but they did substantially increase their share of the world of big business. Large enterprises flourished in the chemical, electrical engineering, motor car, oil, rubber, and aerospace industries, and henceforth formed the very heart of British big business. In these sectors, British firms grew faster than their French counterparts in the three decades following the First World War. They drew nearer to their German counterparts in electricals and chemicals in the inter-war years and overtook them in the aftermath of the Second World War; while they enjoyed from the start a decisive advantage in other 'new' industries such as motor cars, rubber, oil, and aeroplanes.

In 1930 the two largest British industrial companies, whether measured by capital or workforce, were Imperial Chemical Industries (ICI) and Lever Brothers, with respectively £76.7 million and £56.8 million capital and 50,000 and 60,000 employees. ICI was formed in 1926 by the amalgamation of four chemical companies under the joint leadership of Brunner Mond & Co. and Nobel Industries, the latter itself resulting from the earlier merger, in 1918, of the main explosives producers, whose business had greatly expanded during the war.[12] Two weaker companies joined the new combine: United Alkali, the decline of which had been temporarily halted by the war; and British Dyestuffs Corporation (BDC), established under the auspices of the British government in order to ensure the country's supply of dyestuffs during the war. That ICI should often be compared to IG Farben, the giant chemical combine formed a

[9] See M. Collins, *Money and Banking in the U.K.: A History* (London, 1988).
[10] R. Roberts, *Schroders: Merchants & Bankers* (London, 1992), 530.
[11] See a discussion of the issue in B. Alford, 'New Industries for Old? British Industry between the Wars', in R. Floud and D. McCloskey, *The Economic History of Britain since 1700*, ii: *1860 to the 1970s* (Cambridge, 1981), 308–31.
[12] See W. J. Reader, *Imperial Chemical Industries* (Oxford, 1970), i. 448–64.

year earlier in Germany by a similar nation-wide merger, is a tribute to the British chemical industry and its progress during the First World War. ICI undoubtedly provided Britain with a powerful international group. It had a higher share capital than its German rival, but a significantly smaller turnover (some £24 million as against more than £48 million for IG Farben in 1930) and workforce. Twenty-five years later, in 1955, ICI's workforce had more than doubled, to 115,000 employees, exceeding those of Bayer, BASF, and Hoechst combined. Its directors in fact feared that ICI might 'grow too big to be manageable', and considered the possibility of divesting some of its activities, such as metals.[13] But ICI did not only grow in size. It successfully integrated its various constituent parts, invested heavily in research and development, and, despite some misjudgements, positively altered the relative importance of its activities, away from heavy chemicals and explosives and increasingly into dyestuffs, plant protection, fertilizers, pharmaceuticals, plastics, fibres, and petrochemicals.[14]

As for Lever Brothers, its size in the late 1920s resulted from a frenzy of acquisitions of both competitors at home and suppliers of raw materials abroad. This led it to control some 158 associated companies and 60 per cent of the British production of soap by 1921; but it also put the entire business at risk following the foolhardy purchase of the Niger Company for more than £8 million in 1920.[15] In 1929 Lever Brothers merged with the Dutch company Margarine Unie under the name of Unilever. The capital of the new group was nearly £100 million, making it the largest company in Europe, though the two parent companies, Unilever Limited in Great Britain and Unilever NV in Holland, remained legally distinct. Behind these two giants, a number of other large firms emerged in the British chemical industry during this period: Reckitt & Sons in washing additives such as starch and blue; Boots Pure Drug in pharmaceuticals, which combined manufacture with retailing through chain stores and employed 18,000 people in 1935 and more than 35,000 in 1955; British Oxygen Company (BOC) in industrial gas; Fisons in fertilizers, its capital increasing from £520,000 in 1929 to £7.7 million in 1952 following a dynamic campaign of acquisitions of smaller fertilizer concerns and other chemical manufacturers by its chairman Clavering Fison;[16] Beecham, the pill-making business, which extended its activities under the chairman-ship of the financier Philip Hill, acquiring in particular Macleans and the County Perfumery (makers of the hair preparation Brylcream) in

[13] Ibid. ii. 465. This was to be effected in 1962 with the flotation of Imperial Metals Industries.

[14] Ibid., *passim*.

[15] C. Wilson, *The History of Unilever* (London, 1954), i. 247–66.

[16] M. Moss, 'Fison, Sir Frank Guy Clavering, Chemical Manufacturing company Chairman', in D. Jeremy (ed.), *Dictionary of Business Biography*, 5 vols. (London, 1984–6), vol. ii.

1938–9.[17] There was therefore a depth in British chemicals, prefiguring the emergence of giant pharmaceutical companies in the later decades of the twentieth century.

In electrical engineering, five British firms employed more than 10,000 people in 1935, and eleven in 1955. This was a spectacular increase from the pre-1914 situation, even though none of them equalled the size of the two German giants Siemens and AEG during the inter-war years. The two leaders were Associated Electrical Industries (AEI) and General Electric Company (GEC). Like several of the new British industrial giants, AEI was the product of the merger in 1929 of British Thomson-Houston (BTH) and Metrovick, the former British Westinghouse, taken over by Vickers in 1917 and then resold as part the latter firm's restructuring process. At the time of its foundation, AEI was controlled, though secretly, by the American General Electric, but returned to British hands after the war. After the severity of the depression AEI steadily grew during the war and the post-war boom, its workforce increasing from 35,000 in 1935 to 70,000 twenty years later, which put it well ahead of Germany's AEG. It is true that hardly any progress had been made in the integration of BTH and Metrovick, which remained two separate, even antagonistic companies within the same concern.[18] Interestingly, however, their research and development record was one of the best in the country and certainly comparable to that of Siemens or AEG in Germany.[19] GEC's growth was due, like that of AEI, to the innumerable business opportunities successively created by two world wars. But it was also the result of the entrepreneurial drive of Hugo Hirst, chairman from 1910 to 1943, who achieved his early aim to cover the whole electrical domain and 'to build up GEC into the greatest British company'.[20] GEC's workforce increased from 17,500 in 1924 to 24,000 in 1935, 40,000 in 1939, and 60,000 in 1955.

More specialized electrical companies became large firms in the inter-war years: the two cable-making companies British Insulated Cables and Callenders Cable & Construction Company, which merged in 1945 to form British Insulated Callenders Cable Co. (BICC); Electrical and Musical Instruments (EMI), formed in 1931 by the merger between the Gramophone Company and the Columbia Gramophone Co. and capitalized at more than £6 million; Joseph Lucas, maker of electrical parts for the motor industry, including batteries and magnetos, which employed 20,000 people in 1935. They were followed by firms such as Ferranti in transmissions; Standard Telephone and Cable (STC) (a subsidiary of the Amer-

[17] See T. A. B. Corley, 'Hill, Philip Ernest (1873-1944), Property Developer and Industrial Company Chairman', in Jeremy (ed.), *Dictionary of Business Biography*, vol. iii.
[18] R. Jones and O. Marriott, *Anatomy of a Merger* (London, 1970), 146–65.
[19] D. E. H. Edgerton and S. M. Horrocks, 'British Industrial Research and Development before 1945', *Economic History Review*, 47/2 (1994).
[20] Ibid. 79.

ican ITT) in telephone equipment; other generalists, such as Plessey, the workforce of which grew from half a dozen people in 1920 to nearly 16,000 in 1955 under Allen Clark's leadership; and by English Electric, revitalized from the 1930s by American financial and technical assistance, especially Westinghouse, and by George Nelson's dynamic management.

Large firms were less numerous in the other 'new' industries which, given their oligopolistic structure, became rapidly dominated by a handful of giant companies. Motor cars were the only real newcomers to the world of big business after the First World War. Despite rapid growth in the first decade of the century, the largest European firms remained medium-sized companies, none employing as many as 5,000 people in 1913. The war momentarily interrupted the spread of the motor car, though several firms experienced dramatic growth as manufacturers of munitions and other military equipment. In Britain increased demand in the post-war years, and the continuing 33.5 per cent *ad valorem* protective duty introduced during the war, boosted national production.[21] The British motor industry came to be dominated by the so-called 'big three': Ford, Morris, and Austin. The Ford Motor Company (England) had been incorporated in 1911 as a wholly owned subsidiary of the American company, to assemble and then manufacture the Model T. With the introduction of mass production methods, production jumped from 3,000 vehicles in 1912 to more than 6,000 in 1913,[22] making Ford the largest car manufacturer in Europe, ahead of Peugeot and Renault with respectively 5,000 and 4,704.[23] Ford, however, was to lose ground in the 1920s. Its market share fell from 22 per cent in 1921 to 4 per cent in 1929, reflecting the unsuitability of the American Model T to British conditions, in particular after the introduction in 1920 of a tax based on horsepower.

William Morris (later Viscount Nuffield) was the first to take advantage of Ford's decline, and he remained the country's foremost car manufacturer throughout the inter-war period. A car repairer and garage owner, Morris did not start making his own cars until 1913. After the interruption of war, he was able to expand rapidly, his output rising from 387 cars in 1919 to over 20,000 in 1923 and 63,500 in 1929, by which time he was second only to Citroën in Europe. Morris owed his success to a combination of commercial flair, financial caution, and efficient production. He foresaw the demand for cheap, small cars, adopted aggressive pricing

[21] On the British motor industry, see G. Maxcy and A. Silberston, *The Motor Industry* (London, 1959); R. J. Overy, *William Morris, Viscount Nuffield* (London, 1976); R. Church and M. Miller, 'The Big Three: Competition, Management and Strategy in the British Motor Industry, 1922–1939', in B. Supple (ed.), *Essays in British Business History* (Oxford, 1977); R. A. Church, *Herbert Austin: The British Motor Car Industry to 1941* (London, 1979); R. Church, *The Rise and Decline of the British Motor Industry* (Basingstoke 1994).

[22] D. Burgess-Wise, 'Perry, Percival Lee Dewhurst, Lord Perry of Stock Harvard (1878–1956), Motor Vehicle Manufacturer', in Jeremy (ed.), *Dictionary of Business Biography*, vol. iv.

[23] J. M. Laux, *In First Gear: The French Automobile Industry to 1914* (Liverpool, 1976), 199.

policies, and was able to limit his risks by buying out components and assembling them at his Cowley plant. Morris's main competitor was Herbert Austin (later Lord Austin), who had started manufacturing cars as early as 1896, as manager of Wolseley (a subsidary of Vickers sold to Morris in 1927), before setting up on his own in 1905. He was producing 1,500 vehicles and employing 2,300 people in 1913. Unlike Morris, Austin was primarily an engineer and an inventor. These qualities enabled him to rescue his firm from bankruptcy after it had gone into receivership in 1921, and to compete head-on with Morris in the second half of the decade. The company was saved by the huge commercial success of the Austin Seven, a very small car designed by Herbert Austin without the support of his colleagues which went into production in 1923, and the Austin Twelve. Production rose from 2,600 units in 1922 to an estimated 25,000 in 1926 and 50,740 in 1929.

The great depression affected the British motor industry far less than those of the other main producing countries, and expansion continued in the 1930s, with the 'big three' maintaining a market share of over 60 per cent. Ford's recovery followed the introduction of a new light car specifically designed for the British market; its market share rose to 18 per cent in 1938, mostly at the expense of Morris. The motor industry reconverted very rapidly to peacetime activities after the Second World War, and by 1950 Britain was the world's largest car-exporting country, until overtaken by Germany in 1956. However, threatened by the growth of Ford and Vauxhall, their American-owned competitors, Austin and Morris merged in 1952 to form the British Motor Corporation (BMC), from the outset the largest European car manufacturer by a wide margin

The rubber and tyre industry was dominated by one major company in each of the three countries. In Britain, Dunlop had been founded in 1889 and floated in 1896 with £5 million capital by the notorious company promoter Ernest T. Hooley. The company expanded rapidly before the First World War, both at home and abroad, with subsidiaries in France, Germany, the United States, and Japan, and rubber estates in Ceylon and Malaya.[24] In 1921, however, it was brought to the verge of bankruptcy following financial speculations by a leading director, Sir Arthur Du Cros, a member of the founding families. The firm recovered under the chairmanship of Sir Eric Geddes, to become 'good old reliable Dunlop',[25] and the eleventh largest British industrial company (by market capitalization) in 1930. The firm, of course, benefited from the growth of the motor industry, but it established a reputation for reliability, improved managerial control by introducing cost accounting, and diversified its production,

[24] See G. Jones, 'The Growth and Performance of British Multinational Firms before 1939: The Case of Dunlop', *Economic History Review*, 37/1 (1984).

[25] K. Grieves, *Sir Eric Geddes: Business and Government in War and Peace* (Manchester 1989), 108.

mostly into sports equipment, as well as latex foam rubber marketed as Dunlopillo which originated in the company's research centre. By the early 1950s, Dunlop was employing around 100,000 people.

In other sectors, British firms were significantly larger than their Continental competitors. This was in particular the case in the oil industry, where Royal Dutch Shell and Anglo-Persian Oil (which changed its name to Anglo-Iranian Oil in 1935 and to British Petroleum in 1954) were, together with Standard Oil of New Jersey, the 'big three' among the so-called Seven Sisters (the four others being the Gulf Oil Corporation, the Texas Company, Standard Oil of New York, and Standard Oil of California). The newcomer, Anglo-Persian Oil, was formed in 1909 to exploit an oil concession in south-western Iran and secured in 1914 the support of the British government, which became the company's major shareholder. The oil industry enjoyed spectacular growth after the First World War, with the fuel requirements of the expanding motor industry and the progressive replacement of coal by oil as an energy source.[26] By 1930, Shell and Anglo-Persian Oil were already among the top five British industrial companies. Britain also enjoyed European pre-eminence in the aerospace industry, which expanded enormously during the Second World War. Hawker Siddeley employed 70,000 people in 1955; Rolls-Royce, de Haviland, and Bristol Aeroplane's workforces were well over 20,000.[27]

Despite undergoing a structural crisis after the First World War, the staple industries—coal, iron, steel, shipbuilding, textile—did not altogether disappear from the world of big business. The heavy industries remained a major component, in particular as large employers: they contributed fifteen out of thirty-nine companies employing more than 10,000 people in 1935 (including five with more than 20,000); and eleven out of thirty-nine employing more than 20,000 people in 1955. This did not include the coal-mines, which had been nationalized and gathered into the National Coal Board, which then employed more than 700,000 people. The heavy industries remained dominated by shipbuilding, an ascendancy best symbolized by the takeover, between 1919 and 1920, of the entire Scottish iron and steel industry by shipbuilding groups, in sharp contrast to what was then taking place in Germany. The most important initiative came from Lord Pirrie, chairman of Harland & Wolff, the country's, and indeed the world's, largest shipbuilding company; he took control of Colvilles, Britain's largest steel producer, in 1920.[28] Steel and shipbuilding were in turn linked to shipowning, forming a huge network

---

[26] On BP's growth, see J. H. Bamberg, *The History of the British Petroleum Company*, ii. *The Anglo-Iranian Years, 1928-1954* (Cambridge, 1994).

[27] Figures from D. Jeremy, 'The Hundred Largest Employers in the United Kingdom, in Manufacturing and Non-manufacturing Industries, in 1907, 1935 and 1955', *Business History*, 33/1 (1991).

[28] S. Tolliday, *Business, Banking, and Politics: The Case of British Steel, 1918–1939* (Cambridge, Mass., 1987), 32–3, 86–7.

of business relationships, based on the close association between Pirrie's Harland & Wolff and Lord Kylsant's Royal Mail Group, one of the country's leading shipping groups, which was, however, to collapse in 1930.

The shipbuilding and armaments manufacturer Vickers remained the largest company in the sector. Yet the company experienced difficulties in the mid-1920s which brought it to the brink of collapse. Vickers suffered from the post-war depression in the steel, shipbuilding, and armaments industries, but its attempts at diversification were misguided and the firm's management was unable to control its acquisitions.[29] In 1917 Vickers bought the electrical concern British Westinghouse, jointly with Dudley Docker's company the Metropolitan Carriage Wagon & Finance Co. (MCWF); and two years later Docker convinced the Vickers board to buy his own MCWF at the inflated price of nearly £14 million. Vickers had also entered the motor car industry before the war, but its subsidiary, Wolseley, suffered heavy losses in the early 1920s. By 1925 the company was facing a severe crisis, which forced a writing down of its ordinary capital and a thorough reorganization. Vickers became a holding company with interests in three main areas: shipbuilding and armaments, where its works were merged with those of its old rival Armstrong Whitworth and transferred to a new company, Vickers-Armstrong;[30] rolling stocks, where its interests were merged with those of Cammel-Laird into Metropolitan-Cammel, jointly owned by the two companies; and steel, where the English Steel Corporation was formed to rationalize Vickers's steel interests. The electrical and motor businesses were duly disposed of. Vickers was again on a solid footing. With more than 40,000 workers in 1935, it was, even by German standards, a very large company. In terms of capital, whether at nominal or market value, Vickers was larger than any German iron and steel company except the Vereinigte Stahlwerke. The company expanded considerably in the following decades, adding aviation to its major areas of interests and gaining enormous prestige through its contribution to the war effort. Described in 1956 by *The Times* as 'a thriving and well-knit organization',[31] its workforce had reached 70,000, making Vickers one of Europe's largest companies.

The other major company in the heavy industries was Guest, Keen & Nettlefolds (GKN), which also increasingly diversified into engineering during this period.[32] The major step was the acquisition in 1920 of John Lysaght & Co., the steel-making, rolling, and galvanizing group. The merger brought GKN closer to the expanding motor car industry, in par-

---

[29] See J. D. Scott, *Vickers: A History* (London, 1962), and R. P. T. Davenport-Hines, *Dudley Docker: The Life and Times of a Trade Warrior* (Cambridge, 1984).

[30] Armstrong had suffered an even more serious crisis than its old rival, which cost the firm its independence, as the merger was in fact a takeover by Vickers.

[31] Quoted in H. Evans, *Vickers: Against the Odds, 1956–1977* (London, 1978), 19.

[32] See E. Jones, *A History of GKN*, ii. *The Growth of a Business, 1918–1945* (Basingstoke, 1990).

ticular through Lysaght's subsidiary Joseph Sankey & Sons, a leading supplier of electrical stampings and laminations as well as wheels, chassis,
and body pressings. The backward diversification in the early 1920s in
South Wales collieries proved, not surprisingly, less successful, and the
company sold its coal interests to Powell Duffryn in 1935. Likewise,
GKN partly divested from its heavy steel interests: in 1930 it established
with Baldwins a joint company, Guest, Keen & Baldwins Ltd., to run its
steelworks. From 1930 GKN, like Vickers a holding company, could
pay greater attention to the various engineering subsidiaries which it
owned in the Midlands. Its workforce rose from 30,000 in 1935 to 62,000
in 1955.

Concentration also increased in metal-making proper. The top five firms
increased their percentage of total output from 36.4 per cent in 1920 to 47
per cent in 1937.[33] The rationalization of the industry, however, remained
incomplete throughout the period. A new major firm emerged in 1918, the
United Steel Companies. The result of the merger of five companies,
United Steel became from the start the country's third largest steel
producer and had moved to first place by 1929.[34] The second largest producer, Dorman Long, took over the ailing Bolckow Vaughan in 1929. In
Scotland a merger of the five main companies in the late 1930s led to a
near monopoly under Colvilles. The 1920s was the 'black decade' of the
British steel-makers, plagued by over-capacity. They recovered under a
protective tariff in the 1930s, expanded during the war, and prospered
during the post-war boom. The steel industry was nationalized by the
Labour government in 1949, and almost immediately privatized by the
Conservatives in 1953, the major firms retaining their corporate identity
in the process.

The textile industry, by contrast, declined more abruptly in the British
big business hierarchy. There were still large companies in the inter-war
years, but of the big pre-1914 trusts only J. & P. Coats was able to keep its
position at the top of the ranking tables until the 1950s. However, even
before 1914 the textile industry had started its reconversion into artificial
fibres, dominated by one firm, Courtaulds, that reached a position
without equivalent in Europe. Founded in 1816 by Samuel Courtauld,
scion of a Huguenot family, the firm was reasonably prosperous as a silk
manufacturer during the nineteenth century. The turning-point in its fortunes took place in 1904, when it acquired the patent rights to the new
viscose process for making rayon, the first successful man-made fibre.
This was followed in 1909 by the purchase of the American rights to the
viscose process and the setting up of the American Viscose Corporation.
Courtaulds became the world's largest producer of rayon. The company
was floated in 1913 with £2 million capital, which had grown to £20

[33] Tolliday, *Business, Banking, and Politics*, 31.   [34] Ibid. 32.

million ten years later and to £30 million in 1930, making it the fourth largest British industrial company; its workforce then exceeded 20,000. Despite a certain lack of dynamism in the inter-war years, and having in 1941 to sell its subsidiary, American Viscose Corporation, as part of the price of American lend-lease, Courtaulds was still in the 1950s one of the most respected giants of British manufacturing industry, with a director and later chairman, Sir John Hanbury-Williams, also serving as a director of the Bank of England from 1936 to 1963.[35] Another firm to reach a prominent position in artificial fibres was British Celanese, employing more than 13,000 people in 1955. Founded during the First World War by Henry Dreyfus, a Swiss of French Alsatian Jewish origins, it was taken over by Courtauld in 1957. Entrepreneurial initiatives were also taken in the clothing industry. Montague Burton, a Jewish immigrant from Lithuania—his real name was Ossinsky—set up on his own in 1904. He employed 12,000 people in 1929, the year his company was floated, and 20,000 in the early 1950s with £5 million capital. It was then estimated that a fifth of the British male population was clothed by Burtons.[36]

The food, drink, and tobacco industries continued to be well represented within British big business, quite unlike in France and Germany. Imperial Tobacco remained during the entire period one of the country's largest companies, with £64 million capital in 1930 and £72 million in 1953. Measured by market capitalization, Imperial Tobacco was in 1937 the world's second largest company, behind only General Motors.[37] In drinks, the brewers Guinness and Watneys and the whisky manufacturer Distillers all had a share capital in excess of £8 million by 1930. In 1953, Guinness's capital was nearly £15 million, Distillers' nearly £25 million. The only food-manufacturing company to reach this size was the most recent of the large firms, J. Lyons & Co., which had started as a caterer in 1884, opened its first tea-room in 1894, and expanded into a new type of chain of popular restaurants offering reasonably good-quality food in pleasant surroundings. Lyons were soon to add production to distribution, in particular tea, coffee, bread, packaged cakes, and ice-cream.[38] The firm employed 30,000 people in 1935; its capital exceeded £10 million in the early 1950s.

Retail trade reinforced its position in the world of big business with the expansion of chain stores, the size of which far outstripped that of the

[35] See D. C. Coleman, *Courtaulds: An Economic and Social History*, 3 vols. (Oxford, 1969–80).

[36] R. Redmayne (ed.), *Ideals in Industry* (Leeds, 1951), 241, quoted by E. Sigsworth, 'Burton, Sir Montague Maurice', in Jeremy (ed.), *Dictionary of Business Biography*, vol. i.

[37] C. Schmitz, *The Growth of Big Business in the United States and Western Europe, 1850–1939* (Basingstoke, 1993), 32–3.

[38] D. Richardson, 'Gluckstein, Montague (1854–1922), Caterer and Food Manufacturer', 'Lyons, Sir Joseph Nathaniel (1847–1917), Caterer and Food Manufacturer', 'Salmon, Henry (1881–1950), Caterer and Food Manufacturer', in Jeremy (ed.), *Dictionary of Business Biography*, vols. ii, iii, and v.

department stores. Lipton, the early pioneer, was taken over by Unilever in 1927, but chains such as Home & Colonial Stores and W. H. Smith continued their growth, the workforce of the former increasing from 18,000 to 32,000 between 1935 and 1955, that of the latter from 14,000 to 18,000. Other innovators were also soon to make their mark. Woolworths employed 25,000 people in 1935, 60,000 twenty years later. A subsidiary of the American company founded in the 1880s, it inaugurated its first shop in Britain in 1909; 444 of them had been opened by 1930. The success was built on a simple but effective formula: a wide range of cheap ('Nothing over sixpence'), mostly household products were sold in large stores where customers could browse without being pressured to buy. The firm's capital reached £8.75 million at the time of conversion into a public company in 1931, and £20 million in 1953.[39]

Marks & Spencer also took off during this period. Its origins lay in the 1880s as a stall in the Leeds Market, where Michael Marks, a Jewish immigrant from Russia, had the simple idea of selling all his goods for a penny. He opened several 'Penny Bazaars' in the following years and entered in 1894 into a partnership with Thomas Spencer: the two men's capital amounted to £7,500. Marks & Spencer Ltd. was formed in 1907 with a capital of £30,000. Two generations later it had not only become one of the country's largest retail chains, but an institution in British economy and society. The principles on which the company's success was founded, and which have continued to guide it, were devised after the First World War by Simon Marks, Michael's son and inventor of the St Michael trademark: bright and spacious stores, faultless product quality, low prices, long-term but exacting relationships with suppliers, and pleasant working conditions for the employees, the number of which reached 11,000 in 1935 and 28,000 in 1955 with by then more than £10 million capital.[40]

The press barons firmly established their position in the world of big business during this period. Lord Rothermere's Associated Newspapers had a capital of £3.35 million in 1929 and included the *Daily Mail*, launched by his brother Alfred Harmsworth in 1896, whose circulation peaked at nearly 2 million in 1929. Allied Newspapers' capital reached £6.75 million that year. The group was owned by the brothers William and James Berry, later respectively Lords Camrose and Kemsley, and published, among other titles, the *Sunday Times* as well as the *Daily Telegraph*, the latter bought from Lord Burnham in 1927. Film companies followed suit. The Rank Organization owned over 600 cinemas after taking control

[39] M. Dixon, 'Stephenson, William Lawrence (1880–1963), Chain Store Chairman', ibid., vol. v.

[40] C. Shaw, 'Marks, Michael (1859–1907), Chain Store Founder', 'Marks, Simon, 1st Lord Marks of Broughton (1888–1964), Chain Store Chairman', 'Sieff, Israel Moses, Lord Sieff of Brimpton (1889–1972), Chain Store Retailer', ibid., vols. iv and v.

of Gaumont in 1941 and the Odeon Theatres in 1942; its capital reached £7 million in 1953.

In shipping, the leading companies—P. & O., Cunard, the Royal Mail Group—each had more than £8 million share capital in 1930. The Royal Mail Group collapsed in 1930, after it appeared that the company had been trading at a loss since 1921 though it continued to pay a dividend out of hidden reserves, and was liquidated in 1937. White Star, one of the group's major companies, was taken over by Cunard while the others were reorganized into two new operating companies, Royal Mail Lines and Elder Dempster Lines. By the early 1950s, P. & O.'s and Cunard's share capital had both reached £10 million. And companies operating abroad, which had flourished in the age of high imperialism, remained numerous in the City until after the Second World War. However, with a share capital mostly unchanged since pre-1914 days, they no longer belonged to the country's largest undertakings. The exception was British American Tobacco (BAT), founded in 1902 by Imperial Tobacco and American Tobacco to divide world tobacco markets—Britain was exclusively reserved to Imperial and the rest of the world allocated to BAT. In 1911, however, American Tobacco (who originally held two-thirds of the equity) was forced to sell its stake, following the Supreme Court's judgment that it violated anti-trust legislation; and by 1915 British interests had acquired a majority of the company's shares. BAT's capital reached £28 million in 1929.

All this made the diversity and density of British big business from the 1920s to the 1950s. Of course, one should not underestimate the serious difficulties encountered by some industrial sectors, in particular in the staple industries, as well as those of individual companies, to be discussed in a subsequent chapter. There is no doubt, however, that British big business had reached a full-blown, mature stage a generation or two before Germany or France.

THE STABILITY OF GERMAN BIG BUSINESS

In sharp contrast to the political upheavals experienced by Germany between 1918 and 1949, German big business surprisingly displayed a relative stability. The same group of companies continued to dominate the scene, despite huge mergers and demergers, the interference of the Nazi state, and the measures taken by the occupying powers after 1945. These firms were still concentrated in the heavy industries, chemicals, and electrical engineering; motor cars only timidly joined the group of industries dominated by giant firms; while the consumer and service industries remained, apart from a few exceptions, untouched by the rise of the large corporation. If there was a change, it came from the weakening of the position of the banks, the second major component of German big business before 1914.

The big banks suffered from the effects of the First World War, the hyperinflation of 1923, the financial crisis of 1931, and their dismantling by the Allies after 1945. They declined in the hierarchy of German big business, in both quantity and impact. Their number diminished following the disappearance of the large provincial banks, fourteen of which had a capital equal to or in excess of £2 million before 1914. In the inflationary and competitive climate of the early 1920s, the great banks were encouraged to take over the provincial banks with which they were already linked through 'community of interests'.[41] The Deutsche Bank, for example, took over seven banks between 1920 and 1924.[42] As a result the six big Berlin banks were the only banking companies with a capital of £3 million or more. Despite this expansion, the big banks were weakened by the devastation of war and hyperinflation: in 1924 the commercial banks' capital was valued at 30 per cent of its pre-war gold value, their assets at only 21 per cent.

A new large bank emerged from this amalgamation movement, the Commerz- und Privat Bank. It was the result of the merger in 1920 between two provincial banks, the Commerz- und Diskonto Bank (of Hamburg) and the Mitteldeutsche-Privat Bank (of Magdeburg). Another important merger took place in 1922, between the Darmstädter Bank and the Deutsche National Bank under the name of Darmstädter- und National Bank, commonly known as Danat-Bank. Amalgamations on the same grand scale as those which had taken place in Britain in 1918 did not occur before September 1929, when the Deutsche Bank merged with its old rival the Disconto-Gesellschaft, under the name of Deutsche Bank und Disconto-Gesellschaft (later shortened to Deutsche Bank). The directors of the two banks wanted to create a financial institution sufficiently large to deal on equal terms with the leading industrial concerns. The new bank's capital reached £14.25 million. The second big merger, between the Dresdner Bank and the Danat Bank, took place in 1931 under much less favourable auspices, through government compulsion after the failure of the Danat Bank.

The position of the German banks was further weakened by that year's crisis, which affected them much more than their British and French counterparts.[43] The Danat Bank closed its doors on 13 July 1931, and the

---

[41] On the concentration movement in German banking, see M. Pohl, *Konzentration im deutschen Bankwesen* (Frankfurt, 1980).

[42] G. Feldman, 'The Deutsche Bank from World War to World Economic Crisis 1914–1933', in L. Gall *et al.*, *The Deutsche Bank, 1870–1995* (London, 1995), 173, 203.

[43] See K. E. Born, *Die deutsche Bankenkrise 1931: Finanzen und Politik* (Munich, 1967); H. James, 'The Causes of the German Banking Crisis of 1931', *Economic History Review*, 2nd ser. 38 (1984); T. Balderston, 'The Banks and the Gold Standard in the German Financial Crisis of 1931', *Financial History Review*, 1/1 (1994).

government had to intervene directly through a rescue package which included, besides the imposed merger between the Danat Bank and the Dresdner Bank (also severely weakened), the purging of the big banks' management (one-third of the Deutsche Bank's directors, one-half in the Commerzbank, and all but two of the former directors of the Danat and the Dresdner lost their jobs); and a quasi-nationalization of the German banks with 91 per cent of the capital of the new Dresdner Bank, 70 per cent of the Commerzbank, and 35 per cent of the capital of Deutsche Bank (which had been reduced to £7.2 million) being taken into state ownership. The German banks were de-nationalized during the Third Reich, though they remained under state control and lost ground to the savings banks and large state-owned institutions with a privileged legal status.[44]

In the aftermath of the Second World War, the Allies decided that the three big banks should be divided into regional banks. The Deutsche Bank was succeeded by ten separate institutions. The old ties, however, were never really severed. In 1952 the number of successors to each of the 'big three' was reduced to three: one for the *Länder* of the north, one for those of the south, and one for the *Land* of Rhineland-Westphalia. These institutions were in fact working together and published a single balance-sheet, and in 1957 the Deutsche Bank and the Dresdner Bank were reunited, followed a year later by the Commerzbank.

Heavy industry managed to maintain its dominant position despite Germany's loss of production capacity resulting from the territorial clauses of the Treaty of Versailles, which amounted to 44 per cent for iron, 38 per cent for steel, and 26 per cent for coal. The Ruhr industrial élite continued to promote its own interests with little concern for general welfare, putting up prices during the war in order to maximize its profits, and encouraging inflation in the early 1920s in order to facilitate the restructuring and modernization of its plants.[45] The strong man was Hugo Stinnes. His first move was the creation of a 'community of interests', named the Rheinelbe Union, between his own group, Deutsch-Luxemburg, and Gelsenkirchener Bergwerks AG (GBAG), the giant coal concern which pre-war had started diversifying forwards. He then acquired a majority stake in the Bochumer Verein, one of the fifteen largest German iron and steel companies; finally, he completed the whole edifice by uniting forces, on 30 December 1920, with the electrical giant Siemens, under the name Siemens-Rheinelbe-Schuckert-Union. The operation, however, was not a success. The profit-sharing arrangements, in particular, were not favourable to Siemens,[46] and the union was broken up five years later, soon after Stinnes's death.

[44] H. James, 'The Deutsche Bank and the Dictatorship, 1933–1945', in Gall *et al.*, *The Deutsche Bank*.
[45] See G. D. Feldman, *Iron and Steel in the German Inflation 1916–1923* (Princeton, 1977).
[46] W. Feldenkirchen, *Siemens, 1918-1945* (Munich, 1995), 192–3.

A more pragmatic approach succeeded Stinnes's visionary, somewhat adventurous strategy. Faced in 1925 with the urgent need to rationalize and reorganize their industry, leading heavy industrialists entered into negotiations with a view to implementing a vast amalgamation programme. This led to the foundation in 1926 of the Vereinigte Stahlwerke (United Steel). The new trust included four of the five pre-war leading iron and steel concerns: GBAG, Deutsch-Luxemburg, Thyssen, and Phoenix, as well as the Bochumer Verein, the Rheinische Stahlwerke, and the Vereinigte Stahlwerke van der Zypen. Its capital reached 800 million marks (£40 million) and its workforce nearly 200,000 people. However, the foundation of the Vereinigte Stahlwerke did not lead to a fundamental reorganization of the German iron and steel industry.[47] A few big names stayed outside the new combine: not only Krupp, which preferred to preserve its family structure and relied on its traditionally privileged relationship with government, but also Klöckner, created in 1923 by the amalgamation of the various firms acquired over the years by Peter Klöckner, and Gutehoffnungshütte (GHH). Both these opted for integrating forwards by taking over machinery companies—Klöckner took control of Humboldt and of Deutz, while GHH secured, among other acquisitions, a majority stake in the Bavarian giant MAN.[48] Two other major companies remained independent, Hoesch and Mannesmann. In 1929 the seven largest companies produced around 80 per cent of the country's iron and steel, extracted close to 40 per cent of its coal, and more than 70 per cent of its iron ore; a relative deconcentration, however, took place in the 1930s.[49]

Despite its huge size, the Vereinigte Stahlwerke was no longer by the late 1930s and early 1940s the largest concern in German heavy industry. Its place was taken by the Reichswerke Hermann Goering, founded in 1937 by Goering with the full backing of the Nazi state apparatus. The new complex was built around the Salzgitter iron orefields in Prussia taken over from the Vereinigte Stahlwerke. In 1938 the capital of the Reichswerke was increased from 5 million to 400 million Reichsmark. In a few years the complex grew to include 228 subsidiaries, controlled a total capital of 2.5 billion Reichsmark, and employed 600,000 people across the whole of German-occupied Europe.[50] Germany's defeat in 1945 led to a reorganization of its iron and steel industry. The most important change was the dismantling of the Vereinigte Stahlwerke, leaving in its wake, in broad outline, the firms which had merged in the mid-1920s. By the early

[47] See C. Kleinschmidt and T. Welskopp, 'Zu viel "Scale" zu wenig "Scope": Eine Auseinandersetzung mit Alfred D. Chandlers Analyse der deutschen Eisen- und Stahlindustrie in der Zwischenkriegszeit', *Jahrbuch für Wirtschaftsgeschichte* (1993), 2: 251–81.

[48] G. Goldbeck, *Kraft für die Welt: Klöckner-Humboldt-Deutz AG, 1864–1964* (Düsseldorf, 1964), 166–70; E. Maschke, *Es entsteht ein Konzern: Paul Reusch und die GHH* (Tübingen, 1969), 90–161.

[49] G. Mollin, *Montankonzerne und 'Drittes Reich'* (Göttingen, 1988), 31–4.

[50] See Mollin, *Montankonzerne*; R. J. Overy, *Goering: The 'Iron Man'* (London, 1984).

1950s, Thyssen, Phoenix, Rheinische Stahlwerke, Bochumer Verein, and GBAG had reappeared alongside Klöckner, Hoesch, Mannesmann, Gutehoffnungshütte and Krupp, which had also been reorganized. Heavy industrial companies remained the largest single group within German big business after the Second World War, with 15 among the 30 employing 10,000 people or more, and 30 companies among the 71 with a capital of £5 million or more, though the proportion was starting to diminish.

However spectacular, the merger leading to the foundation of the Vereinigte Stahlwerke was not a first in German manufacturing industry. It had been preceded a year earlier by the big merger of the chemical industry, even more wide-ranging as it involved the three largest firms, BASF, Bayer, and Hoechst, as well as five smaller companies with which they were linked in a 'community of interests'. In terms of capital, at both its nominal and market values (respectively £55 and £147 million), IG Farben was Germany's largest company in 1929, with 114,000 employees one of the three biggest employers in Europe. IG Farben alone represented one-third of the German chemical industry, with a monopoly in dyestuffs, even though its importance was decreasing in the firm's overall activities; and it held a dominant position in the production of most products at the leading edge of the chemical industry, such as pharmaceuticals, photographic films, nitrogen, magnesium, and plastics.[51]

The huge size of IG Farben tends to mask the existence of other large firms in the German chemical industry. A tenth of IG Farben's capital was more than enough to warrant inclusion in the world of big business in the late 1920s. This was the case with five other companies. The two largest, Burbach-Kaliwerke and Kali-Industrie, were potash producers. The latter, however, diversified into crude oil, synthetic oil, nitrogen, chemicals, explosives, and magnesium,[52] changing its name to Wintershall in 1929. Kokswerke & Chemische Fabrike also diversified from coke and coke gases into pharmaceuticals and fine chemicals as well as dyeing, washing, and cleaning products, by taking control of a number of companies in 1922–3, including Schering and Kahlbaum. Rütgerswerke was engaged in building materials, basic chemicals, and plastics and synthetics, while Deutsche Solvay-Werke successfully competed in the alkali trade.[53]

As is well known, IG Farben was to play a major role in Germany's war effort, in the manufacture of synthetic rubber and fuel as well as the supply of gas chambers. Twenty-three of its senior executives went on trial before the Nuremberg tribunal in 1947–8, and thirteen received

---

[51] A. Chandler, *Scale and Scope* (Cambridge, Mass., 1990), 586. In 1937, IG Farben accounted for 98% of the dyestuffs produced in Germany, 50% of the pharmaceuticals, 60 to 70% of photographic films, 70% of nitrogen, and 100% of magnesium.

[52] P. Hayes, *Industry and Ideology: IG Farben in the Nazi Era* (Cambridge, 1987), 154–5.

[53] Chandler, *Scale and Scope*, 584–6.

prison sentences. The firm was dismantled, although the deconcentration remained limited, as 90 per cent of what remained of the firm in West Germany was transferred to the three successor firms, BASF, Bayer, and Hoechst.[54] By 1950 output had reached its 1936 level, and in 1953 the three successor firms were among the largest in the country, with Hoechst capitalized at over £20 million and Bayer at over £30 million.[55] Far behind the big three, large chemical companies included Wintershall and Chemische Werke Hüls, one of the smaller firms demerged from IG Farben.

Fewer institutional changes took place in electrical engineering. The industry itself suffered from the war and its consequences, especially the loss of plants and patents abroad, the closing of foreign markets to German goods, and the competition from newly formed electrical industries; its share of world exports fell from almost half in 1913 to between 25 and 30 per cent for most of the inter-war years.[56] However, unlike the chemical and heavy industries, there was no merger between the largest firms after the First World War (although such a possibility was seriously considered, especially from AEG's point of view, between 1925 and 1932), and there was no demerger following the Second World War. Siemens and AEG maintained the dominance which they had established before the war. They were present, directly or indirectly, in all the aspects of the industry and accounted for more than 50 per cent of Germany's overall production. With 116,000 employees in 1929, Siemens was the second largest German employer, and AEG, with 70,000, the fourth. Other companies of some significance invariably fell into these firms' sphere of influence. Thus in 1931 Siemens and AEG took control of Bergmann Elektrizitäts-Werke, a manufacturer of insulating and wiring conduits which employed some 12,000 people, leading to a reduction of Bergmann's activities. The exception was Robert Bosch GmbH, manufacturer of dynamos and other motor car electrical appliances, which controlled about 70 per cent of this niche, with as much as 90 per cent for sparking plugs. The firm expanded with the growth of the motor car industry, rising to third place among German electrical companies in the 1930s; it employed 12,000 employees in 1929 and more than 20,000 in 1953. Firms also reached huge proportions in electricity supply, though most were wholly or partly owned by local authorities. The giant among them was the Rheinisch-Westfälisches Elektrizitätswerk (RWE): measured by total assets (over £200 million), it was the country's largest company in 1953.

The German motor car industry lagged behind those of France and

[54] Hayes, *Industry and Ideology*, 377.
[55] On the rebirth of the three German chemical giants, see R. Stokes, *Divide and Prosper* (Berkeley, n.d.).
[56] Feldenkirchen, *Siemens, 1918–1945*, 101–2, 647. The exception was the early 1930s, when the German share of world exports reached 32.7% in 1932, and 34.9% in 1932.

Britain before the 1930s. The two leading manufacturers, Daimler-Benz and Opel, did not enjoy the spectacular rise of their most successful French and British competitors. Daimler-Benz, formed in 1926 by the merger of Daimler and Benz, was a large company, employing some 14,000 people in 1929, but concentrated on the production of luxury models. The largest producer, Adam Opel, was taken over by General Motors in 1929. Opel grew rapidly under American ownership to become Europe's largest manufacturer in the 1930s: it produced 122,856 cars in 1935, as against 96,512 by Morris.[57] The situation was transformed in the early 1950s by the arrival of a newcomer, Volkswagen.[58] The origins of the firm had little to do with commercial logic. The initiative to launch a low-priced people's car (*Volkswagen*) had been taken by Hitler after his seizure of power. The car was designed by Ferdinand Porsche, vast sums of money were invested in its development, and a huge integrated plant was built at Wolfsburg, though only a limited number of cars were produced before the war. Contrary to widely held assumptions, the plant survived the war almost intact. Production was revived by the occupying British authorities, and ownership transferred to the German state in 1949. Four years later, Volkswagen was the second largest European car producer behind the British Motor Corporation. Also in the automobile industry, Germany had, in Continental, a global competitor in rubber and tyres. German oil companies, by contrast, were severely weakened by defeat in the First World War. In the mid-1920s Shell and Standard Oil controlled half the German market, and Deutsche Erdöl, in no position to compete, reached agreements with Anglo-Persian Oil.[59] The production of synthetic fuel during the Nazi period was mostly a state enterprise, and in the early 1950s the two major German oil companies were Esso AG and Deutsche Shell, among the country's twenty largest companies measured in terms of nominal capital.

In other industrial sectors big business remained, as before 1914, a rarity. In textiles, Nordwolle with a 24,500-strong workforce in 1929 belonged to the country's top ten employers and weighed heavily enough in the German economy to cause its bankers serious difficulties when it collapsed in June 1931, thus contributing to the outbreak of the banking crisis a few months later. In artificial fibres, the Vereinigte Glanzstoff-Fabriken (VGF), founded in 1911, experienced rapid growth and soon established itself as the country's leading producer, second only to Courtaulds in Europe. VGF, however, was heavily indebted, and under the aus-

---

[57] Figures from Overy, *William Morris*, and A. Sloan, *My Years with General Motors* (New York, 1954).

[58] On the origins of Volkswagen, see S. Tolliday, 'Enterprise and State in the West German Wirtschaftswunder: Volkswagen and the Automobile Industry, 1939–1962', *Business History Review*, 63/3 (1995).

[59] J. Gillingham, *Industry and Politics in the Third Reich: Ruhr Coal, Hitler and Europe* (London, 1985), 73, Chandler, *Scale and Scope*, 520–1.

pices of the Deutsche Bank it merged in 1929 with the Dutch synthetic fibre manufacturer Nederlandsche Kunstzidje to form the Algemeene Kunstzijde Unie (AKU). In the food, drink, and tobacco industries, the Berlin brewery Schultheiss, which acquired its rival Patzenhofer in 1920, alone reached the lower limit of big business, with £2 million capital and 7,000 employees in 1929. It no longer met these requirements by the early 1950s, when the only two large companies were the sugar refinery Süddeutsche Zucker and Unilever's German subsidiary Margarine-Union. In trade, big business remained confined to department stores. The most striking success was that of Rudolf Karstadt, who began in the 1880s with a shop selling ready-made clothes, opened five branches in the next decade, took over his brother's thirteen shops in 1900, opened his first department store in Hamburg in 1912, and merged in 1920 with the department store chain Althoff. Karstadt's capital reached £4 million in 1929 and £5 million in 1953.

Newspapers and publishing remained dominated by the three groups which had emerged before the war: Mosse, Ullstein, and Scherl. Their actual size, however, is difficult to evaluate. Ullstein Verlag was the largest group.[60] Not only did it own four daily newspapers, including the *Vossische Zeitung*, with some 400,000 copies Germany's highest-circulation newspaper, and several weekly magazines; but it also owned printing presses, was engaged in book publishing (one of their best-selling authors was Erich Maria Remarque), ran a news service and a photo agency, and owned five cinemas and a film studio. The group employed 9,198 people, including 203 journalists, in 1929; its capital, however, was only £600,000, probably because it was still a family-owned private limited company, until the Ullstein were dispossessed in 1939. The Scherl group was controlled from 1915 by Alfred Huggeberg, a former Krupp director, who became leader of the German National Party in 1928. In addition to the newspapers he took over from Scherl, Huggenberg established a number of companies in order to provide the myriad of small provincial newspapers with specific services: the Vera Verlaganstalt offered them financial advice; and the Allgemeine Anzeiger took charge of advertising. Huggenberg was also able to procure capital through his own finance companies; and the publishers who received his assistance were obliged to subscribe to his news agency, Telegraph Union. He completed the edifice in 1927 by taking a controlling interest in the Universum Film AG (UFA), the largest film-producing company in Germany, which had run into serious financial difficulties. Scherl's capital was £1.5 million in 1927, but the concern appears to have been more a political than a commercial enterprise. During the Nazi period, the biggest newspaper was the party's official organ, the *Völkischer Beobachter*, with a circulation approaching

[60] On the Ullstein and Scherl publishing groups, see M. Eksteins, *The Limits of Power: The German Democratic Press and the Collapse of Weimar Democracy* (Oxford, 1975), 74–115.

600,000 in 1939, and reaching 1,700,000 in 1944. By the early 1950s no press, publishing, film distribution, or similar type of leisure group belonged to the world of German big business.

The two major shipping companies, HAPAG and Norddeutscher Lloyd, remained among the country's top twenty companies in the 1920s. Their prestige was high enough, and Wilhelm Cuno, HAPAG's managing director, sufficiently representative of the world of big business for him to become Reich Chancellor in a non-party-dominated government in 1922. At just over £8 million, HAPAG's capital in 1930 was about the same as that of P. & O. or the Royal Mail Group. The position of the two German companies had considerably deteriorated by the early 1950s.

STRENGTHS AND WEAKNESSES OF FRENCH BIG BUSINESS

As in Britain, big business in France broadened from the 1920s to include the 'new' industries of the second industrial revolution. Companies in electrical engineering, chemicals, motor cars, oil, and rubber crossed the threshold of the large corporation. Their growth, however, was slower than in Britain, where big business remained significantly larger and far more diversified. From the 1920s to the 1950s, French big business came in fact closer to the German model, dominated by a cluster of large companies mostly involved in the production of capital goods. The major difference was that France did not possess a handful of truly giant firms. To a large extent this was due to the absence of far-reaching mergers. More generally, however, the severity of the economic depression of the 1930s, which affected France more than most industrialized countries, followed by defeat and occupation in the 1940s, interrupted the brief expansion enjoyed by French firms in the 1920s.[61]

Another common feature of French and German big business was the decline of the big banks. Like their German counterparts, the French big banks lost their position as the country's largest companies after the First World War, while in the international league table they suffered from the devaluation of the franc in the 1920s. No major merger took place during this period, whether between the four large *banques de dépôts* (Crédit Lyonnais, Société Générale, Comptoir National d'Escompte de Paris, and Banque Nationale de Crédit) or even between a major deposit bank and one of the larger provincial banks. The latter enjoyed a relative expansion in the 1920s, but from a European perspective they were slipping out of

---

[61] See M. Lévy-Leboyer, 'La grande entreprise française: Un modèle français?', in M. Lévy-Leboyer and J.-C. Casanova, *Entre l'état et le marché: L'Économie française des années 1880 à nos jours* (Paris, 1991).

the world of big business; the capital of the largest of them, Crédit du Nord, was a mere £1.2 million in 1930 and its total assets £20 million. From the onset of the depression, the share of deposits held by publicly owned institutions, above all the savings banks, far outstripped that held by the commercial banks. Their deposits slightly more than doubled from 30 to 67 billion francs between 1920 and 1937, while those in the savings banks increased more than sevenfold, from 15 to 113 billion.[62] The old-established private banks forming the Parisian *haute banque* remained influential in the inter-war years. However, the semi-nationalization of the Banque de France in 1936, and that of the railway companies the following year, undoubtedly diminished their control over the financial sector of the French economy; it was further eroded by the nationalization of the commercial banks and the insurance companies in 1946. Unlike the deposit banks, however, the *banques d'affaires* were left in private hands. The most prominent of them, the Banque de Paris et des Pays-Bas, remained a major power in the French economy, though it emerged considerably weakened at the Liberation. In 1953, only one bank featured among France's twenty largest companies measured by capital, whereas they had occupied the five first places before 1914. The big nationalized deposit banks had become mere dwarfs in comparison with their British rivals, having competed on equal terms less than half a century before.

The motor car industry was the most successful of the new industries in France. From 1890 to 1904, French production of motor cars was the highest in the world, and between 1904 and 1930 it was second only to that of the United States. Three firms dominated the French industry after the First World War, with a 63 per cent market share in the late 1920s: Peugeot, Renault, and Citroën. Peugeot and Renault were already in 1913 the second and third largest European car manufacturers—behind the British Ford Motor Company—though they were still medium-sized companies. The Peugeots were an old provincial business dynasty, established in the Montbéliard area, in eastern France, since the eighteenth century. They started as millers, moved to textiles, and later to small metal goods such as springs, saws, planes, pitchforks, coffee mills, and corset-busks, as well as crinolines when they were all the rage during the Second Empire. In 1886 they embarked on the production of bicycles, soon becoming leaders in France, and a few years later took up motor cars. The entrepreneurial drive came from Armand Peugeot, with only hesitant support from the rest of the family. Armand Peugeot presented his first steam tricycle at the Paris exhibition of 1889, and established a separate company, the Société Anonyme des Automobiles Peugeot, in 1896. In 1901 he

[62] A. Gueslin, 'Banks and the State in France from the 1880s to the 1930s: The Impossible Advance of the Banks', in Y. Cassis (ed.), *Finance and Financiers in European History, 1880–1960* (Cambridge, 1992), 78.

launched the successful 'Bébé Peugeot', a two-seater. Impressed by Armand's success, Peugeot Frères launched their own car, the 'Lion Peugeot', in 1906. As there was no acrimony between the cousins, an agreement was soon reached and the two firms merged in 1911.[63]

Louis Renault entered the automobile business a little later. He built his first car in 1898, at the age of 21, and the following year created with his two brothers the company Renault Frères. Ten years later he was the country's largest producer. Renault owed his early success to his participation in motor races, to his cars' reputation for durability and easy maintenance, and also to his innovative abilities, especially the direct drive mechanism which he perfected for his first car. During the pre-war decade, Renault diversified his production into taxis, vans, and buses, and gradually integrated all stages of the production and distribution of motor cars. The real expansion, however, came with the First World War. Renault's workforce rose from 4,400 to 22,000 by 1918. With the experience gained in the production of commercial and military vehicles, increased integration, and the investment of war profits, Louis Renault was able thereafter to build a huge concern, by 1929 employing 30,300 people and producing 54,117 motor cars.[64] Peugeot's growth was slower, with 32,000 vehicles being produced in that year, and a 20,000-strong workforce. Both firms, however, had already been overtaken by a relative newcomer, and the most forceful French entrepreneur of his day, André Citroën.

Citroën was already involved in the motor industry before the war: he was head of his own gear company, which he established in 1905; but in 1908 he also joined the board of the Mors company, a small motor manufacturer (it produced 800 cars in 1913) facing liquidation, and led a team of directors that managed to keep the company afloat.[65] The war was Citroën's great opportunity. In a newly established factory at the quai de Javel in Paris, he manufactured shells on a mass production basis; his total output had reached 26 million at the end of the war, and his workforce grew from 3,500 to 11,700 between 1915 and 1918. After the war, Citroën was the first to apply the American methods of mass production to the French motor industry, not only in production (assembly-lines were introduced in 1919, three years earlier than Renault) but also in distribution (Citroën set the pace in car advertising; he pioneered sole dealers and hire purchase). His output rose from about 1,000 cars in 1919 to 20,000 in 1920, 67,000 in 1924, and to a peak of 96,000 in 1929, with 33,000 employees.[66]

[63] See R. Sédillot, *Peugeot: De la crinoline à la 404* (Paris, 1960); Laux, *In First Gear*.

[64] P. Fridenson, *Histoire des usines Renault*, i. *Naissance de la grande entreprise* (Paris, 1972).

[65] Laux, *In First Gear*, 39–40, 129–32; S. Schweitzer, *André Citroën* (Paris, 1992), 30–40.

[66] S. Schweitzer, *Des engrenages à la chaîne: Les Usines Citroën 1915–1935* (Lyons, 1982); Fridenson, *Histoire des usines Renault*.

In contrast to Britain and Germany, the three major firms in the French motor car industry were among the country's very largest companies, a reflection of both the vigour of the French car industry and the relative weakness of the other sectors. Things changed with the depression. Output fell from 211,000 vehicles in 1929 to 136,000 in 1932, as France lost her European leadership to Britain and was later pushed to third place by Germany. Renault and Peugeot increased their market share at the expense of Citroën, which nevertheless still remained France's largest manufacturer despite its failure in 1934. In defiance of the world economic depression, André Citroën had entirely rebuilt his Javel plant in 1933. Overcome by debts, the company went into receivership and was taken over by Michelin. The French automobile industry recovered quickly after the Second World War. A major change in the ownership structure was of course the nationalization of Renault in 1945, following accusations of collaboration with the German war effort made against Louis Renault, and his death in controversial circumstances on 24 October 1944.[67]

Large corporations also emerged in the industries linked to motor manufacturing. In rubber, Michelin belonged from the beginning, with Dunlop and Continental, to the industry's 'global oligopoly'. In oil, France attempted to enhance her position after the First World War through the Compagnie Française des Pétroles (CFP).[68] The CFP was created in 1924 to exploit the French concession in the Turkish Petroleum Company, which consisted of the German share (25 per cent) in this company confiscated after the war. The intention of the French government was to create a global national oil company, involved in production, transportation, refining, and distribution. In order to implement this policy and overcome the hesitations of many of the shareholders, the state took a 30 per cent stake in the company in 1930 (and 40 per cent voting rights); the government also appointed two directors and had to approve the others. A subsidiary company, the Compagnie Française de Raffinage, was created in that year and granted a 25 per cent market share. The rest was in the hands of the Anglo-Saxon 'trusts' (Standard Oil, Royal Dutch Shell, Anglo-Iranian) linked to various French interests. Supported by the French government, the CFP became the main company in the French oil industry. In the early 1950s the five largest oil companies in France were, besides the CFP and its sister company the Compagnie Française de Raffinage, Esso Standard, Shell Française, and the Société Générale des Huiles de Pétrole, a subsidiary of Anglo-Iranian Oil. All belonged, in terms of capital, to the country's ten largest companies.

[67] Louis Renault was incarcerated in September 1944, and though already ill (he suffered from aphasia and uraemia), he was badly beaten up during the night of 3 October, leading to suspicions that this might have contributed to his death. See G. Hatry, *Louis Renault: Patron absolu* (Paris, 1982), 401–8.

[68] See J. P. Daviet, *Un destin international: La Compagnie de Saint-Gobain de 1830 à 1939* (Paris, 1988), 510–19; E. Faure, *La Politique française du pétrole* (Paris, 1938).

In electrical engineering, the First World War gave a boost to the Compagnie Générale d'Électricité (CGE), which attained big business status. By 1930 the group employed 20,000 people and controlled fifty companies, with a majority stake in forty of them. Electrical equipment had become the group's dominant activity, with 43 per cent of its turnover to metallurgy's 27 per cent; electricity supply accounted for 18 per cent.[69] Thomson-Houston, however, was determined to maintain its leadership.[70] With the technological assistance of the American General Electric Company, the group in the 1920s considerably expanded its activities in electrical engineering, especially in heavy equipment, through a mixture of mergers, joint ventures, and investment in new plants. But expansion also meant restructuring, in particular divestment from its holdings in tramway companies, one of Thomson's major interests before 1914. Electricity generating companies, however, remained part of the group, though they became increasingly autonomous. The most ambitious step was taken in 1928, when Thomson and the Société Alsacienne de Constructions Mécaniques merged their heavy electrical equipment businesses into a newly formed company, Alsthom. The new company, the largest in the sector in France, had a capital of £3.6 million (£2 million of which was jointly taken up by the two mother companies) and employed 12,000 people.

The Compagnie Générale d'Électricité was able to weather more successfully than Thomson and Alsthom the years of depression, war, and occupation, and emerged as the leading French company in electrical engineering by the early 1950s. However, the major French firms obviously enjoyed a far slower growth than their British competitors during this period. Besides electrical engineering powerful groups controlled electricity supply in France. They had close links, through minority shareholdings and interlocking directorships, with the manufacturers of electrical equipment as well as with other public utility companies. One of the largest, the Énergie Électrique du Littoral Méditerranéen, had a capital of £2.4 million in 1928 and was closely linked to Thomson-Houston. The other leading group was the Union d'Électricité, formed in 1919 by the merger of six regional companies and led by Ernest Mercier, one of France's leading inter-war industrialists.[71] The Union d'Électricité was linked to 75 other companies, including the Lyonnaise des Eaux, the Compagnie Parisienne de Distribution d'Électricité, and the Société d'Électricité de Paris. Its share capital of £2.2 million in 1928 is thus a poor indicator of its true size. Electricity supply was nationalized in 1946.

The large corporation also became a common feature in the chemical

---

[69] *Alcatel Alsthom: Histoire de la Compagnie Générale d'Électricité* (Paris, 1992).

[70] See P. Lanthier, 'Les Constructions électriques en France: Financement et stratégies de six groupes industriels internationaux, 1880–1940', unpub. Ph.D. thesis (University of Paris-X (Nanterre), 1988), 624–751.

[71] See R. F. Kuisel, *Ernest Mercier: French Technocrat* (Berkeley and Los Angeles, 1967).

industry. The biggest firm remained Saint-Gobain, employing 15,000 people in 1928, but as before the war its activities were divided between glass and chemicals. Glass-making was in fact more successful than chemicals in the inter-war years. Saint-Gobain's diversification into nitrogen and oil proved disappointing, and its share of the French chemical industry declined after the First World War.[72] The Produits Chimiques et Électrométallurgiques d'Alais, Froges et Camargue, which changed its name to Pechiney in 1950, developed into a large corporation, with a 9,000-strong workforce in 1928; its activities, however, were divided between chemicals and aluminium.[73] Kuhlmann's growth was not hampered by the loss of its plants in northern France during the war—rather, that loss stimulated the redeployment of its activities. To the production of super-phosphates the firm added that of dyes after merging with the Compagnie Nationale des Matières Colorantes in 1924. This dye company had been established in 1917 on the state's intitative, as France, like Britain, had depended on German imports before the war. Kuhlmann reached a near monopoly in dyestuffs in the following years by taking over a number of smaller competitors.[74]

The principal weakness in the French chemical industry was the absence of a major merger on the lines of ICI in Britain or IG Farben in Germany. Negotiations were entered into, but a merger between Saint-Gobain and Kuhlmann failed to materialize in 1926–7; the main opposition came from Saint-Gobain which felt that the project was favouring Kuhlmann and feared bank interference.[75] This failure deprived the country of a significant international player and reduced the scale of investment in major research and development projects. In 1928, however, two medium-sized firms, the Société Chimique des Usines du Rhône and Poulenc Frères, merged under the name of Rhône-Poulenc. The new company, which was to become the French 'national champion' in the chemical industry, was still of a comparatively modest size, with 4,500 employees and £288,000 capital by the following year. Rhône-Poulenc, which invested in promising markets such as artificial textiles (through its subsidiary Rhodiaceta), plastics, and pharmaceuticals, was little affected by the depression. By 1938 it was vying with Kuhlmann for top position in the French chemical industry, with a larger turnover but a smaller workforce (just over 10,000 as against Kuhlmann's 15,000).[76] And

[72] See Daviet, *Un destin international*, and *Une multinationale à la française: Saint-Gobain 1665–1989* (Paris, 1989).

[73] See C. J. Gignoux, *Histoire d'une entreprise française* (Paris, 1955).

[74] See J. F. Léger, *Une grande entreprise dans la chimie française: Kuhlmann 1825–1982* (Paris, 1988).

[75] J. P. Daviet, 'An Impossible Merger? The French Chemical Industry in the 1920s', in Y. Cassis, F. Crouzet, and T. Gourvish (eds.), *Management and Business in Britain and France: The Age of the Corporate Economy* (Oxford, 1995).

[76] Ibid. 186–7. See also P. Cayez, *Rhône-Poulenc, 1895–1975* (Paris, 1988).

by 1959, on the eve of a fundamental restructuring of the French chemical industry, Rhône-Poulenc's market share had reached 20 to 25 per cent (though the company was only a quarter ICI's size) as against around 10 per cent each for Kuhlmann, Saint-Gobain, and Pechiney.[77]

Whatever the rise of the 'new' industries, the heavy industries remained, from the 1920s to the 1950s, the backbone of French big business. In 1929 France was the world's second largest producer of cast iron, ahead of Germany, and the third largest producer of steel, ahead of Great Britain, despite the constraints posed by a small internal market and insufficient coal resources exacerbated by excess capacity following the recovery of Alsace and Lorraine. However, production increase failed to lead to larger firms. The number of companies employing 10,000 people or more was not much higher than in the pre-war years. Moreover, the number of giant firms hardly grew, in contrast to Germany and even Britain. Schneider, which increasingly diversified into mechanical and electrical engineering, and the reunited de Wendel still dominated the industry. Behind these two giants, however, the majority of the sector's large corporations were the collieries of northern France (Mines d'Anzin, Mines de Lens, Mines d'Aniche, etc.): nine of them employed 10,000 workers or more as against three other iron and steel companies (Marine-Homécourt, Châtillon-Commentry, Longwy). Such a weight to the coal-mining companies remained a French peculiarity. Some of them assumed control of major iron and steel companies: the Mines de Lens, for example, took a controlling stake in Nord-Est in 1923.[78]

Despite the absence of mergers between major companies, the complex network of joint ownerships which characterized French heavy industry must be taken into account when assessing the size of the leading groups. Take the German mining and industrial properties in dis-annexed Lorraine. They were sequestrated and divided into five coal, iron, and steel concerns, each acquired by a group of several companies.[79] Marine-Homécourt, Micheville, and Pont-à-Mousson, for example, were linked by cross shareholdings and joint interests in various companies, forming a powerful group known as Mar-Mich-Pont. In 1919, they jointly acquired (together with the Forges d'Alais and the Aciéries de France) for 125 million francs the Société Lorraine des Aciéries de Rombas, which included mines and plants formerly belonging to Rombacher Hütte and Deutsch-Luxemburg. A looser association including Schneider, de Wendel, Châtillon-Commentry, and Denain-Anzin acquired the Société Métallurgique de Knutange.

---

[77] Daviet, Une multinationale à la française, 214–15.
[78] O. Hardy-Hémery, 'Croissance et marché en sidérurgie: Les Avatars des forges et aciéries du Nord-Est (1817–1948)', in P. Fridenson and A. Straus (eds.), Le Capitalisme français, 19e–20e siècles: Blocages et dynamismes d'une croissance (Paris, 1987), 125.
[79] See C. Prêcheur, La Lorraine sidérurgique (Paris, 1959).

While the 1930s was a period of recovery for the British steel industry, the depression led to a collapse of French production, stagnating at some 50 to 60 per cent of capacity. Changes ensued in the aftermath of the Second World War. The coal industry was nationalized in 1946, while major consolidations took place in iron and steel. Usinor (short for Union Sidérurgique du Nord) was formed in 1946 to merge the iron and steel interests of Denain-Anzin and Nord-Est; while Sidelor (Sidérurgie de Lorraine) was established in 1950 to merge those of the Mar-Mich-Pont group (Marine-Homécourt, Micheville, Pont-à-Mousson, and Rombas). Finally, Lorraine-Escaut was created in 1953 through the merger of five companies, including Longwy which held a majority stake in the new concern. The fourth leading group was de Wendel, converted into a limited company in 1952. By then these four groups of about equal size together accounted for 54 per cent of French steel output. In terms of workforce, capital, and output, the largest firms in the iron and steel industry had become comparable in size to their German counterparts.

In textiles, Saint-Frères was one of the largest French companies in the 1920s, with £2.4 million capital and 9,000 employees in 1928. In artificial fibres, production was concentrated through a complex network of relationships rather than in a single large firm as in Britain and Germany. The Comptoir des Textiles Artificiels (CTA) had been founded in 1911 by the two major producers, the Gillet and Carnot groups, in order to market the products of their various companies, as well as to co-ordinate and rationalize their industrial activities. Both groups consolidated their interests in 1936: the Gillet companies were merged into Givet-Izieux, and the Carnot companies into the Viscose Française;[80] each had a capital of more than £2.5 million in 1952, and together they employed far in excess of 10,000 people.[81] The other major component of the network was Rhodiaceta, a joint subsidiary of CTA and Rhône-Poulenc, created in 1922.[82]

The large corporation remained absent from the food, drink, and tobacco industries, while no breakthrough occurred in the service industries. Retail trade remained dominated by the department stores, which increasingly operated on a national scale after the war. They also developed new sales techniques, in particular with the creation of fixed-price stores. In 1931 Uniprix was launched by the Nouvelles Galeries and Prisunic by Le Printemps; the Galeries Lafayette followed with Monoprix in 1932. The traditionally dominant Bon Marché came up against fierce competition and was overtaken by the Galeries Lafayette in the 1920s and by Le Printemps in the 1930s.

In newspapers, no press baron was able to build an empire on the scale of those existing in Britain. Of the leading groups of the pre-war years,

[80] M. Laferrère, *Lyon ville industrielle* (Paris, 1960), 210–12.
[81] J. Houssiaux, *Le Pouvoir de monopole* (Paris, 1956), 248–54.
[82] See Cayez, *Rhône-Poulenc*.

only the Société du Petit Parisien et d'Éditions Pierre Dupuy & Cie maintained its position. The circulation of *Le Petit Parisien* fluctuated around 1.5 million from 1919 to 1935. Thereafter, it increasingly lost ground to *Paris-soir*, launched in 1931 by Jean Prouvost, a textile manufacturer. Abundantly illustrated and with an extensive sports coverage, its circulation reached 1,800,000 by 1939. In its wake Prouvost launched *Marie-Claire* in 1937 and *Match* in 1938, each with sales of a million or more. Political propaganda could also reach big business dimensions. In the 1920s the perfumer François Coty bought several newspapers, including *Le Figaro* and *L'Action française*, in order to spread his extreme right political views. In 1928 he launched *L'Ami du peuple*, whose circulation soon reached 1 million. Newspapers, however, proved a heavy drain on Coty's dwindling resources, especially after 1929, and his empire was liquidated in 1933.[83] Finally, as in the pre-war years, big business in the service industries included a few colonial companies (Gafsa, SCOA), shipping companies (Chargeurs Réunis, Messageries Maritimes), and newspaper distribution (Hachette), a reflection of the contrasted progress made by the large firm in France during this period. However, despite having been weakened by the depression and German occupation, French big business grew in fact closer to its British and German counterparts, especially the latter, paving the way for further convergence in the following decades.

[83] See C. Bellanger *et al.* (eds.), *Histoire générale de la presse française*, iii. *De 1871 à 1940* (Paris, 1972), 511–43.

3

Recent Developments

NEW DIMENSION

During the thirty years of sustained economic growth which followed the Second World War, European big business likewise grew, in both size and scope. In the first place, the number of large companies increased considerably, especially during the 1960s. This is clearly discernible in the light of the yardstick of 10,000 employees or more. From exceptional, this size became if not common, at least fairly widespread. The surge took place almost entirely between 1953 and 1972, when the number of companies employing 10,000 people or more rose from 65 to 160 in Britain, from 20 to 62 in France, and from 26 to 102 in Germany; subsequently (1972–89) the numbers hardly increased, remaining more or less the same at 162 in Britain, rising to 81 in France, and actually falling to 80 in Germany, where a polarization between giant firms on one hand and small and medium-sized firms on the other took place. Inevitably the post-war proliferation of large companies has modified perceptions of the phenomenon. Attention has tended to focus on the largest, truly gigantic firms. Do we need therefore a new definition of the large company, increasing the threshold to, say, 20,000 employees? Here a distinction should be made between large firms and big business, which can no longer be equated in the later part of the century. The level of managerial sophistication required to manage firms employing between 10,000 and 20,000 people still justifiably categorizes them as large companies. On the other hand, big business is primarily a matter of power. It is, by its very nature, exclusive and can thus only consist of the leading firms.

The more so as, from the 1960s, big business took on a new dimension in Europe. Hitherto, companies employing more than 100,000 people had been very much the exception. But by the early 1970s their number had risen to twenty-two (nine in Britain, eight in Germany, and five in France), only increasing to twenty-six (nine in Britain, eleven in Germany and six in France) over the next two decades as recession and rationalization led to widespread downsizing. Siemens was by far the largest employer in Europe in 1972 with 301,000 employees, followed by GEC (211,000), ICI (199,000), Volkswagen (192,000), and British Leyland (191,000).[1] Three companies employed more than 300,000 in 1989: Daimler-Benz (368,226),

[1] *Fortune*, Sept. 1973.

Siemens (365,000), and Unilever (300,000); and only three others more than 200,000: Volkswagen (250,616), British Telecom (237,400), and Alcatel Alsthom, the former Compagnie Générale d'Électricité (210,300).[2]

This gigantism was largely the result of far-reaching mergers—often encouraged if not prompted by the state and aimed at creating companies sufficiently large to compete successfully in the world markets. The threat of the 'American challenge' as well as American direct investments in Europe also contributed to this spurt. The embodiment of this policy of 'national champions' was most spectacularly, though by no means exclusively, expressed in France in the late 1960s and early 1970s. More than elsewhere, mergers took place between firms which already were among the very largest in their respective sectors. In chemicals, state-originated attempts to concentrate the industry around two major companies of 'international' dimensions led to the merger between Ugine and Kuhlmann in 1966, joined by Pechiney in 1971 to form Pechiney-Ugine-Kuhlmann (PUK). In 1969 Rhône-Poulenc, the other major company in the sector, took over Péchiney-Saint-Gobain, formed a few years earlier to merge and rationalize the chemical activities of these two companies. In building materials, Saint-Gobain, which had divested from chemicals, merged in 1970 with Pont-à-Mousson, an iron and steel company specializing in drain pipes, in which it had established a commanding position in international markets.[3] The iron and steel industry underwent major restructuring with, among others, the merger between de Wendel, the legendary family concern, and Sidelor, leading by the early 1970s to the formation of two major groups, Usinor and Sacilor.[4] In the motor car industry, Peugeot took over Citroën in 1974. In banking, the Banque Nationale pour le Commerce et l'Industrie and the Comptoir National d'Escompte de Paris merged in 1966 under the name of Banque Nationale de Paris (BNP), which became the country's largest bank.

In Britain, major consolidations took place in electrical engineering, with the takeover in 1967 and 1968 of English Electric and the Associated Electrical Industries by the General Electric Company; in the motor car industry with the merger in 1968 between Leyland and British Motor Holdings to form British Leyland; while in banking, the two smallest banks among the 'big five', the National Provincial Bank and the Westminster Bank, amalgamated in 1968 under the name of National Westminster Bank. Other mergers were implemented through nationalization. In the steel industry, for example, the British Steel Corporation, formed in 1967, included the fourteen steel producers and was organized from 1969 on a product rather than on a regional basis, thus obliterating the old

[2] *Fortune*, 30 July 1990.
[3] See P. Allard *et al.*, *Dictionnaire des groupes industriels et financiers en France* (Paris, 1978); M. Bauer and E. Cohen, *Qui gouverne les groupes industriels?* (Paris, 1981).
[4] See H. d'Ainval, *Deux siècles de sidérurgie française* (Grenoble, 1994).

company structures. The aircraft industry was nationalized and consolidated into British Aerospace in 1977. Major reorganization also took place in Germany, especially in the iron and steel industry. Thyssen, under Günther Sohl, for all intents and purposes recreated the old Vereinigte Stahlwerke, taking over Phoenix in 1962, Oberhausen in 1967, and Rheinstahl in 1973; while Krupp took over the Bochumer Verein in 1958 and Hoesch merged with the Dortmunder Union in 1966. Most of the coal-mining industry, however, came together in 1968 in the state-owned Ruhrkohle. Other significant mergers took place in engineering, with the takeover of Demag by Mannesmann in 1973, in motor cars with the takeover of Auto-Union by Volkswagen in 1964, and in chemicals with the takeover of Wintershall by BASF.

These well-known and highly publicized cases were only part of the reorganization process. Several large companies lost their independence in these years. In Britain, for example, 28 of the 100 largest companies were taken over between 1957 and 1969.[5] Business concentration increased in the 1970s and 1980s, but mergers between the largest industrial and financial companies became more difficult in countries claiming to abide by the rules of competitive capitalism, at least within national frontiers. Illustrious names were nevertheless to disappear, most often falling into the hands of huge conglomerates, the rise of which has been one of the main big business developments in the last thirty years. Imperial Tobacco, the second largest industrial company in the world in 1937 (behind General Motors),[6] and still ranked eleventh in Britain in 1972, was taken over by Hanson Trust in 1986; Hanson, a consummate example of the new conglomerates, propelled itself into Britain's top ten companies in the late 1980s by buying and restructuring a number of companies on both sides of the Atlantic.[7] In Germany, the once mighty AEG, one of the world's most powerful electrical concerns before the First World War, and still ranked seventh in Germany in 1972, was taken over by Daimler-Benz in 1985 after being put under bankruptcy protection in 1982. The famous motor car manufacturer thus became the largest industrial company in Europe through diversification into engineering and aeronautics, though this policy had run into difficulties by the early 1990s.

CONVERGENCE

Convergence in the productivity and income levels of the major industrialized countries has been a major feature of the last fifty years. Emerging

[5] L. Hannah, *The Rise of the Corporate Economy* (1st edn. London, 1976), 167.
[6] C. Schmitz, *The Growth of Big Business in the United States and Western Europe, 1850–1939* (Basingstoke, 1993), 32–3.
[7] See A. Brummer and R. Cowe, *Hanson: A Biography* (London, 1994).

from the devastation caused by the war, the German and French economies enjoyed an average growth rate of their real GDP of respectively 4 and 4.3 per cent between 1950 and 1973; this enabled them to catch up with, and then overtake, Britain, which experienced a slower rate of 2.5 per cent.[8] By 1973 West Germany had become Europe's largest economy, but the difference between the three countries was much narrower than twenty years earlier, West Germany's GDP being 11 per cent higher than that of Britain and 16.5 per cent higher than that of France. Growth rates slowed down in all three countries between 1973 and 1989 and the respective positions of the three countries were very slightly modified. On the eve of the fall of the Berlin Wall, the overall size of the West German economy was about 12.5 per cent larger than that of Britain and France.[9] This convergence at the macro-economic level was to a large extent reflected in the world of big business. In the three countries, big business had by then penetrated all major domains of economic activity, whether in industry, finance, or services; while abnormal differences between the size of the largest companies, especially those operating in the same industries, had mostly disappeared.

The number of *giant* companies was becoming more similar in the three countries. In 1972, 23 British, 18 German, and 15 French industrial companies had a turnover of $1 billion or more. Britain, however, still had a significantly higher number of *large* companies, whether measured by turnover (60 companies with a turnover of more than $400 million, the minimum to be included in the 300 largest American industrial companies, as against 38 in Germany and 29 in France), or, as already seen, by workforce. This was partly due to the higher level of concentration in British industry, where the share of the top 100 firms in manufacturing output had reached 40 per cent in 1970, as against 30 per cent in Germany and 23 per cent in France.[10] This trend continued in the 1970s and 1980s. In 1989, there were 43 British, 32 German, and 29 French companies among the world's 500 biggest *industrial* corporations, all with a turnover of $2.5 billion or more. Among those with a turnover of $5 billion or more, however, 19 were British, 17 German, and 13 French. And with the exception of the two giant oil companies Shell and BP, the *largest* industrial companies were once again German: whether measured by turnover or workforce, Daimler-Benz, Volkswagen, and Siemens were significantly larger than other British and French companies. Moreover, with 11 companies among the top 100 in 1989, Germany was ahead of Britain and

    [8] A. Maddison, *Dynamic Forces in Capitalist Development* (Oxford, 1991), 49.
    [9] Gross Domestic Product in 1985 US relative prices was, in $ million, 565,655 for Britain, 537,997 for France, and 626,607 for Germany in 1973; and 770,420 for Britain, 777,081 for France, and 867,194 for Germany in 1989; ibid. 198–9.
    [10] Estimates by L. Hannah, 'The Joint Stock Company: Concentration and the State 1894–1994', in A. Allan (ed.), *Proceedings of the Annual Conference 1994*, Business Archives Council (London, 1995).

France who had 9 each.[11] Market capitalization, however, shows Britain largely maintaining her historical lead: on that measure, 36 of the 100 largest European companies in 1993 were British, as against 16 German and 18 French.[12]

The sectoral distribution of the British, French, and German leading companies displayed increasing similarity, probably reaching its highest point in the early 1970s (Table 3.1). This was the period when neat parallels could be established between the handful of companies which dominated the major industries of their respective country: British Leyland, Renault, Peugeot, and Citroën, and Volkswagen in motor cars; ICI, PUK and Rhône-Poulenc, and BASF, Bayer, and Hoechst in chemicals; GEC, Thorn and Plessey, CGE and Thomson, and Siemens and AEG-Telefunken in electricals; Barclays, Natwest, Midland, and Lloyds, BNP, Crédit Lyonnais, and Société Générale, and Deutsche, Dresdner, and Commerzbank in banking, and so on, as can be seen in Table 3.1. The exceptions were in the over-representation of British companies in consumer goods and services. A quarter of a century later, big business remains concentrated in the same broad sectors. The main change has been the disappearance of an independent British-owned motor car industry. British Leyland was nationalized in 1975 to avoid its collapse, though this did not stop its continuing decline; the company's much shrunken car division, renamed Rover, was sold to British Aerospace in 1988, which in turn sold it to BMW in 1994. In both France and Germany, motor manufacturers—Renault and Peugeot Citroën; and Volkswagen, Daimler-Benz, and BMW, the latter enjoying a spectacular growth in the last fifteen years—still formed the backbone of their respective countries big business. Imbalances have also occurred in the electrical industry where GEC, the sole remaining British giant company in the field, has become much smaller than Alcatel Alsthom or even Thomson in France, and of course Siemens in Germany. There has been convergence, however, in the common failure by the three countries to meet the challenge of American and Japanese competition in semiconductors and computers.

This convergence, however, should not conceal the persistence of deep-rooted national characteristics. Take the iron and steel industry. By the early 1970s it was well into its long-term decline, with the diminished role of steel in the armaments industry in the age of electronics and nuclear power, the attractiveness of substitutes such as aluminium or plastics, and the competition from steel-makers in south-east Asia and southern Europe. Nevertheless, the heavy industries still exercised an unusually preponderant weight in German big business. Only in Germany did they still form the single largest group of giant companies in 1972: 9 of the 33

---

[11] *Fortune*, 30 July 1990.
[12] *Financial Times*, 20 Jan. 1995.

Table 3.1. The leading British, French, and German firms in selected industries, 1972 (measured by turnover, in $ billion)

	Britain		France		Germany	
	Company	Turnover	Company	Turnover	Company	Turnover
Motor cars	BL	3.248	Renault	3.537	Volkswagen	5.017
			Peugeot	2.134	Daimler-Benz	4.157
			Citroën	2.089		
Electrical equipment	GEC	2.514	CGE	2.164	Siemens	4.713
	Thorn	1.028	Thomson	1.521	AEG	3.151
					R. Bosch	1.808
Engineering	GKN	1.559			GHH	2.329
					Mannesmann	2.054
Metals	RTZ	1.471			Metallgesellschaft	1.341
Chemicals	ICI	4.236	PUK	2.662	Hoechst	4.076
			Rhône-Poulenc	2.396	BASF	3.720
					Bayer	3.315
Iron and steel	British Steel	3.630	Usinor	1.246	Thyssen	3.060
			Wendel-Sidelor	1.099	Krupp	2.108
					Rheinstahl	1.648
Banking (total assets)	Barclays	21.592	BNP	22.345	Deutsche	18.724
	Natwest	20.570	CL	20.586	Dresdner	15.391
	Midland	13.845	SG	17.910	Commerz	11.342
	Lloyds	13.428				

Note: The oil, food and drink, and tobacco industries have not been included because of their weak representation in France and Germany.

Source: Fortune, Sept. 1973.

with a workforce of 20,000 or more, or with a turnover of $500 million or more. Their number as well as their economic muscle had undoubtedly diminished, but Thyssen, Krupp, Klöckner, and Hoesch remained major forces in German big business. Other firms, such as Mannesmann or Gutehoffnungshütte, while divesting from iron and steel, stayed in the production of heavy capital goods such as machinery, engineering, non-ferrous metals, or chemicals. Since then iron and steel industry has undergone further rationalization, so that the French firm Usinor-Sacilor has become Europe's largest steel producer; but significantly, Germany still had more large firms in the sector than Britain and France in 1989, though their number was later reduced by the merger between Krupp and Hoesch in 1993.

In chemicals and allied products, German firms regained their pre-war pre-eminence, Hoechst, BASF, and Bayer becoming the three largest European firms in the sector by the 1980s. The gap with Britain, however, should not be overstated. While each of the German 'big three' companies became larger than ICI even before it divested its pharmaceutical activities with the creation of Zeneca in 1993, giant firms have emerged in the British pharmaceutical industry (Glaxo, Smithkline Beecham, Wellcome, the latter taken over by Glaxo in 1994), with no equivalent in Germany. Large chemical companies were less successful in France, PUK in particular being forced to abandon its activities in chemicals while the national champion Rhône-Poulenc never quite managed to match ICI's achievements, let alone those of the great German firms.

In consumer goods, large firms were still more commonly found in Britain. Indeed, food and drink were to a great extent responsible for the inordinately high number of large British companies in the late twentieth century. In textiles, British firms retained some of their old supremacy (though this did not reflect a competitive advantage in the industry); three firms (Courtaulds, Coats Patons, and English Calico) had a turnover of more than $400 million in 1972, as against none in France and Germany. Britain also maintained her predominance in services, partly as a result of her substantially larger tertiary sector.[13] In 1972, 28 British companies in various service industries had a turnover in excess of £150 million, as against 8 in France and 9 in Germany.[14] A more significant difference was that the French and German companies were mostly department and chain stores (the major exceptions being Hachette and the Lyonnaise des Eaux in France, HAPAG-Lloyd, Haniel, and Axel Springer in Germany). British firms, on the other hand, were engaged in a much broader range of activities, including commodity brokers and trading companies

---

[13] 53.5% of employment as against 46.8 in France and 41.9 in Germany; and 54.4% of GDP, as against 45.6 in France and 44.6 in Germany. D. F. Channon, *The Service Industries: Strategy, Structure and Financial Performance* (London, 1978), 4.
[14] *The Times 1000* (1973), and *Entreprise*, Nov. 1973.

(Czarnikow, Inchcape, Dalgety), shipbrokers and shipping companies (CT Bowring, Shipping Industrial Holdings, P. & O.), hotels (Trust House Forte), cinema and leisure (Rank Organization), as well as a number of retailers.[15]

The number of large service companies increased in all three countries in the 1980s, though they were still far smaller and less numerous than in America. In 1989, 30 of them in Britain, 26 in France, and 21 in Germany had a turnover of £1.5 billion or more.[16] However, the same differences remained, as 69 per cent of the French and 67 per cent of the German large service companies were in retailing, as against only 43 per cent in Britain where new firms in press and communication, advertising, hotel and leisure, business services, and others had attained big business status. They were joined by the newly privatized utility companies, some of them, such as BT (British Telecom), being among the country's largest companies. And last, but by no means least, from the 1960s the City of London regained its position as the leading (with New York) international financial centre by seizing the opportunities to become the centre of new markets, in particular for Eurobonds. As in earlier periods, this predominance of the financial sector was not based on the size of the largest British banks, but on the activities of the City as a whole, a large proportion of which were by then controlled by foreign banks.

National characteristics may well have persisted, but they have become less clearly reflected in the sectoral distribution of the largest companies. Such classifications themselves have lost much of their meaning, following the rise of conglomerates and the diversification of most large enterprises in activities far remote from their original core business, blurring the distinctions not only between industries but also between manufacturing and services.[17] Furthermore, the formidable expansion since the 1960s of foreign direct investment has made large firms increasingly independent from their national economy, especially British firms: in 1990 the stock of outward foreign investment of the United Kingdom was $244.8 billion, representing 25.1 per cent of GDP, as against $155.1 billion for Germany and $114.8 billion for France, representing respectively 10.4 and 9.6 per cent of GDP.[18] Aggregate figures, however, conceal the higher level of multinational expansion reached by the largest firms.

Are recent divergences a simply transitory phenomenon, attributable to the necessarily different rhythm at which firms in each country have

---

[15] See Channon, *The Service Industries*.

[16] *The Times 1000* (1989–90); *L'Expansion*, Nov.–Dec. 1990; M. Bauer and B. Bertin-Mourot, *'Les 200' en France et en Allemagne* (Paris, n.d. [1992]).

[17] Increased product differentiation has led some authors, in the first place Michael Porter, to analyse competitiveness at the level of very narrowly defined industries, and even segments within industries. See M. Porter, *The Competitive Advantage of Nations* (London, 1990).

[18] G. Jones, 'British Multinationals and British Business since 1850', in M. Kirby and M. Rose (eds.), *Business Enterprise in Modern Britain* (London, 1994), 174.

responded to the challenges of global competition? Or will they prove to be more fundamental, resulting from a divorce between two types of capitalism, as recently argued by some commentators?[19] These are not questions for the historian to answer. What is particularly striking in the light of the historical experience is first that the general trend of the century has been towards convergence and secondly that cross-European mergers between large companies have remained so far the exception, though foreign direct investment has increased among European countries. Should such mergers become more common, as has been predicted for some time, they would no doubt increase convergence, by giving birth to European, rather than British, French, or German large companies; but they might also be organized on the basis of national specializations and reinforce them in the process.

[19] See in particular M. Albert, *Capitalisme contre capitalisme* (Paris, 1991).

PART II

PERFORMANCES

What matters, in the end, is performance: the object of business history is to explain the success or failure of a company, an entire industry, or, at a more global level, the relationship between business and economic performances. Yet, surprisingly, the analysis of performances is not really at the core of comparative business history. We simply do not know which were the most successful companies in Europe in the early or mid-twentieth century, whether they were German, French, or British, in which sector they were involved, and what have been their fortunes in the following decades. Comparative studies have chiefly centred around such themes as the strategy and structure of the firm,[1] technological innovation,[2] multinational development,[3] business concentration,[4] state intervention,[5] industrial relations,[6] and social and cultural attitudes.[7] These are all factors which can explain business success or failure; but they do not by themselves represent a measure of business performance, even though they are often treated as such. The separation between ownership and management, for example, or the existence of productive facilities abroad, are usually considered as marks of business success, whether at the level of a firm, a sector, or an economy as a whole. Conversely, a classical education or a marriage into the aristocracy has tended to be seen as inducing business failure.

Are these assumptions, and many others, corroborated by the actual performances of the companies concerned? The task of answering this question in a comparative historical perspective is certainly not easy, and the theoretical and methodological problems

[1] See in particular A. Chandler and H. Daems (eds.), *Managerial Hierarchies* (Cambridge, Mass., 1980); A. Chandler, *Scale and Scope* (Cambridge, Mass., 1990); W. Lazonick, *Business Organization and the Myth of the Market Economy* (Cambridge, 1991).
[2] D. C. Mowery and N. Rosenberg, *Technology and the Pursuit of Economic Growth* (Cambridge, 1989); D. E. H. Edgerton and S. M. Horrocks, 'British Industrial Research and Development before 1945', *Economic History Review*, 47/2 (1994), 213–38.
[3] M. Casson (ed.), *The Growth of International Business* (London, 1983); A. Teichova, M. Lévy-Leboyer, and H. Nussbaum (eds.), *Multinational Enterprise in Historical Perspective* (Cambridge, 1986); G. Jones and P. Hertner (eds.), *Multinationals: Theory and History* (Aldershot, 1986); G. Jones, *The Evolution of International Business: An Introduction* (London, 1996).
[4] H. Pohl (ed.), *The Concentration Process in the Entrepreneurial Economy since the Late Nineteenth Century* (Stuttgart, 1988).
[5] See for example A. Prost (ed.), 'Les Nationalisations d'après guerre en Europe occidentale', *Le Mouvement social* (special issue), 134 (1986); M. Chick (ed.), *Governments, Industries and Markets* (Aldershot, 1990).
[6] See for example H. Gospel and C. Littler (eds.), *Managerial Hierarchies and Industrial Relations: An Historical and Comparative Study* (London, 1983); S. Tolliday and J. Zeitlin (eds.), *The Power to Manage? Employers and Industrial Relations in Comparative Historical Perspective* (London, 1991).
[7] K. Nakagawa (ed.), *Social Order and Entrepreneurship* (Tokyo, 1977); B. Collins and K. Robbins (eds.), *British Culture and Economic Decline* (London, 1990); Y. Cassis (ed.), *Business Elites* (Aldershot, 1994).

act as a powerful deterrent. A first problem is, how do we define business performance? There exist, of course, a variety of possible measures. Size, as we have seen, is one of them, though an insufficient one. Productivity, market share, and exports are also only aspects of business performance. Added value has recently, and convincingly, been put forward by John Kay as 'the key measure of corporate success',[8] but its calculation is impracticable for a large part of the century. In a long-term perspective, *sustained profits and profitability* remain the most palpable evidence of business success.

Four measures of business performance will be examined. The first two, discussed in Chapter 4, are concerned with the net profits achieved by the leading British, French, and German companies. The third and fourth measures, discussed in Chapter 5, consider these companies' ability to survive and grow in the long term. Net profits will be compared in both absolute and relative terms. Absolute figures are of course largely dependent on size, but they are essential to gauge a firm's economic power. Of the various rates of profits which could be taken into consideration, return on shareholders' funds has seemed the most appropriate for this study. Finally, to the extent that we define performance as *sustained* profits and profitability, this will be measured in terms of longevity and growth.

This analysis works of course on the assumption that performances in general, and profits in particular, can differ widely between firms, even within the same industry. Comparisons can be made at different levels: between firms, or between sectors; between firms or sectors of the same country; between firms or sectors of different countries; or between the overall business performances of various countries. All possibilities will be examined in the next two chapters. However, given the general purpose of this book, the emphasis will be on comparisons between countries.

[8] J. Kay, *Foundations of Corporate Success* (Oxford, 1993), 19. The value added created by a firm is defined as a measure of 'the difference between the market value of its output and the cost of its inputs' (p. 23).

4

Profits and Profitability

Comparing profits raises a number of problems. There is first the question of the reliability of the sources of information and their compatibility for comparative purposes. Analysing the profits of a large sample of companies, in three different countries and over a long period of time, rules out the possibility of systematically consulting companies' internal records, to the extent of course that such records are available. One has thus to rely on published balance-sheets and profit and loss accounts. The risk that published figures are distorted cannot be ruled out, in particular for earlier periods when legislation concerning companies' financial statements was relatively lax, and many a historical study has revealed differences between published and actual profits.[1] Furthermore, in a comparative analysis, this risk is compounded by the differences between the accountancy practices in each country which, despite increasing convergence, have persisted to this day. Published accounts, however, should not be readily dismissed. They provide for all countries at best a fairly accurate picture, at worst a rough idea of a company's state of affairs, and there is no reason a priori to believe that discrepancies between published and real profits were more pronounced in one country than in another. In addition, even if 'untrue', published profits do reflect the image a company wishes to project.

A second problem arises from the specific conditions in which firms operate in different countries. Protective tariffs, cartel agreements, monopoly positions, captive markets—all are likely to have affected company profits in varying degrees from one country to another. On the other hand, these varying conditions were part of the real world in which big business operated, and must therefore be integrated in any meaningful comparison of business performance.

The purpose of this chapter is modest but important: modest because, despite the abundance of figures, it does not pretend to offer much more than an *order of magnitude* of what has been the comparative evolution of corporate profits in Britain, France, and Germany; important because even

---

[1] See for example J. Bouvier, F. Furet, and M. Gillet, *Le Mouvement du profit en France au XIXe siècle* (Paris, 1965); Y. Cassis, *City Bankers, 1890–1914* (Cambridge, 1994); G. Jones, *British Multinational Banking, 1830–1990* (Oxford, 1993); R. Church, T. Baldwin, and B. Berry, 'Accounting for Profitability at the Consett Iron Company before 1914: Measurement, Sources and Uses', *Economic History Review*, 47/4 (1994). M. Spörrer, 'What New Estimates of Industrial Profitability Can Tell us about the Weimar and the Nazi Economy', *Diskussionsbeiträge aus dem Institut für Volkswirtschaftslehre (520) Universität Hohenheim*, 125 (1996).

an order of magnitude is still missing from most debates about the relative business performances of the major European countries. Rather than
the last word, this chapter is thus conceived as a beginning, a point of
departure for further refinements in comparative analysis.

The analysis is based on the net published profits of a sample of top
British, French, and German companies. All the companies included in
the sample are large, according to the criteria defined in Part I. However,
they were not necessarily each country's largest thirty or fifty companies
at the selected benchmark years. The sample has rather been established
in order to reflect the specific composition of the world of big business in
each of the three countries. It was not necessary, for example, to include
all the iron and steel concerns in the sample of pre-1914 German companies before reaching for a smaller, though still large, food or textile
company. Lists of companies included in the sample can be found in the
Appendix. In order to iron out possible distortions caused by occasional
erratic results, profits and profitability have been compared on the basis
of a three-year average. The following years have been taken into account:
1911–13, 1927–9, 1953–5, 1970–2, and 1987–9.[2] Given the relative lack of
synchronization between the trade cycle of the three countries, few other
years, apart from the long boom of the 1960s, would have presented
broadly similar economic conditions. Comparing the depression years of
the 1930s, for example, or the periods of upheaval following the two
world wars (the early 1920s and late 1940s) would have increased the risks
of distortion, as countries were affected at different times and with
varying degrees of intensity.

PROFITS

In absolute terms, profits are to a large extent a matter of size, so it is not
surprising to find that the highest profits have consistently been generated by British firms (Tables 4.1 to 4.5). Let us first, though, consider the
period before 1914, when the pre-eminence of British companies had not
yet been firmly established. The average profit of the top British companies was only fractionally higher than that of their German counterparts,
at respectively £613,000 and £584,000; France was somewhat behind with
£314,000. Similarly, nine British companies made more than £1 million
profit in 1911–13, as against eight in Germany and only one in France. On

[2] For 1911–13, 1927–9 and 1953–5, figures have been collected from the *Handbuch der
Aktiengesellschaften* and the *Saling Börsen Handbuch* for Germany, from the *Cote Desfossé* and
annual reports kept in the Crédit Lyonnais historical archives for France, and from the
Investor's Monthly Manual, *The Economist*, and annual reports kept at the Guildhall Library
for Britain. For 1970–2 and 1987–9, I have used the figures provided by the business magazine *Fortune*.

the other hand, the net profits of three British firms (Imperial Tobacco; the Glasgow thread manufacturer J. & P. Coats; and the South African diamond combine De Beers Consolidated) approached £3 million, while the highest profits achieved by a German firm (Krupp, Deutsche Bank) or by a French firm (Crédit Lyonnais) did not reach the £2 million mark (Table 4.1).

The general trends observed in the distribution of the largest companies are reflected in profit figures. One is the strength of the German electrical, chemical, and heavy industries. The profits of the largest German iron and steel concerns (Krupp, Phoenix, GBAG),[3] for example, were not matched by those of any of their British and French competitors, including Vickers and Armstrong in Britain. The gap was even wider in electrical engineering. AEG's £1.4 million profits were thirteen times as high than those of the British GEC (£108,000), and seven and a half times as high as those of the French CGE (£190,000). In chemicals, however, the profits of the British firm Brunner Mond were of the same order of magnitude as those of Hoechst, Bayer, and BASF. The diversity of British big business can be perceived through the impressive profits of companies in both capital and consumer goods industries. In all three countries, banks made large profits. Interestingly, three German banks (Deutsche, Dresdner, and Disconto-Gesellschaft) and a French one (Crédit Lyonnais) were ahead of the three leading British clearers (Westminster, Lloyds, and Midland). In France, banks were not only far ahead of industrial companies, but they were the only large companies of any kind whose profits reached levels comparable to those of their British and German counterparts. Finally, and somewhat surprisingly, the only firms in services with profits rivalling those of banks and industrial companies were the two German shipping companies HAPAG and Norddeutscher Lloyd, with respectively £728,000 and £648,000. By comparison, P. & O.'s profits were only £366,000, Cunard's £215,000, and those of the Compagnie Générale Transatlantique £107,000.

From the 1920s to the 1950s the gap between the British companies on the one hand, and the German and French on the other, widened considerably. In 1927–9 the average profit of British companies was £1.54 million as against £576,000 for their German and £267,000 for their French counterparts. Imperial Tobacco was by far the most profitable company in Europe, with £9.6 million, followed by another tobacco company, British American Tobacco, with £6.4 million; three other British companies topped £5 million (Lever Brothers, Shell, and ICI) as against a single

---

[3] The figures given in Table 4.1 are published profits. For the German iron and steel companies, however, real profits extracted from the companies' internal records can be found in W. Feldenkirchen, *Die Eisen- und Stahlindustrie des Ruhrgebiets 1879–1914: Wachstum, Finanzierung und Struktur ihrer Grossunternehmen* (Wiesbaden, 1982).

Table 4.1. Highest company profits in Britain, France, and Germany, 1911–1913 (£000s)

	Great Britain		France		Germany	
	Company	Profits	Company	Profits	Company	Profits
1	De Beers	2,920	Crédit Lyonnais	1,576	Krupp	1,762
2	J. & P. Coats	2,833	Société Générale	856	Deutsche Bank	1,726
3	Imperial Tobacco	2,718	Comptoir d'Escompte	709	AEG	1,424
4	Rio Tinto	1,613	Paribas	616	Phoenix	1,422
5	Shell	1,537	Banque de l'Union Parisienne	511	Siemens	1,299
6	Guinness	1,166	Châtillon-Commentry	495	Dresdner Bank	1,268
7	Westminster Bank	1,054	Gafsa	458	Disconto-Gesellschaft	1,252
8	Lloyds Bank	1,036	Longwy	455	GBAG	966
9	Midland Bank	1,011	Marine-Homécourt	455	Hoechst	852
10	Lever Brothers	829	Saint-Gobain	341	Bayer	787
11	Vickers	809			HAPAG	728
12	Brunner Mond	772			BASF	722
13	National Provincial Bank	753			Norddeutscher Lloyd	648
14	Armstrong	639			Deutsch-Überseeische Elektricitäts-Gesellschaft	642
15	Barclays Bank	625			Deutsch-Luxemburg	608
16	Burmah Oil	625				

German one (IG Farben). Altogether, twenty-two British companies made profits in excess of £1 million as against only five in Germany and none in France. Table 4.2 further illustrates these differences. British banks, for example, had by now firmly moved ahead of their European rivals, while the French banks lost ground at both national and international level. The Midland Bank's profits were almost double those of the Deutsche Bank and five times those of the Crédit Lyonnais.

Traditional German strength in electrical, chemical, and heavy industries persisted. However, despite a larger turnover, IG Farben's profits were only fractionally higher than those of ICI. As for the Vereinigte Stahlwerke, its profits undoubtedly dwarfed those of its British counterparts (just under £1 million for GKN and Vickers, a mere £93,000 for Dorman Long and £216,000 loss for United Steel). However, despite its nearly 200,000-strong workforce, Vereinigte Stahlwerke made far less profits than the British textile companies Courtaulds and J. & P. Coats. Moreover, with £516,000 profits in 1927–9, Krupp, the most profitable German company before 1914, was no longer among the country's top ten. In electrical engineering, the profits of GEC (£662,000) and AEI (£211,000) in Britain, and CGE (£197,000) and Thomson (£168,000) in France, did not match those of Siemens and AEG, though GEC was getting nearer. And the Gramophone Company's staggering £1 million profits were actually higher than those of AEG, though it was to lose similarly vast amounts of money in the early 1930s. French companies' profits were inevitably depressed by the devaluation of the franc. Only one company, Michelin, would have ranked among the German top ten, with profits five times as high as those of its German counterpart Continental (£163,000), though only half those of its British counterpart Dunlop. In services, British companies' earnings were on the whole higher than those of their Continental counterparts, even though only one of them, Associated Press, was among the country's top twenty. In shipping, P. & O. and Cunard's profits were respectively £804,000 and £673,000 while Allied Newspapers' stood at £636,000. In retailing, Home & Colonial Stores' £524,000 were slightly lower than the £602,000 of the German department store chain Karstadt; the latter, however, was to encounter serious difficulties in 1931. In France, profits of the Bon Marché and the Galeries Lafayette were in the £350,000–£400,000 range.

By 1953–5 the average profit of the top British companies had outgrown that of their German and French counterparts by a factor of six to seven. The figures were respectively £5.6 million, £765,000, and £898,000, Germany having fallen behind France. BP's earnings, £32.7 million, were by then the highest in Europe, more than ten times those of Siemens, Germany's highest, with £2.98 million.[4] No German or French company

[4] These profits are those of Siemens & Halske and Siemens Schuckertwerke together.

Table 4.2. Highest company profits in Britain, France, and Germany, 1927–1929 (£000s)

	Great Britain		France		Germany	
	Company	Profits	Company	Profits	Company	Profits
1	Imperial Tobacco	9,598	Michelin	879	IG Farben	5,603
2	BAT	6,425	Crédit Lyonnais	503	Vereinigte Stahlwerke	2,636
3	Lever Bros.	5,626	Mines de Lens	467	Deutsche Bank	1,425
4	Shell	5,409	Pechiney	448	Siemens	1,387
5	ICI	5,145	Saint-Gobain	447	Wintershall	1,072
6	Courtaulds	3,950	Banque de l'Indochine	447	AEG	800
7	J. & P. Coats	3,950	Société Générale	444	Disconto-Gesellschaft	769
8	Anglo-Persian	3,159	Comptoir d'Escompte	427	Mannesmann	760
9	Midland Bank	2,626	Mines d'Anzin	418	Danat Bank	746
10	Lloyds Bank	2,515	Paribas	403	Norddeutscher Lloyd	669
11	Barclays Bank	2,296			Dresdner Bank	632
12	Guinness	2,262			Karstadt	602
13	Distillers	2,230				
14	De Beers	2,214				
15	Westminster Bank	2,147				
16	National Provincial Bank	2,131				
17	Dunlop	1,956				
18	Watneys	1,221				
19	Associated Press	1,207				
20	Rio Tinto	1,117				
21	Morris	1,079				
22	Gramophone	1,008				

Table 4.3. Highest company profits in Britain, France, and Germany, 1953–1955 (£000s)

	Great Britain		France		Germany	
	Company	Profits	Company	Profits	Company	Profits
1	BP	32,668	CFP	6,146	Siemens	2,979
2	ICI	25,299	Renault	2,735	Bayer	2,655
3	BAT	22,057	Esso Standard	2,615	BASF	2,525
4	Unilever	19,641	Rhône-Poulenc	1,916	GBAG	2,164
5	Imperial Tobacco	11,723	L'Air Liquide	1,510	Hoechst	2,131
6	Shell	10,708	Pechiney	1,449	Rheinstahl	1,296
7	Courtaulds	9,751	Michelin	1,359	Mannesmann	1,997
8	BMC	9,157	Saint-Gobain	1,287	Continental	836
9	Woolworths	9,101	CGE	1,206	Wintershall	716
10	Distillers	8,133	Ugine	1,116	Deutsche Erdöl	689
11	GUS	6,775	Citroën	976	Daimler-Benz	680
12	Stewarts & Lloyds	6,587	Kuhlmann	890	Vereinigte Glanzstoff	674
13	GKN	5,444	Say	788	AEG	658
14	P. & O.	5,427	Tréfileries Havre	754		
15	Steel Co. of Wales	5,070	SNECMA	739		
16	Burmah Oil	4,702				
17	Dunlop	4,662				
18	AEI	4,470				
19	United Steel	4,438				
20	Marks & Spencer	4,147				
21	BICC	4,051				
22	Hawker Siddeley	4,007				

would have ranked among the top twenty-five British companies,[5] with the sole exception of the Compagnie Française des Pétroles which would have ranked twelfth.

In all sectors, British companies' profits were far higher than those of their German or French counterparts. The gap was huge in the traditional British strongholds: oil, food, drink and tobacco, and services. Even in chemicals, ICI's profits were three times as large as those of Bayer, BASF, and Hoechst put together. The profits of the German chemical companies were in fact closer to those of their French counterparts, especially Rhône-Poulenc, and to a lesser extent l'Air Liquide or Saint-Gobain (Table 4.3). French and German companies' profits were also closer in motor cars (compare BMC with Renault and Citroën, and Daimler-Benz), and even electrical engineering: putting Siemens aside, the CGE's profits had actually moved ahead of those of AEG, while Althom's £628,000 was not far

[5] In addition to the companies listed in Table 4.3, another five British firms had net profits in excess of £3 million: Vickers and Dorman Long (£3.9 million each), GEC (£3.4 million), and Tube Investments and J. & P. Coats (£3.3 million each).

Table 4.4. Highest company profits in Britain, France, and Germany, 1970–1972 ($ million)

	Great Britain		France		Germany	
	Company	Profits	Company	Profits	Company	Profits
1	Shell	424	CFP	101	Hoechst	97
2	BP	252	SGPM	68	BASF	94
3	ICI	217	Elf	63	Bayer	93
4	BAT	185	Rhône-Poulenc	54	Daimler-Benz	89
5	Unilever	127	PUK	54	Siemens	81
6	GEC	112	Peugeot	44	VW	70
7	Imperial Tobacco	110	CGE	27	Mannesmann	31
8	Courtaulds	95	Usinor	25	Thyssen	29
9	Distillers	83	L'Air Liquide	24	R. Bosch	21
10	Burmah Oil	73	BSN	22	Henckel	21
11	Allied Breweries	62				
12	Bass	60				
13	RTZ	60				
14	GKN	57				
15	Thorn	57				
16	Beecham	54				
17	Reed International	42				
18	Glaxo	35				
19	Ass. British Food	34				
20	British Leyland	33				
21	Coats Patons	33				
22	Hawker Siddeley	32				
23	Plessey	30				

Note: Industrial companies only. The total profits of Royal Dutch Shell and Unilever have been halved.

behind. Banks continued to fall in the hierarchy of size and profits. Even in Britain, banks' earnings were no longer among the country's highest (Barclays Bank's profits were just under £2.5 million), although they outstripped those of their French and German competitors. The distance separating the leading British companies from their Continental counterparts might appear excessive, and must no doubt be kept in perspective. Though normal economic conditions were by then prevailing in the three countries, France and Germany were still in the process of catching up with Britain. Nevertheless, such a gap was also a reflection of the new dimension attained by British big business in the aftermath of the Second World War.

A certain convergence inevitably took place in the following decades. However, it narrowed rather than filled the gap. Performances of large corporations are far better documented since the late 1960s, with interna-

Table 4.5. Highest company profits in Britain, France, and Germany, 1987–1989 ($ million)

	Great Britain		France		Germany	
	Company	Profits	Company	Profits	Company	Profits
1	Shell	2,742	Peugeot	1,406	Daimler-Benz	1,836
2	BP	2,655	Renault	1,189	Bayer	999
3	BAT	1,690	Elf	1,011	Hoechst	944
4	Hanson	1,580	Saint-Gobain	605	BASF	819
5	ICI	1,490	Rhône-Poulenc	541	Siemens	731
6	Grand Metropolitan	1,257	CGE	481	VW	395
7	RTZ	1,070	Michelin	395	R. Bosch	352
8	Glaxo	992	Orkem	389	Thyssen	310
9	BTR	902	BSN	350	BMW	240
10	Unilever	845	LVMH	340		
11	GEC	777	Pechiney	327		
12	Guinness	700	Lafarge-Coppée	304		
13	British Steel	652				
14	Bass	542				
15	Reed International	520				
16	Allied Lyons	460				
17	ABF	339				
18	BOC	318				
19	Hillsdown Holdings	308				
20	Racal	307				
21	Beecham	306				

Note: Industrial companies only. The total profits of Royal Dutch Shell and Unilever have been halved.

tional comparative tables readily available in the financial press. In 1970–2 the average profit of the top ten British industrial companies was $155.8 million, which was substantially higher than the $62.7 million of their German and the $48.2 million of their French counterparts.[6] As can be seen from Table 4.4, seven British industrial companies had profits exceeding $100 million as against only one in France and none in Germany. British companies' profits were also higher in every industrial sector except motor cars. This trend continued until the late 1980s. In 1989 the average profit of the ten largest industrial companies was $1,577 million in Britain, $831 million in France, and $917 million in Germany.[7] Although Daimler-Benz was by then achieving the biggest profits, seventeen British industrial companies had profits exceeding $500 million, as against seven in France and six in Germany (Table 4.5). The difference from the previous decades was that the leading British companies were, on the whole, no

[6] Calculated from *Fortune*, Sept. 1973.
[7] Author's calculations from *Fortune*, 30 July 1990, p. 75.

longer larger than their French and German counterparts, which raises the question of profitability.

PROFITABILITY

A number of ratios are available in order to measure a company's profitability: dividend (which is a ratio of distributed profits to share capital), ratio of net profits to capital employed, ratio of net profits to shareholders' funds, ratio of operating profits to net assets, ratio of cash flow to total assets, and so on. All have their value, though they are not all workable for earlier periods. From our perspective—a broad comparison of the performance of the leading British, French, and German companies throughout this century—they are all likely to provide similar results. Return on shareholders' funds is a good indication of managerial success, measuring how efficiently the funds belonging to the company's owners have been used by those in charge of the company's affairs. It is a ratio widely used by economic historians in the three countries, though possibly more in continental Europe than in Britain.[8] Shareholders' funds can also be reconstituted from the companies' published balance-sheets in each of the three countries.

One must, however, be aware of the limitations of such a ratio: net profits are affected by taxation while shareholders' funds are not necessarily valued at current cost. A high profit rate can result from an inordinately low share capital rather than from strong business results. Such distortions do happen. Nevertheless, return on shareholders' funds remains, and is seen by companies themselves as, a useful measure of performance. In their 1995 report to shareholders, the directors of the French banking group Paribas declared 'an ambitious target of profitability', which was 'to reach a 15 per cent return on shareholders' funds' —from an admittedly low rate of 5 per cent.[9] Interestingly, investors in the iron and steel industry in nineteenth-century Britain also considered a 15 per cent return on shareholders' funds as a fair expectation.[10] Here therefore is a useful yardstick of business profitability, though, as we shall see, a return of 15 per cent or more has been achieved by only a handful of companies throughout the century. On the basis of actual performances, 10 per cent appears much more realistic.

Analysis of profitability reveals a picture at once similar to and differ-

[8] See the recent inquiry by Jacques Marseille, Institut d'Histoire Économique, University of Paris I-Sorbonne, on the performance of French companies since the 1930s, which uses a similar approach. Preliminary results in 'Les Entreprises stars du XXe siècle', *L'Expansion*, 9/19 Dec. 1993.

[9] *Le Monde*, 10 Apr. 1995.

[10] Church, Baldwin, and Berry, 'Consett Iron Company', 716.

Table 4.6. Average rate of profit of the leading British, French, and German companies, 1913–1989 (%)[a]

	1911–13	1927–9	1953–5	1970–2	1987–9
Britain	12.8	10.6	8.3	8.6	17.2
France	8.3	9.8	5.8	5.4	14.4
Germany	10.7	7.2	3.0	7.2	10.5

[a] For 1972 and 1989, industrial companies only.

ent from that already sketched by the study of profits. Similar in the sense that, on average, British companies have proved consistently more profitable than their Continental counterparts, France and Germany alternating in second place (Table 4.6). Different in the sense that, as one would expect, the most profitable companies were not always those with the highest level of profits; while behind national averages lay huge differences between sectors and individual companies.

Before 1914 the most profitable companies were those operating in colonial empires or abroad (Table 4.7). The highest rate of return, not only of the pre-war but of all the benchmark years, was reached by the Compagnie des Phosphates et Chemin de Fer de Gafsa with an average of 47.3 per cent for the years 1911–13,[11] followed by Rio Tinto, the copper mining company, with 38 per cent, and by De Beers Consolidated, the South African diamond mining concern, with 33.6 per cent. A wider sample would no doubt have revealed several other highly profitable colonial companies, in line with findings that rates of returns were generally higher on overseas than on home investments,[12] though the Consolidated Gold Fields of South Africa, for example, did not reach 7 per cent. Two other groups of companies were inordinately profitable. One, not surprisingly, consisted of the three German chemical companies Hoechst, Bayer, and BASF, which fully exploited their dominance of world markets in dye products. Taken together their profit rate was nearly 26 per cent, with Hoechst itself approaching 30 per cent. Rates of profit reached 14.7 per cent at Brunner Mond and 7.3 per cent at the more mature Saint-Gobain.

---

[11] Established in 1897, the Compagnie des Phosphates et Chemin de Fer de Gafsa mined phosphates, operated a railway between Gafsa and Sfax, cultivated some 74,000 acres of land, and owned two oilworks. Smaller French colonial companies, such as the Compagnie des Mines d'Ouasta or the Charbonnages du Tonkin, were even more profitable. See J. Marseille, *Empire colonial et capitalisme français: Histoire d'un divorce* (Paris, 1984), 110–11.

[12] See in particular M. Edelstein, *Overseas Investment in the Age of High Imperialism: The United Kingdom, 1850–1914* (London, 1982); L. Davis and R. A. Huttenback, *Mammon and the Pursuit of Empire: The Political Economy of British Imperialism, 1860–1912* (Cambridge, 1987).

Table 4.7. The most profitable British, French, and German companies, 1911–1913 (rate of return on shareholders' funds higher than 10 per cent)

	Great Britain		France		Germany	
	Company	Profits	Company	Profits	Company	Profits
1	Rio Tinto	38.0	Gafsa	47.3	Hoechst	29.5
2	De Beers	33.6	Châtillon-Commentry	33.0	Bayer	25.5
3	Dunlop	20.9	Longwy	24.0	BASF	22.7
4	Amalgamated Press	19.6	Marine-Homécourt	20.2	Phoenix	21.2
5	Shell	18.5	Nord-Est	18.4	Krupp	15.8
6	J. & P. Coats	15.9	Schneider	13.9	Berliner Elektricitäts-Werke	14.9
7	Burmah Oil	15.7	Générale des Eaux	13.1	Siemens	14.1
8	Brunner Mond	14.7	Banque de l'Union Parisienne	12.6	Gutehoffnung	13.6
9	National Provincial Bank	14.5	CGE	11.6	AEG	13.1
10	Lloyds Bank	14.4	Galeries Lafayette	10.1	Schultheiss	11.9
11	Metropolitan Amalgamated	14.1			Bochumer Verein	11.4
12	Guinness	13.9			Deutsche Bank	10.9
13	Imperial Tobacco	13.7			Rombacher	10.7
14	Westminster Bank	13.6			Hohenlohe Werke	10.3
15	Vickers	13.4			Kattowitzer	10.3
16	Midland Bank	12.9				
17	Howard & Bullough	12.9				
18	Barclays Bank	12.6				
19	GEC	11.3				
20	Harrods	11.2				
21	Dorman Long	10.7				
22	Home & Colonial	10.4				
23	Stewarts & Lloyds	10.3				
24	Calico Printers	10.1				

The second, perhaps more unexpected group consisted of the French iron and steel companies. The average return on shareholders' funds of the five companies included in the sample was as high as 21.6 per cent; Châtillon-Commentry, Longwy, and Marine-Homécourt were especially profitable. Such high profits might have derived, at least in part, from sales of iron ore from Meurthe-et-Moselle,[13] though this explanation needs to be substantiated at the level of individual firms. By comparison, the average rate of return of the eighteen German heavy industry companies included in the sample was 10.4 per cent; and that of the ten British companies 9.2 per cent. The north of France coal-mining companies, which did not publish their balance sheets, could not be included in the analysis of profits; but the indications are that they were highly profitable.[14] The consequence of this omission, however, is the under-representation of the heavy industries in the sample of French companies, which might well have held down the average rate of profits of French big business.

British banks were distinctly more profitable than their Continental counterparts (13.8 per cent as against 8.3 per cent for the French banks and 9.1 per cent for the German banks). Their results, however, did not reach the heights of the German chemical or the French iron and steel companies. Other sectoral comparisons are difficult, because large companies tended to operate in different areas in each of the three countries. There were no German or French equivalents to the large British companies in consumer durables, textiles, or oil, while comparisons tend to be meaningless in electrical engineering, the size of Siemens and AEG being about ten times that of GEC and CGE. No sector of British business was exceptionally profitable, i.e. exceeded a 20 per cent return on shareholders' funds. What is more striking in the British case is the number of companies realizing a satisfactory rate of profit: 54.5 per cent of them reached 10 per cent or more as against 38.5 per cent of both French and German companies. On the other hand, the only large corporation in the sample to record a loss was British: Palmers Shipbuilding lost £32,000 in 1912, resulting in a meagre average rate of return of 0.6 per cent for the three years 1911–13. Other poor performers included the brewers Watney, Combe & Reid, one of the largest British companies, with 2 per cent, mainly as a result of over-capitalization;[15] Oberschlesische Eisen-Industrie, with 2.1 per cent;[16] and British Westinghouse, the extravagant venture of the American George Westinghouse, which had obviously been

[13] M. Rust, 'Business and Politics in the Third Republic: The Comité des Forges and the French Steel Industry, 1896–1914', unpub. Ph.D. thesis (Princeton University, 1973), 205.

[14] See Bouvier, Furet, and Gillet, *Le Mouvement du profit en France*.

[15] T. Gourvish and R. Wilson, *The British Brewing Industry 1830–1980* (Cambridge, 1994), 296–8. Other London brewers were in a similar position.

[16] Heavy industries from Upper Silesia were on the whole less profitable than their counterparts in the Ruhr. See T. Pierenkemper, 'Entrepreneurs in Heavy Industry: Upper Silesia and the Westphalian Ruhr Region 1852 to 1913', *Business History Review*, 53/1 (1979), 65–78.

built on too large a scale in 1903, with 2.9 per cent, due in large part to the company's improved results in 1913.[17]

Differences were narrower in the late 1920s, in particular between British and French big business. The average rate of return on shareholders' funds was 10.6 per cent for the British, 9.8 per cent for the French, and 7.2 per cent for the German leading companies. The profitability of German big business clearly deteriorated in the 1920s,[18] though the profit squeeze must have been tighter for German industry as a whole.[19] France's big business was undoubtedly successful, with 48.9 per cent of the country's top companies achieving a rate of profit higher than 10 per cent, as against 46.3 per cent of British companies and only 19 per cent of German companies (Table 4.8). However, the performance of the French companies cannot be solely attributed to their dynamism in a booming economy. The devaluation of the franc also meant that their share capital remained in part, and sometimes in full, at its pre-1914 value, while profits were expressed at current price, a combination which in some cases produced a slightly inflated ratio.

The most significant divergence between the three countries concerned the respective performances of their heavy industries. As in the pre-1914 years, French companies were more successful than their British and German counterparts, thanks at least partly to the windfall of sequestrated German properties acquired from the government at exceptionally favourable prices.[20] Coal-mining companies from the north of France such as the Mines de Marles, the Mines d'Aniche, and the Mines d'Anzin which had diversified into steel-making were particularly successful, with rates of return in the 14 to 16 per cent range; and at 8.9 per cent the average rate of profit of all major companies in this sector (including iron and steel), which accounted for over a quarter of French top companies' shareholders' funds, was not far from the national average. This was in sharp contrast to both Britain and Germany, where profit rates were respectively 3.2 and 5.1 per cent. The predicament of the British heavy industries in the 1920s is well known.[21] A coal-mining company such as Powell Duffryn

[17] See R. Jones and O. Marriott, *Anatomy of a Merger: A History of GEC, AEI and English Electric* (London, 1970), 43–58.

[18] On the low profit rates in Weimar Germany, see in particular K. Borchardt, 'Zwangslagen und Handlungsspielräume in der grossen Weltwirtschaftskrise der frühen dreissiger Jahre: Zur Revision der überlieferten Geschichtsbildes', in Bayerische Akademie der Wissenschaften, *Jahrbuch 1975* (Munich, 1975); H. James, *The German Slump: Politics and Economics 1924–1936* (Oxford, 1986); T. Balderston, *The Origins and Course of the German Economic Crisis: November 1923–May 1932* (Berlin, 1993).

[19] See Spörrer, 'New Estimates of Industrial Profitability'.

[20] C. Prêcheur, *La Lorraine sidérurgique* (Paris, 1959), 207–8.

[21] For the steel industry, see S. Tolliday, *Business, Banking, and Politics: The Case of British Steel, 1918–1939* (Cambridge, Mass., 1987). For the coal industry, see B. Supple, *The History of the British Coal Industry, iv. 1913–1946: The Political Economy of Decline* (Oxford, 1987), and M. Dintenfass, *Managing Industrial Decline: The British Coal Industry between the Wars* (Columbus, Oh., 1992).

Table 4.8. The most profitable British, French, and German companies, 1927–1929 (rate of return on shareholders' funds)

	Great Britain		France		Germany	
	Company	Rate of return (%)	Company	Rate of return (%)	Company	Rate of return (%)
1	Gramophone	35.4	Banque de l'Indochine	31.7	Schultheiss	17.9
2	Austin	19.4	Say	29.5	Karstadt	13.9
3	Marks & Spencer	19.4	Michelin	23.9	Danat Bank	12.4
4	Guinness	18.3	Havas	21.8	Siemens	12.0
5	BAT	18.2	Gafsa	17.3	Süddeutsche Zucker	11.3
6	Rio Tinto	18.0	Bon Marché	16.8	Wintershall	11.2
7	Imperial Tobacco	17.1	Hachette	16.5	Deutsche Bank	11.2
8	Morris	17.1	Mines de Marles	16.1	Commerzbank	10.5
9	Shell	16.5	Mines d'Aniche	15.7	Stollwerck	9.8
10	Boots	16.0	Dollfuss-Mieg	15.5	Dresdner Bank	9.5
11	De Beers	15.8	Peñarroya	14.1	Ostwerke	9.5
12	Distillers	14.7	Mines d'Anzin	13.8	IG Farben	9.3
13	BIC	13.4	Galeries Lafayette	13.2		
14	Watneys	13.2	Peugeot	12.6		
15	Dunlop	12.5	CGE	11.7		
16	J. & P. Coats	12.3	Longwy	11.5		
17	J. Lucas	12.3	SCOA	11.5		
18	Babcock & Wilcox	12.2	Sarre et Moselle	11.5		
19	Home & Colonial	11.4	Paribas	11.3		
20	Tate & Lyle	11.2	Fives-Lille	11.1		
21	Westminster Bank	11.2	Pechiney	10.5		
22	Callenders Cable	11.1	Comptoir d'Escompte	10.1		
23	Midland Bank	10.8				
24	Bass	10.7				
25	Lloyds Bank	10.1				

lost on average £53,000 a year between 1927 and 1929, United Steel
£216,000 (respectively 1.2 and 2 per cent of shareholders' funds). Dorman
Long's and Harland & Wolff's rate of profit was a meagre 1 per cent. Only
Stewarts & Lloyds, Vickers, and Guest, Keen & Nettlefolds were above 6
per cent.[22] In Germany, coal was also an industry in crisis.[23] Harpener
Bergbau only managed a 3.4 per cent return on shareholders' funds, and
the giant steel concern Vereinigte Stahlwerke, which was also Germany's
largest coal producer, 4.5 per cent. Krupp, which faced near collapse in
1925, was even less profitable with 4.4 per cent; and Hoesch and Klöckner only fractionally more with respectively 5 and 5.6 per cent.[24]

The consequences, however, were not the same for the two countries as
German big business, unlike British, was still dominated by the coal, iron,
and steel industries. In Britain the heavy industries accounted for less than
10 per cent of the shareholders' funds of the large corporations, as against
more than a third in Germany. Other industries could thus offer little com-
pensation in Germany. The chemical industry, for example, was far less
profitable than in the pre-war years: IG Farben's 9.5 per cent profit rate
paled in comparison with Hoechst's 29.5 per cent or even BASF's 22.7 per
cent in 1911–13, even though it compared favourably with ICI's 6.7 per
cent. In the late 1920s the most profitable German companies were, surprisingly, in the food and drink industry (Schultheiss in brewing, Süddeutsche Zucker in sugar-refining, Stollwerck in confectionery, and
Ostwerke in distilling) and in retailing (Karstadt), which counted for very
little within German big business. Siemens and the big banks were the
only major representatives of German big business among the ten most
profitable companies.

In Britain, by contrast, the poor performance of the heavy industries
had a limited impact, because of the diversification of big business and
the strong showing of most other sectors. Textiles, for example, was
another staple industry in crisis, but its two leading firms, J. & P. Coats
and Courtaulds, were making healthy profits, respectively 12.3 and 9.6
per cent. The Bleachers' Association was not far behind with 8.5 per cent,
having been able to improve on its pre-war levels of profitability, despite
a diminution in the volume of its business, largely as a result of its
dominant market position.[25] Despite Fine Cotton Spinners' and British
Celanese's weaker results (respectively 6 and 5 per cent), the largest firms
in the industry reached an average rate of profit of 9.5 per cent, compared

[22] Rates of return on shareholders' fund were 7.3% for Vickers, 6.8% for Stewarts & Lloyds,
and 6.2% for GKN.
[23] See J. Gillingham, *Industry and Politics in the Third Reich: Ruhr Coal, Hitler and Europe*
(London, 1985), 5–31.
[24] The highest rates of profit in the German heavy industries were those of Rheinbraun
(8.4%), Mannesmann (7.7%), and the Mitteldeutsche Stahlwerke (6.6%).
[25] J. Bamberg, 'The Government, the Banks and the Lancashire Cotton Industry,
1918–1939', unpub. Ph.D. dissertation (University of Cambridge, 1984), 13.

with a 1.1 per cent *loss* for the admittedly much smaller German firms.[26] In electrical engineering, the Gramophone's profits were spectacular; but the good results of the cable-makers British Insulated Cables and Callenders Cables, and of the maker of car electrical accessories Joseph Lucas (12.3 per cent as against 7.4 per cent for its German counterpart R. Bosch), also contributed to the sector's overall performance (12.2 per cent as against 9.1 in Germany and 8 in France). Food, drink, and tobacco was even more impressive with 15.6 per cent, while the two car manufacturers, Austin and Morris, were highly profitable in the late 1920s.[27] Banks partly lost in profitability what they had gained in size through the mammoth amalgamations of 1918 and were at about the national average. Chemicals, including pharmaceuticals (Boots) and other allied products (Unilever), were lower at 8.5 per cent.

Comparisons are more difficult for the mid-1950s, mainly because of the huge difference between the average rates of profits of British and German companies (respectively 8.3 and 3 per cent), France being in between with 5.8 per cent (Table 4.9). Not a single German company reached a 10 per cent rate of profit in 1953–5, as against 27 per cent of British and 19 per cent of French companies. The highest rate achieved by a German company was much lower, at only 6 per cent, a level attained or surpassed by 79 per cent of British companies and 42 per cent of French companies.

These figures undoubtedly reflect the delayed recovery of some sectors of German big business after the Second World War. This was especially the case with the heavy industries, the least profitable sector of German industry (2.2 per cent). The dismemberment of the huge conglomerates by the Allies proceeded slowly. It was only between 1951 and 1953 that seventeen companies were eventually formed to succeed the giant Vereinigte Stahlwerke. The last to be set up was August Thyssen Hütte, at first consisting of a single steel plant in Hamborn and reconstructed with funds from the Marshall Plan after having been completely dismantled. All the companies in the sector were newly formed (or re-formed), and had emerged from a period of factory dismantlements and other measures originally designed to eradicate the Ruhr's huge military potential.[28] Iron and steel production only reached its pre-war level in 1952, two years later than sectors such as machine tools or chemicals. Taking 1936 as base 100, the index of iron and steel production had risen to 129.7 by the end of 1954, as against 248.8 for machine tools and 222.0 for chemicals.[29]

---

[26] This was the result of Vereinigte Glanzstoff's £2.9 million loss in 1929.

[27] See R. Church, *Herbert Austin: The British Motor Car Industry to 1941* (London, 1979); R. Overy, *William Morris, Viscount Nuffield* (London, 1976).

[28] See J. Gillingham, *Coal, Steel and the Rebirth of Europe, 1945–1955* (Cambridge, 1991).

[29] Figures from R. Stokes, *Divide and Prosper: The Heirs of I. G. Farben under Allied Authority 1945–1951* (Berkeley n.d.), 165.

Performances

Table 4.9. The most profitable British, French, and German companies, 1953–1955 (rate of return on shareholders' funds)

	Great Britain		France		Germany	
	Company	Rate of return (%)	Company	Rate of return (%)	Company	Rate of return (%)
1	Woolworths	20.0	Hachette	18.3	Gutehoffnung	6.0
2	BMC	15.0	Banque de l'Indochine	15.8	Continental	5.8
3	GUS	14.4	Crédit Lyonnais	13.4	Felten & Guilleaume	4.9
4	Steel Co. of Wales	13.9	L'Air Liquide	13.0	Vereinigte Glanzstoff	4.7
5	BP	13.1	Comptoir d'Escompte	12.6	Karstadt	4.6
6	Stewarts & Lloyds	12.9	Paribas	12.3	Süddeutsche Zucker	4.5
7	Hawker Siddeley	12.0	Société Générale	10.9	Degussa	4.4
8	BAT	11.4	Rhône-Poulenc	10.1	Siemens & Halske	4.4
9	Rolls-Royce	11.3	CFP	9.6	Rheinstahl	4.4
10	Dorman Long	11.2	Say	9.3	Deutsche Erdöl	4.3
11	Marks & Spencer	10.8	Nord-Est	9.0	Hoechst	4.2
12	Guinness	10.1	Renault	9.0	Bayer	4.0
13	BICC	9.8				
14	Unilever	9.5				
15	Imperial Tobacco	9.4				
16	Distillers	9.2				
17	Metal Box	9.0				

Dismantlement may have worked in the long-term interests of the German iron and steel industry, but short-term profits were undoubtedly affected. Moreover, iron and steel required huge amount of capital investment. Thyssen made no profits between 1953 and 1955, the Bochumer Verein lost 5 million marks in these three years, while Klöckner only started to operate at a profit in 1954, making an average return on its shareholders' funds of only 1.3 per cent. Deconcentration could thus be beneficial to firms left with the processing end of a formerly vertically integrated concern, such as the Gutehoffnungshütte (though the separation from its former coal and iron and steel subsidiaries was mainly formal[30]), where return on share-holders' funds reached 6 per cent. Results were uneven in the other major fields of German big business activity. Rates were around 4 per cent in chemicals, and only 3 per cent in electrical engineering, while the large banks were still divided into a number of regional units.

Rates of profits were substantially higher in most sectors of British busi-ness. Strong results were achieved in motor cars, BMC benefiting from the rapid conversion to peacetime activities and the surge in the production of motor vehicles of the late 1940s and early 1950s;[31] in aircraft, with Hawker Siddeley and Rolls-Royce (de Haviland suffered £663,415 loss in 1954 after writing off £4,732,538 of redundant Comet stock following the withdrawal of the Comet's certificate of airworthiness); and in retailing (Woolworths, Great Universal Stores, and Marks & Spencer), as well as in food, drink, and tobacco (Guinness, Distillers, Imperial Tobacco). Apart from motor cars, these were all areas where big business still hardly oper-ated in Germany.

Interestingly, there was much less difference in the more traditional fields of big business activity, especially in the chemical and electrical industries. Large firms such as AEI, GEC, or ICI were not among Britain's most profitable companies. And with profit rates of respectively 6.8, 7.2, and 6.7 per cent, they were only fractionally more profitable than their German counterparts Siemens (4.4 per cent), Hoechst (4.2 per cent), or Bayer (4 per cent), or for that matter the CGE (4.7 per cent) and Kuhlmann (5.3 per cent) in France. The same can be said of Dunlop, Continental, and Michelin, and to a lesser extent of Courtaulds and Vereinigte Glanzstoff-Fabriken.[32] British banks, whose activities had become increasingly regu-lated and cartelized, slipped further down the scale with an average rate of profit of 7 per cent. The most spectacular difference was in the iron and steel industry, with rates of profits well over 10 per cent for companies such as Stewarts & Lloyds, Dorman Long, or Steel Company of Wales.

[30] H. Joly, 'L'Élite industrielle allemande: Métier, pouvoir et politiques 1933–1989', unpub-lished Ph.D. thesis (École des Hautes Études en Sciences Sociales, Paris, 1993), 316–17.
[31] See G. Maxcy and A. Silberston, *The Motor Industry* (London, 1959).
[32] Dunlop's rate of profit was 7.1%, Continental's 5.8%, Michelin's 7.8%, Courtaulds' 8.1%, and Vereinigte Glanzstoff's 4.7%.

This was a result of both the earlier start of British post-war expansion and the decision by the new Conservative government in 1951 to privatize the steel industry which had been nationalized a few years earlier by Labour. The steel companies had thus to be made attractive to potential private investors.[33]

The French iron and steel companies were hardly more profitable than their German counterparts, with an average rate of profit of 2.7 per cent.[34] The financing of the reconstruction and modernization plans required massive investment. Other sectors, however, did better; especially, and somewhat paradoxically, the banks, whether the nationalized deposit banks (Crédit Lyonnais, Société Générale, Comptoir National d'Escompte de Paris), or the investment banks (Banque de Paris et des Pays-Bas, Banque de l'Indochine) which remained in the private sector. However, with the exception of the Banque de l'Indochine, which remained profitable during the war years,[35] these results must be attributed to the very low level to which their shareholders' funds had fallen by the early 1950s. At the Banque de Paris et des Pays-Bas, for example, shareholders' equity reached its lowest value at constant prices in 1952.[36] Strong performances by firms in chemicals (L'Air Liquide, Rhône-Poulenc), oil (CFP, Esso Standard), and motor cars (Renault) also contributed to improve the overall profitability of French big business in the early 1950s.

Twenty years later, with Germany having accomplished her *Wirtschaftswunder*, France nearing the end of the *Trente Glorieuses*, and Britain on the threshold of a troubled economic decade, British big business remained comfortably more profitable than its Continental counterparts. The gap with Germany did narrow. The average rate of profits of the top *industrial* companies for the years 1970–2 were respectively 8.6 and 7.2 per cent. French companies were behind with 5.4 per cent, mostly as a result of the heavy losses incurred by such major firms as Renault and Citroën, the giant iron and steel concern Wendel-Sidelor, as well as the smaller textile group Agache-Willot.[37] British companies outperformed their German counterparts in all sectors apart from motor cars and steel (Table 4.10). In the motor industry, Daimler-Benz and BMW were especially successful, while Volkswagen's more modest return was higher than the newly formed, and still profitable, British Leyland. British Steel, on the other hand, was the only loss-maker among major British companies,

---

[33] See K. Burk, *The First Privatisation: The Politicians, the City and the Denationalisation of Steel* (London, 1988).

[34] The rates of profit of the two largest companies, Usinor and Sidelor, were respectively 3.3 and 0.4%.

[35] See M. Meuleau, *Des pionniers en Extrême-Orient: Histoire de la Banque de l'Indochine, 1875–1975* (Paris, 1990), 407–39.

[36] E. Bussière, *Paribas* (Antwerp, 1992), 303–6.

[37] Ratio of net profits to shareholders' equity of 43 British, 26 French, and 32 German industrial companies with more than $500 million turnover in 1972 listed in *Fortune* magazine, Sept. 1973.

Table 4.10. The most profitable British, French, and German companies, 1970–1972 (rate of return on shareholders' funds)

	Great Britain		France		Germany	
	Company	Rate of return (%)	Company	Rate of return (%)	Company	Rate of return (%)
1	Beecham	21.2	L'Oréal	19.7	Daimler-Benz	17.2
2	Glaxo	20.1	L'Air Liquide	15.5	Varta	15.2
3	Thorn	18.3	Thomson	13.1	BMW	14.1
4	Courtaulds	14.7	Michelin	10.4	Deutsche Babcock	11.0
5	Associated British Foods	14.5	Hachette	10.0	Henckel	9.7
6	BAT	12.7	Peugeot	9.8	Mannesmann	9.7
7	Distillers	11.9	Dassault	9.6	R. Bosch	9.6
8	Unilever	11.8	CFP	9.4	Bayer	9.5
9	Allied Breweries	11.6	Gervais-Danone	8.6	Schering	9.3
10	Imperial Tobacco	11.3	Perrier	8.5	Hoechst	8.8
11	Reckitt & Colman	11.1	BSN	7.6	BASF	8.8
12	GEC	11.0			Degussa	8.5
13	Metal Box	10.9			Siemens	8.1
14	Johnson Matthey	10.5				
15	Lonrho	10.4				
16	Bass Charrington	10.4				
17	British Oxygen	10.0				
18	Hawker Siddeley	9.8				
19	ICI	9.5				
20	Coats Patons	9.5				
21	Shell	9.0				

Note: Industrial companies only.

while returns on shareholders' equity were between 4.5 and 6.5 per cent at Thyssen, Krupp, Hoesch, and Klückner, as well as Usinor and Creusot-Loire in France. In chemicals, rates of profits were comparable between ICI and BASF, Bayer, and Hoechst (Rhône-Poulenc was far behind); but they were substantially lower than those of the emerging British pharmaceutical giants Beecham and Glaxo, making the entire sector (including pharmaceuticals, detergents, cosmetics, etc.) more profitable in Britain with 11.4 per cent as against 8.8 per cent in Germany and 6.3 per cent in France, where l'Air Liquide and L'Oréal stood out. Electrical engineering displayed similar differences,[38] while British big business profitability was enhanced, as in earlier periods, by its powerful food, drink, and tobacco industry. Services have not been included in the national averages of rates of profit for 1972. As we have seen, they accounted for a larger part of big business in Britain; they were also more profitable. The largest of them, with $400 million turnover or more, made an average rate of return on shareholders' funds of 14.8 per cent in Britain (with rates as high as 30 per cent for Marks & Spencer and 22 per cent for Tesco), as against 6.2 in France (despite Carrefour's 43.7 per cent), and 8.6 per cent in Germany (with a top of 23.7 per cent for the mail order company Otto Versand).[39] In all three countries, large companies were more profitable in services than in manufacturing. The difference, however, was significantly larger in Britain (72 per cent) than in France (15 per cent) and Germany (19 per cent).

Comparative analyses of business performance have flourished since the 1980s, providing historians with a wealth of data, which all confirm the trend of the previous eighty years. British top companies have remained more profitable than their German and French counterparts. The three countries' companies that were ranked among the world's top 500 in 1989 (45 British, 29 French, and 32 German) provide a striking illustration. The average rate of return on shareholders' equity for the years 1987–9 was 17.2 per cent for the British, 14.4 for the French, and 10.5 per cent for the German companies.[40] Twenty British companies reached a rate of profit of 20 per cent or more, with a record 54 per cent for Hanson Trust. Only one French (Peugeot, with 27.5 per cent) and one German company (Daimler-Benz, with 25.3 per cent) achieved such rates (Table 4.11).

Why has British big business consistently been more profitable than its German and French competitors? A complete answer to this question will have to wait until a detailed, archive-based comparative study is undertaken, which of course represents a huge research agenda. Case studies

---

[38] The respective average rates of return were 10.5% for the British, 7.6% for the German, and 5.3% for the French companies.
[39] Percentages calculated from figures in 'Les 1.000 premières entreprises de l'Europe des neuf', *Les Dossiers d'Entreprise* (Nov. 1973), 371–3.
[40] Percentages calculated from figures given in *Fortune*, 30 July 1990.

Table 4.11. The most profitable British, French, and German companies, 1987–1989 (rate of return on shareholders' funds)

	Great Britain		France		Germany	
	Company	Rate of return (%)	Company	Rate of return (%)	Company	Rate of return (%)
1	Hanson	54.1	Orkem	35.5	Daimler-Benz	25.3
2	Hillsdown Holdings	36.3	Peugeot	27.5	Hoechst	15.8
3	BTR	36.2	Lafarge-Coppée	19.5	Bertelsmann	15.1
4	Glaxo	33.3	LVMH	18.6	Thyssen	14.4
5	Racal	31.9	Péchiney	17.9	Bayer	11.5
6	RTZ	29.6	Saint-Gobain	17.7	Continental	11.5
7	Grand Metropolitan	28.7	Matra	17.0	Hüls	11.3
8	Reed International	28.6	Rhône-Poulenc	16.3	Henckel	11.0
9	Cadbury	28.3	L'Oréal	16.3	Degussa	10.9
10	Unilever	28.1	Hachette	15.8	BASF	10.8
11	BICC	26.2	CEA-Industrie	14.4	BMW	10.0
12	Unigate	25.8	Valeo	14.2	R. Bosch	10.0
13	Courtaulds	25.7	CGE	14.0		
14	RMC	23.6				
15	BAT	23.6				
16	Reckitt & Colman	22.3				
17	Tate & Lyle	22.2				
18	STC	21.8				
19	ICI	20.6				
20	Dalgety	20.1				
21	Thorn	19.5				
22	BOC	18.8				
23	Pilkington	18.7				
24	Guinness	16.7				
25	GEC	15.7				
26	Rolls-Royce	15.4				

Note: Industrial companies only.

concentrating on the long-term profits of a limited number of British, French, and German companies operating in the same sector would undoubtedly be helpful and throw some light on at least part of the question. In the meantime, three factors can be put forward to explain the *overall* performance of British big business.

The first is structural and concerns the very nature of big business in Britain, far more diversified in the first part of the century than in France and Germany. And this diversification included from an early stage new and often highly profitable fields of activity, especially in the consumer and service industries. As we have seen, old-established large corporations in iron and steel, chemicals, and electricals often displayed similar rates of profit in two countries, or even in the three countries. In Britain, however, more profitable industries could compensate for more mature, or temporarily depressed, sectors. Low rates of profit in the heavy industries, for example, had far less impact on British than on German big business in the late 1920s. British businessmen might also have been quicker at shedding less profitable undertakings. The second factor is the result of specific circumstances, and mainly concerns the period extending from the 1920s to the 1950s when differences, in particular between Britain and Germany, were at their sharpest. In both the late 1920s and mid-1950s, although Germany had recovered from the war, British (and to a lesser extent French) business was operating in a sounder and more stable economy. At the other benchmark years, in particular pre-1914, the gap was much narrower and cannot be considered as really significant.

The third, and more controversial, factor is cultural. The long-standing, and rather odd, assumption that British capitalists were not sufficiently motivated by profits must obviously be rejected. It is rather a case of the alleged priority given by British business leaders to short-term profits over long-term development.[41] As an explanation of Britain's relative economic decline, it has recently enjoyed a certain vogue in the context of the high profits and takeover mania of the 1980s. But it is an old one: company promoters (who were responsible for most domestic industrial flotations) were accused of the same evils at the turn of the century—of overcapitalizing the companies they were selling to the public in order to make a fast buck, with little concern for their long-term or even mid-term prospects.[42] The respective merits of the capital markets and the univer-

[41] See for example H. W. De Jong, 'European Capitalism: Between Freedom and Social Justice', *Review of Industrial Organization*, 10 (1995), 399–419, who suggests 'that the Anglo-Saxon type of corporation, even though it achieves a remarkably better profitability than the Continental firm, has a lesser degree of value productivity and also a lower growth rate'.

[42] See J. Armstrong, 'The Rise and Fall of the Company Promoter and the Financing of British Industry', in J. J. Van Helten and Y. Cassis (eds.), *Capitalism in a Mature Economy: Financial Institutions, Capital Exports and British Industry, 1870–1939* (Aldershot, 1990), 115–38; D. Kynaston, *The City of London*, ii. *Golden Years 1890–1914* (London, 1995), 142–5, 179–83, 211–14; H. O. O'Hagan, *Leaves from my Life*, 2 vols. (London, 1929).

sal banks in the financing of industry will be discussed in a subsequent chapter, with other aspects of business leadership. One way of testing the 'short-termism' hypothesis, however, is to consider another criterion of business performance: companies' long-term survival.

5

Survival

Profits are not the only measure of corporate success. They are an end.
But they are also a means, for only sustained profits can allow a company
to overcome periods of crisis, to adapt to new conditions, to meet competition—in other words, to stand the test of time. Survival is an unquestionable, perhaps the ultimate, mark of success. Business history has often
been accused of being a 'success story' discipline, of being primarily interested in companies which have survived to the present day and celebrate
the event with an appropriate jubilee volume. This is an unfair accusation: business history has long freed itself from this genre. But the accusation is in itself revealing of the criterion by which corporate success is
spontaneously judged: survival and longevity.

Business leaders also cherish their company's independence and have
rarely failed to fight pugnaciously a hostile takeover bid. Selling a large
company might be in the shareholders' best interests; it might save jobs
or be part of an industry's necessary reorganization. It is only occasionally seen as a success for the leaders of the company surrendering its independence.[1] For those advocating market discipline, takeover bids are
seen as the best sanction against a failing management. Longevity is thus
a useful complement to profitability, and gives a good measure of a
company's long-term performance.[2] Of course, other factors than strictly
managerial contribute to a company's long-term survival. A firm's destiny
is largely determined by the sector in which it is engaged: the large textile
companies, some dating from the early days of the industrial revolution,
could hardly have been expected still to count among the world's largest
in the late twentieth century. Even the iron and steel companies, epitome
of the large corporation in the early to mid-twentieth century, have
declined to but a minor part of big business in post-industrial economies.
Protective tariffs or cartel agreements can also artificially maintain alive
a company which would have otherwise succumbed to competition,
while privileged relationships with political power can provide a decisive

[1] A rare example is Dudley Docker's sale of his company, Metropolitan Carriage Wagon
& Finance Co., to Vickers in 1919 referred to in Ch. 2. See R. P. T. Davenport-Hines, *Dudley
Docker: The Life and Times of a Trade Warrior* (Cambridge, 1984).

[2] For a similar approach, considering what had become in 1995 of the world's 100 largest
industrial companies of 1912 in terms of survival and stockmarket capitalization, see L.
Hannah, 'Marshall's "Trees" and the Global "Forest": Were "Giant Redwoods Different"?',
paper delivered at the NBER Conference on Organisational Learning and Corporate Capability, October 1996.

advantage over rivals. Business life, and business performances, are also affected by major international upheavals, especially world wars and their after-effects. These exogenous factors vary greatly from one country to another, and can thus be considered as decreasing, or on the contrary increasing, the value of survival as a mark of business success; this will depend on one's point of view. Survival in this context will be but a poor indicator of a firm's intrinsic competitiveness, a notion which in any case only exists in the abstract. On the other hand, survival encapsulates most determinants of business success, including chance, which extend beyond a firm's own capabilities, and can thus be seen as a 'real' measure of business performance.

LONGEVITY

Survival can be defined as a company's ability to remain both *independent* and sufficiently *large* still to enjoy big business status. Big business status has been defined in Part I; a turnover of at least £150 million in 1973 and £1 billion in 1989 has been considered as the minimum required for the more recent years. In order to be of any analytical use, independence requires a flexible definition. Mergers between equals, for example, pose a problem, as in the case of BASF, Bayer, and Hoechst and the formation of IG Farben in 1925. In such cases, the two or several firms involved have been considered as having survived, in order to avoid a bias against companies for which a merger was a dynamic step rather than a penalty for managerial failure. Nationalizations pose another problem. While they undoubtedly mean a loss of independence, a distinction should be made between firms which have kept their corporate identity and those which were merged into wider conglomerates. The former have been considered as having survived; they include the British iron and steel companies nationalized by Labour in 1949 and de-nationalized by the Conservatives in 1953; or the French deposit banks, nationalized by de Gaulle in 1946 and privatized (with the exception so far of the Crédit Lyonnais) four decades later. The latter include the public utility companies (electricity, gas), as well as the coal-mining companies nationalized after the Second World War in Britain and France; or the British steel companies, after they were renationalized by Labour in 1967 and merged into British Steel. On the basis of these admittedly arbitrary definitions, the destiny of the leading British, French, and German companies has been examined in both the medium and long term, using the same sample as for the analysis of profits.[3] The results can be seen in Table 5.1, which shows what

---

[3] Companies lacking sufficient information to be included in the analysis of profits have been added. The sample for the year 1973 includes the leading companies in industry, finance, and services.

Table 5.1. Survival of the largest British, French, and German companies, 1907–1989 (%)

	1929			1953			1972			1989		
	GB	F	D	GB	F	D	GB	F	D	GB	F	D
1907	86	96	75	73	67	42	50	44	25	37	42	19
1929	—	—	—	92	79	57	73	56	46	56	46	35
1953	—	—	—	—	—	—	79	70	76	64	50	58
1972	—	—	—	—	—	—	—	—	—	77	74	73

Notes: The table should be read as follows: percentage of leading companies active in 1907 which were still independent and large companies in 1929, 1953, 1972, and 1989, and so on.
GB = Great Britain, F = France, D = Germany in this and subsequent tables.

percentage of the leading companies of each of the benchmark years were still independent and large at each of the following benchmark years.

The French large firms of the pre-1914 years were the most successful, both in the medium and in the long term. Ninety-six per cent were still in existence twenty-five years later, in the late 1920s, as against 86 per cent of British firms and 75 per cent of German firms. And 42 per cent of them were still independent and large some eighty years later, in the late 1980s, as against 37 per cent of their British and 19 per cent of their German counterparts. New large firms, however, emerged after the First World War and their performances have to be taken into account. Of the large European corporations of the late 1920s, the British have proved the most resilient, again both in the medium and in the long term. Ninety-two per cent survived until the mid-1950s, as against respectively 79 and 57 per cent of the French and German firms; and 56 per cent until the late 1980s, as against 46 per cent of the French and 35 per cent of the German companies. Rates of survival increasingly converged after the Second World War, though the large British companies of the early 1950s proved somewhat more resilient than their Continental counterparts.

Contrary to conventional wisdom, conditions were not unfavourable to large firms in France in the first part of the century. There were, to be sure, difficult moments in the 1930s and 1940s, but they proved, on the whole, survivable. In contrast to Germany, very few firms' disappearance was due to liquidations during the depression of the 1930s. Citroën was in fact the only major casualty: the firm went bankrupt in 1934 but continued to trade under new ownership. Major disappearances between the late 1920s and early 1950s were due to the nationalization of the collieries (Mines d'Anzin, Mines de Lens, etc.) and of the electricity supply companies

(Union d'Électricité, Énergie Électrique du Littoral Méditerranéen, etc.). The particular configuration of French business partly explains their survival. Big business consisted of a comparatively small number of truly large companies, which reduced the possibility of being absorbed by a larger competitor. Such amalgamations did not really take place before the restructuring of the 1960s and 1970s,[4] hence the sharp decline of survival rates between 1953 and 1972. French big business has also traditionally maintained a close relationship with the state. In the inter-war years, most large corporations belonged to what used to be called the 'secteur abrité', or protected sector, i.e. firms which were protected from the rigours of the market by the fact that they belonged to cartelized industries and that they sold the bulk of their products to the state,[5] while the 1960s opened the era of the 'national champions'.

War and depression had a greater effect on German big business. The loss of Upper Silesia after the First World War resulted in the disappearance of a number of large-scale companies, such as the Hohenlohe Werke and the Oberschlesische Eisen-Industrie in the iron and steel industry, or Vulkan in shipbuilding. Resounding failures took place in the early 1930s. They included one of the great Berlin banks, the Danat Bank, which suspended payments in July 1931; an insurance company, the Frankfurter Allgemeine Versicherung, which went into liquidation in 1931–2; and the largest firm in the textile industry, the Nordwolle, which collapsed in 1931 after losing 200 million Reichsmark in speculative transactions. Nazi anti-Semitism also took its toll: the Hamburg private bank M. M. Warburg & Co. was 'Aryanized' in 1939 and changed its name to Brinckmann, Wirtz & Co.; the iron and steel company Kattowitzer AG was confiscated in the same year on the grounds that it was a Jewish property. On the other hand, the short-term failure of IG Farben and the Vereinigte Stahlwerke, which did not survive the Second World War, did not jeopardize the long-term survival of their leading constituent companies (BASF, Bayer, Hoechst, Thyssen). And several lesser companies which had been taken over and integrated into the giant iron and steel and chemical combines recovered their independence and survived in the medium or even the long term. Nevertheless, concentration was higher in German than in French industry. From an earlier stage, major companies were absorbed by even larger competitors, in particular in the iron and steel industry. Thus a firm of the size of the Union AG of Dortmund, which employed more than 12,000 people, was taken over by Deutsch-Luxemburg in 1910; the Bochumer Verein was taken over by the Rheinelbe Union in 1920. As in France, however, takeovers of major firms markedly increased in the 1960s.

[4] See Ch. 3, p. 64.
[5] See I. Kolboom, *La Revanche des patrons: Le Patronat français face au Front Populaire* (Paris, 1986); R. Vinen, *The Politics of French Business 1936–1945* (Cambridge, 1991).

British firms' rate of survival is more surprising given the level of industrial concentration in Britain, which was the highest in Europe and mainly
resulted from waves of mergers, especially at the turn of the century, in
the 1920s, and in the 1960s.[6] There is no doubt that a wider sample of large
companies, consisting of the top 500 or 1,000 companies, would show a
much higher rate of disappearance in Britain than in France and Germany,
especially in the last thirty years.[7] However, as we have seen, big business was far more extensive in Britain, and even though mergers did take
place between large companies, those in the top fifty were less likely to
be taken over than their counterparts in France or Germany. Nationalizations played a part in the disappearance of large firms, though to a lesser
extent than in France, as coal-mining and public utility companies never
weighed as heavily in British as in French big business. On the other hand,
major firms have been weakened by the nationalization of some of their
activities, such as steel. Vickers is a major case in point: the old armament
giant successively lost its steel, shipbuilding, and aircraft interests.[8] This
high level of stability in the upper reaches of British big business has,
however, been marred by a few spectacular failures, with no real equivalent in either Germany or France. The most striking example is undoubtedly the collapse of British Leyland in 1975 and the disappearance of the
British-owned motor industry. But there are others, such as the decline
and eventual takeover of Dunlop (while Michelin rose to number one in
the world); the failure of Rolls-Royce, rescued by the government in 1971;
or, though it was no longer a large company, the resounding collapse of
Barings in 1995. These events, and others, have crystallized the public
imagination, often to the detriment of a more balanced view of the overall
performance of British big business.

GROWTH

The question remains, however, whether profitability and survival have
been achieved at the expense of growth. Companies which have remained
independent and large over a twenty-year period may well have grown
at very different rates, some shooting up to the top of the rankings, others
only managing to maintain their status. A simple measure of such differences is the comparison of the growth of assets. This has been done for
the *surviving* companies included in the sample, by calculating the growth
of total assets, at constant prices, from one benchmark year to the other.
The resulting ratios are only intended to complement and qualify the rates

[6] See L. Hannah, *The Rise of the Corporate Economy* (2nd edn. London, 1983).
[7] See for example D. C. Mueller (ed.), *The Dynamics of Company Profits: An International
Comparison* (Cambridge, 1990), 169–71.
[8] See H. Evans, *Vickers: Against the Odds, 1956–1977* (London, 1978).

of survival discussed above, *not* to provide any overall measure of big business growth, which would of course require a different type of sample. Nor are they designed to propose an alternative measure of business performance. Fast growth, as is well known, is not necessarily the best strategic course, though, in the expanding world of big business, leading companies cannot afford to lose ground over a long-term period.

Of the pre-war companies which survived as independent and large until 1929, the British ones enjoyed the most sustained growth, whether taken collectively or individually (Table 5.2). Total assets of non-financial companies[9] increased by 56 per cent in real terms between 1911 and 1929, as against 16 per cent for the French and 2 per cent for the German companies. Not surprisingly, growth was faster in the so-called 'new industries' (with GEC, though pre-war only on the fringes of big business, Dunlop, Lever Brothers, and Shell) as well as in services (Amalgamated Press, Harrods, Home & Colonial Stores). At the other end of the scale, the textile conglomerates actually shrank, though not sufficiently to be excluded from the world of big business. A similar though less pronounced development can be observed in France, where electrical engineering (CGE), electricity supply (Parisienne de Distribution d'Électricité, EELM), and service (Galeries Lafayette) companies enjoyed the fastest growth. Thomson's contraction was due to the creation of Alsthom, which received parts of its assets. The new industries had less scope for growth in Germany. However, the aggregate assets of the companies which merged into IG Farben increased almost threefold between 1911 and 1929. Otherwise, the fastest-growing German companies were in the traditional textile (Nordwolle) and food (Schultheiss) industries, in sharp contrast to Britain. On the whole German companies suffered more from the losses following the First World War. This is most emphatically exemplified by Krupp, whose total assets in 1929 were only 55 per cent of their pre-war level; Krupp had to undertake an almost complete reconversion from the manufacture of military equipment, which it had dominated before the war, to the production of civilian goods. Finally, it must be stressed once again that these figures *do not* include newly formed companies, or companies which were not large enough to be included in the 1907 sample, some of which, especially in the motor car industry, grew at a much faster rate than those considered in Table 5.2.

The large British companies of the late 1920s combined higher survival with faster growth rates. By the early 1950s their combined total assets had grown by 70 per cent in real terms, as against 27 per cent for the French and 4 per cent for the German companies (Table 5.3). Marks & Spencer enjoyed by far the fastest growth, underlining the dynamism of services in British business (P. & O., Home & Colonial, Gaumont). As in

---

[9] Banks cannot be included in such averages because of the far larger amount, and different nature, of their assets and liabilities.

Table 5.2. Growth of assets of surviving companies, 1911–1929: ratio of total assets, 1929 (1911 = 100)

	Great Britain		France		Germany	
	Company	Ratio of assets	Company	Ratio of assets	Company	Ratio of assets
1	GEC	529	Parisienne Distribution Électricité	206	IG Farben[b]	296
2	Dunlop	435	CGE	185	Nordwolle	211
3	Lever Brothers	414	Galeries Lafayette	184	Darmstädter Bank	177
4	Shell	366	Énergie Électrique du Littoral Méditerranéen	172	Schultheiss	167
5	ICI[a]	365	Longwy	159	Siemens[c]	127
6	Barclays Bank	362	Banque de l'Indochine	151	Vestag[d]	110
7	Dorman Long	357	Saint-Gobain	141	AEG	107
8	Amalgamated Press	337	Générale Transatlantique	115	Dresdner Bank	107
9	National Provincial Bank	271	Paribas	114	Deutsche Bank[e]	105
10	Harrods	265	Schneider	111	Norddeutscher Lloyd	103
11	Midland Bank	254	Marine-Homécourt	103		
12	Burmah Oil	252	Comptoir d'Escompte	92	Stoehr	93
13	Lloyds Bank	251				
14	Home & Colonial	242	Crédit Lyonnais	80	GHH	90
15	Westminster Bank	232	Société Générale	76	HAPAG	82
16	P. & O.	231	Thomson	72	Harpener	76
17	Imperial Tobacco	196	Say	63	Felten & Guilleaume	74

18	Stewarts & Lloyds	191			
19	GKN	160			
20	Cunard	156			
21	Vickers	127			
22	Bass	114			
23	Rio Tinto	105			
24	De Beers	104			
25	Guinness	100			
26	Bolckow Vaughan	98			
27	Whitley	92			
28	J. & P. Coats	87			
29	Watneys	86			
30	Cotton Spinners	83			
31	John Brown	75			
32	Rylands	74			
33	Calico Printers	66			
34	Bleachers	63			
35	Consolidated Gold Fields	42	Châtillon-Commentry	42	Stollwerk	60
36	United Collieries	34	Messageries Martimes	24	Krupp	55
					Laurahütte	39
					Oberschlesische Eisenbahnbedarfs	27

[a] Combined total assets of Brunner Mond, Nobel Dynamite Trust, and United Alkali.
[b] Combined total assets of BASF, Bayer, Hoechst, Grisheim Elektron, Agfa.
[c] Siemens & Halske and Siemens Schuckertwerke.
[d] Combined total assets of Thyssen, GBAG, Deutsch-Luxemburg, Phoenix, Rheinische Stahlwerke, Bochumer Verein.
[e] Combined total assets of Deutsche Bank and Disconto-Gesellschaft.

Table 5.3. Growth of assets of surviving companies, 1929–1953: total assets 1953 (1929 = 100)

	Great Britain		France		Germany[a]	
	Company	Assets	Company	Assets	Company	Assets
1	Marks & Spencer	652	CFP	688	Mannesmann	273
2	Lucas	437	SCOA	306	R. Bosch	204
3	AEI	433	Huiles de Pétrole	255	Klöckner	199
4	Stewarts & Lloyds	385	Fives-Lille	250	Süddeutsche Zucker	182
5	Anglo-Persian	366	Jeumont	230	Daimler-Benz	179
6	Vickers	300	Alsthom	213	Continental	154
7	P. & O.	288	Pechiney	171	Siemens[c]	134
8	BAT	286	Générale Transatlantique	164	Deutsche Erdöl	137
9	BICC[b]	284	Longwy	141	AG Weser	126
10	Austin/Morris	251	Saint-Gobain	137	C. Dierig	116
11	GEC	251	Hachette	130	Hoesch	112
12	Distillers	243	SACM	128	Ilseder Hütte	111
13	Babcock & Wilcox	219	Banque de l'Indochine	121	AEG	81
14	United Steel	214	Say	119	Vereinigte Glanzstoff	58
15	Dunlop	205	Agache	109	Gutehoffnung	48
16	Home & Colonial	198	CGE	109	Wintershall	47
17	GKN	197	Thomson	109	Karstadt	34
18	Gaumont	197	Dollfus-Mieg	101	HAPAG	27
19	Cunard	193	Peugeot	99	Burbach Kaliwerke	26
20	United Dairies	183	Crédit Lyonnais	93		
21	Barclays Bank	180	Société Générale	83		
22	Midland Bank	176	Kuhlmann	78		
23	Platt Bros.	168	Comptoir d'Escompte	66		

Rank	Company	Value		Company	Value
24	ICI	160		Chargeurs	61
25	National Provincial Bank	146		Bon Marché	60
26	Dorman Long	141		Michelin	59
27	Imperial Tobacco	135		Schneider	57
28	Lloyds Bank	134		Paribas	56
29	Shell	132		Saint-Frères	50
30	Westminster Bank	130		Galeries Lafayette	25
31	J. & P. Coats	126			
32	Bass	116			
33	Allied Newspapers	115			
34	Unilever	107			
35	J. Lyons	106			
36	Tate & Lyle	105			
37	Boots	101			
38	Courtaulds	101			
39	British Celanese	99			
40	Associated Newspapers	89			
41	Guinness	89			
42	Elder Dempster	82			
43	Cotton Spinners	75			
44	Watneys	73			
45	Harland & Wolff	62			
46	EMI	49			
47	Bleachers	44			

[a] The small number of German companies is due to the fact that the successor companies to IG Farben and Vereinigte Stahlwerke cannot be included, and that the three big banks were divided into regional companies until 1957.

[b] Combined assets of British Insulated Cables and Callenders Cables.

[c] Siemens & Halske and Siemens Schuckertwerke.

the 1920s, electricals (Lucas, AEI, BICC, GEC) and oil (especially the more recently formed Anglo-Persian) were the fastest-growing industries. Seven other firms more than doubled their total assets between 1929 and 1953, though their subsequent fortunes were to prove rather disappointing. They included the two iron and steel companies, Stewarts & Lloyds and United Steel, the merged motor manufacturers Austin and Morris, the armaments combine Vickers, the tyre and rubber giant Dunlop, the drink conglomerate Distillers, and the engineering company Babcock & Wilcox.

Among French companies, the Compagnie Française des Pétroles stands out, with an almost sevenfold increase of total assets, making it one of the country's largest companies. Two electrical engineering companies, Fives-Lille and Jeumont, more than doubled their assets, while nearly half of them had fallen behind their 1929 level, including the three nationalized deposit banks as well as the privately owned *banque d'affaires*, the Banque de Paris et des Pays-Bas. The picture is distorted for German big business, as the two major industrial companies, IG Farben and Vereinigte Stahlwerke, which were liquidated and dismantled, and the three big banks, which were temporarily divided into regional institutions, cannot be taken into consideration.

In all three countries, large companies grew at a much faster rate from the early 1950s to the early 1970s. German big business, however, outpaced its French and British counterparts. From a level of 100 in 1952, the index of total assets of that year's largest German companies had reached 562 in 1972, as against 415 for the French and 315 for the British companies (Table 5.4). Three main, and not necessarily unrelated, reasons explain this unprecedented surge. First, the very low starting-point of several compa-

Table 5.4. Growth of assets of surviving companies, 1953–1972: total assets 1972 (1953 = 100)

	Great Britain		France		Germany	
	Company	Assets	Company	Assets	Company	Assets
1	Burmah Oil	926	Crédit Lyonnais	1267	Thyssen	1802
2	Boots	913	Rhône-Poulenc	1149	Hoechst	1118
3	GEC	781	Société Générale	1135	Daimler-Benz	1071
4	Shell	680	Peugeot	807	Karstadt	819
5	Lucas	575	Paribas	767	R. Bosch	701
6	BMC	516	Thomson	710	Siemens	593
7	Beecham	479	Printemps	699	Bayer	588
8	J. Lyons	475	Renault	699	AEG	576
9	Marks & Spencer	460	L'Air Liquide	638	KHD	500

Table 5.4. *Continued*

	Great Britain		France		Germany	
	Company	Assets	Company	Assets	Company	Assets
10	Tate & Lyle	436	Usinor	590	Hoesch	490
11	Metal Box	434	Vallourec	585	Degussa	394
12	BP	420	Pechiney	565	Demag	364
13	Courtaulds	366	CFP	505	MAN	359
14	GKN	354	Saint-Gobain[b]	381	Rheinstahl	356
15	Reckitt & Colman	328	SNECMA	379	Mannesmann	346
16	GUS	327	Say	369	Continental	324
17	M. Burton	308	Michelin	364	Enka-Glanzstoff	265
18	Cadbury	296	Huiles de Pétrole	313	Klöckner-Werke	213
19	Barclays Bank	293	Esso Standard	312	Süddeutsche Zucker	212
20	BICC	292	CGE	309		
21	Hawker Siddeley	291	Creusot	303		
22	ICI	258	Hachette	298		
23	Tube Investments	253	Alsthom	268		
24	Guinness	239	Banque de l'Indochine	244		
25	Dunlop	232	Citroën	237		
26	Natwest[a]	220	Lesieur	185		
27	Lloyds Bank	218	Astra	130		
28	Distillers	213	Chargeurs	127		
29	Woolworths	213	Messageries Maritimes	97		
30	BAT	210	Jeumont	55		
31	Imperial Tobacco	208				
32	Midland Bank	181				
33	J. & P. Coats	171				
34	Unilever	112				
35	P. & O.	105				
36	Vickers	62				

[a] Combined assets of National Provincial Bank and Westminster Bank.
[b] Combined assets of Saint-Gobain and Pont-à-Mousson.

nies which had only started their post-war recovery in the early 1950s; this was the case with the French banks and the German iron and steel companies. Secondly, the wave of mergers which, as already discussed, often brought together the largest firms in an industry: Thyssen, for example, almost reconstituted the old Vereinigte Stahlwerke, Rhône-Poulenc and Pechiney brought together the bulk of the French chemical industry, GEC the bulk of British electrical engineering. And thirdly, a period of sustained economic growth, from which big business benefited, while rising standards of living gave a boost to the all-important motor car industry. The trend continued, though at a slower pace, in the 1970s and 1980s: the total assets of the German largest companies reached an index of 264 in 1989, from a 100 basis in 1972, as against 192 for their French and 136 for their British counterparts (Table 5.5).

Table 5.5. Growth of assets of surviving companies, 1972–1989: total assets 1989 (1972 = 100)

	Great Britain		France		Germany	
	Company	Assets	Company	Assets	Company	Assets
1	Tesco	391	Paribas	699	BMW	962
2	Sainsbury	367	CGE	441	VEBA	765
3	Beecham	337	Casino	333	Daimler-Benz	675
4	Lonhro	300	Schneider	306	Preussag	651
5	Natwest	243	Crédit Lyonnais	282	Volkswagen	506
6	P. & O.	238	Michelin	277	Deutsche Bank	457
7	Marks & Spencer	233	Société Générale	267	Dresdner Bank	417
8	Unilever	233	Renault	235	Commerzbank	400
9	Dalgety	219	Rhône-Poulenc	230	Metallgesellschaft	333
10	Barclays Bank	209	SNECMA	215	Degussa	295
11	Midland Bank	202	Hachette	197	Schering	272
12	BP	195	Carrefour	192	Continental	256
13	Bass	194	Thomson	185	Stinnes	247
14	Lloyds Bank	192	Saint-Gobain	181	R. Bosch	243
15	BAT	184	Peugeot	168	Siemens	235
16	BOC	176	L'Air Liquide	162	BASF	198
17	Thorn	156	CFP	120	Thyssen	179
18	Cadbury	146	Printemps	115	Hoechst	170
19	Inchcape	145	SCOA	107	Mannesmann	165

Table 5.5. *Continued*

	Great Britain		France		Germany	
	Company	Assets	Company	Assets	Company	Assets
20	Shell	145	Pechiney	101	RWE	161
21	GUS	137	Nouvelles Galeries	91	Deutsche Babcock	159
22	Allied Lyons[a]	133			Kaufhof	139
23	Woolworths	126			Klöckner-Werke	137
24	Reckitt & Colman	122			Deutsche Shell	130
25	Tate & Lyle	119			Bayer	127
26	J. Lucas	118			Krupp	110
27	Hawker Siddeley	117			Karstadt	105
28	RTZ	110			KHD	79
29	RHM	110			Esso AG	71
30	Coats Viyella	108			Horten	58
31	BICC	99				
32	GEC	98				
33	ICI	92				
34	Reed	77				
35	Unigate	75				
36	GKN	64				
37	Bowater	38				
38	Courtaulds	34				
39	Burmah Oil	20				

[a] Combined assets of Allied Breweries and J. Lyons.

As indicated in previous chapters, several German and also French companies had huge potential to catch up on their British competitors in the early 1950s, especially in chemicals, motor cars, and banking. In chemicals the three German giants BASF, Bayer, and Hoechst each became fractionally larger than ICI, whereas taken together they had been smaller than the British firm in the early 1950s; while despite its impressive growth, Rhône-Poulenc never entirely caught up. That some of the British companies should have been left behind by their German, and even French, competitors is, however, another matter. The collapse of the British motor industry is a case in point. Electrical engineering is more complex. GEC managed to hold its own in the 1950s and 1960s, so as to become larger than Siemens, in terms of turnover, after its takeover of AEI and English Electric in 1967 and 1968. By the late 1980s, however, GEC had been clearly outdistanced, in terms of size, by its leading German and French competitors (with the exception of AEG, which was put under bankruptcy protection before being taken over by Daimler-Benz), though it remained, by a significant margin, the most profitable company.[10]

Survival in the long term has not been uncommon among European leading firms. Twenty-four companies in Britain, nine in France, and ten in Germany have remained large and independent for most of the century—from 1910 to 1990 (Table 5.6). A hardly less distinguished group of eleven British, eight French, and ten German companies maintained this status for about sixty years, from the 1930s to 1990 (Table 5.7).[11] Though past performances are no guarantee of future success,[12] these companies must be considered, from a historical point of view, as the cream of big business in twentieth-century Europe. Beyond its anecdotal interest, this long-term view encapsulates some of the main differences between Britain on the one hand, and France and Germany on the other. The first is, not surprisingly, the larger share of banks and insurance companies among British long-lived large companies. In the three countries, however, the survival of large banks has been *de facto* guaranteed by the state. The second difference concerns the long-lived industrial companies. In France and Germany, most were among their country's largest companies by 1989. In Germany, twelve out of sixteen were in the top twenty, and eight in the top ten.[13] In France, ten out of fourteen were in the top twenty, and as many as eight were in the top ten.[14] The main difference between the two countries is that the core of German big business was formed before 1914, whereas it was established in the 1920s in France— and not in the 1960s as is often assumed. In Britain, by contrast, no more than eight (out of twenty-seven) long-lived industrial companies were in the top twenty, and five in the top ten.[15]

Such a contrast is a reflection of both the strengths and weaknesses of British big business. Its strong points have been, besides high profitability, its density and diversity, extending to sectors (such as food or textile)

[10] GEC's turnover was $2.16 billion in 1968, as against $2.01 billion for Siemens and $969 million for the French GEC. In 1989, the figures were $7.8 billion for GEC, $27.5 billion for Siemens, and $21.2 billion for CGE.

[11] These two groups of companies still had an unbroken record in 1989, unlike a third group of distinguished casualties which, despite having survived at least sixty years—from the early century to the early 1970s—had disappeared (or were no longer large enough) in the following years. Such a group includes the likes of Imperial Tobacco, Dunlop, and Vickers in Britain, de Wendel in France, or AEG in Germany.

[12] The Midland Bank was acquired by the HSBC group in 1992.

[13] In this order: Daimler-Benz, Siemens, BASF, Hoechst, Bayer, Thyssen, Bosch, RWE. The other two were Volkswagen and VEBA, ranked respectively three and four.

[14] Renault, Peugeot, CFP/Total, CGE, Générale des Eaux, Péchiney, Thomson, Saint-Gobain.

[15] Shell, BP, Unilever, BAT, ICI.

Table 5.6. Companies which remained large for eighty years (1910–1990)

	Britain	France	Germany
Banks	Barclays Lloyds Natwest[a] Midland Hongkong & Shanghai	Crédit Lyonnais Société Générale Paribas	Deutsche Bank Dresdner Bank
Insurance	Prudential Royal Commercial Union		
Metal, machinery	GKN RTZ	Schneider	Thyssen Krupp Hoesch Mannesmann
Electrical engineering		Thomson	Siemens
Chemicals	ICI[b] Unilever Reckitt		BASF Bayer Hoechst
Oil	Shell Burmah Oil		
Glass	Pilkington	Saint-Gobain	
Food, drink, tobacco	Guinness Bass BAT		
Textiles	Coats		
Services	P. & O. Dalgety W. H. Smith Cable & Wireless[c]	Générale des Eaux Galeries Lafayette Hachette	

[a] The National Provincial Bank and the Westminster Bank were both large companies in 1910.

[b] The forerunners of ICI, Brunner Mond and Nobel Explosives, were both large companies in 1910.

[c] Eastern Telegraph, one of Britain's largest companies before 1914, was with Marconi one of the two leading protagonists in the 1929 merger which gave birth to Cable & Wireless.

Table 5.7. Companies which remained large for sixty years (1930–1990)

	Britain	France	Germany
Banks			Commerzbank
Insurance			Allianz
Metal, machinery		Péchiney	Klöckner Metallgesellschaft
Electrical engineering	GEC BICC Lucas	CGE	R. Bosch
Chemicals	Boots		
Motor cars		Renault Peugeot	Daimler-Benz Opel
Oil	BP	CFP	
Rubber, tyres		Michelin	Continental
Food	Tate & Lyle Cadbury		
Textiles	Courtaulds Burton		
Services	Marks & Spencer Woolworths	Printemps Chargeurs	RWE Karstadt

where companies could not expect to rank among the very first; and its dynamism, leading to a turnover at the top and to the advent of new-comers. Its major weakness has been the decline, and even the total disappearance, of a number of domestically owned industries, especially motor cars, and to a lesser extent electrical engineering, where the bulk of German and French largest companies remained concentrated in the late 1980s. This has not greatly affected British big business's overall profitability. Whether it has affected the overall performance of the British economy is of course another matter which remains to be seen.

PART III

BUSINESS LEADERSHIP

Few would dispute that a company's success owes a great deal to the quality of its leadership. Good business leadership, or the ability to make the right strategic choices, results from a combination of individual abilities—the actual skills which business leaders put at their company's disposal—and collective capability—the organizational structure through which these skills can be applied. Individual competence and collective capability are obviously influenced by the overall conditions prevailing in each country. The notions of 'business organization', of 'business systems', and of 'business culture' have recently been put forward as explanatory frameworks.[1]

Chapter 6 looks into the shaping of businessmen's individual skills (through family background, education and training, and career patterns), while Chapter 7 examines the process of decision-making (through the functioning of company boards, the structure of the firm, multiple directorships, and the relationships between finance and industry). Some of these issues have become fertile ground for global explanations of national business 'success' or 'failure': the persistence of family capitalism has often been seen as one of the main factors explaining Britain's 'decline' and France's 'backwardness'; many observers have attributed the early advantage taken by Germany in the 'second' industrial revolution to her business leaders' technical training and higher level of professionalism; the strategy and structure of the firm has dominated the research agenda in business history in the last three decades; and the respective merits of bank-oriented and 'market-oriented' systems have stirred some of the liveliest controversies in economic history.

It is usually assumed that the differences in economic and business performances observable between countries can be explained by certain *national* characteristics of business leadership, formed by a specific institutional and cultural environment. But how much can they really explain, especially when dealing with countries broadly similar in terms of socio-cultural values and level of economic development? This is the major question addressed in the third part of this book. The conclusions reached in the previous two parts suggest that the discussion's usual starting-point—how to explain Britain's 'entrepreneurial failure' in comparison with German, and even recent French, successes—might not be appropriate. What has been missing so far is a direct comparison of British, French, and German

[1] See for example W. Lazonick, *Business Organization and the Myth of the Market Economy* (Cambridge, 1991); R. Whitley (ed.), *European Business Systems: Firms and Markets in their National Contexts* (London, 1992); M. Casson, *The Economics of Business Culture: Game Theory, Transaction Costs and Economic Performance* (Oxford, 1991).

business leaders. The analysis which follows has been based on compatible samples, established on the same criteria for the three countries. This should help to avoid some of the biases deriving from the reliance on an in-depth analysis for one country and secondary material for the others. For the purpose of this study, business leaders have been defined as the chairmen and managing directors (sometimes the general managers) of the major British, French, and German companies, using the same sample of companies and the same benchmark years as for the analysis of performance in Part II.

6

Competence

Were European business leaders properly qualified to carry out their duties? Did their competence increase in the course of the twentieth century? Were there significant differences in this respect between top British, French, and German businessmen? These are the basic questions addressed in this chapter. The acquisition of business competence should be seen as a lengthy process, as the entire path leading to the top of a large corporation. It is a process which starts at birth, often by being born in a business family; it then continues through secondary or even university education; and is finally shaped by the decisive steps in career development. These three major moments will be examined in turn.

FOUNDERS, INHERITORS, AND MANAGERS

There is little doubt left about the narrow social recruitment of business élites. Recent studies—the earliest dating back to the 1950s—in both Europe and the United States have destroyed all myths surrounding the opportunities of spectacular upward social mobility offered by business life, not least the legendary rise from rags to riches in one generation. This popular perception rested on a few exceptional cases, the most famous being probably Andrew Carnegie, the son of a Scottish weaver who became America's steel king and one of the world's richest men. Cold statistical analyses of large cohorts are far more prosaic. In their overwhelming majority, business leaders have been recruited among the privileged classes—landowners, businessmen, senior civil servants, professionals—at all times, even during the industrial revolution which witnessed the rise of a new social class, the bourgeoisie; and everywhere, including in the United States of America, a new country and the land of individual enterprise. Furthermore, up to the generations active in the 1960s, more than half of the business leaders of the industrialized world were themselves sons of businessmen. The signs of the passage from family capitalism to managerial capitalism were slow to emerge. The massive increase of the number of salaried managers hardly widened the social background from which managers were recruited: a working-class background has remained exceptional within the business élite.

Such is the broad consensus which has emerged from the various inquiries undertaken in the last thirty to forty years into the social origins

Table 6.1. Social origins of business leaders (%)

Father's occupation	1907			1929			1953			1972			1989		
	GB	F	D	GB	F	D	GB	F	D	GB	F	D	GB	F	D
Landowner	9	10	0	5	0	2	5	6	3	7	2	3	0	4	0
Businessman	64	48	65	57	73	73	56	44	44	45	58	32	29	33	44
Politician, civil servant	4	16	15	3	8	3	3	26	21	4	4	18	0	16	6
Professional	12	10	8	18	8	9	13	16	21	24	27	30	26	29	22
Junior executive	0	0	4	1	0	3	0	4	5	2	2	10	6	5	22
Small businessman	8	6	4	10	3	2	7	0	3	7	4	3	0	4	0
Worker, employee	3	10	4	6	8	8	16	4	3	11	2	5	39	9	6
Total	100	100	100	100	100	100	100	100	100	100	100	100	100	100	100
No. of cases	86	46	53	104	56	73	87	77	71	63	55	51	50	57	51
No data	19	15	5	25	20	10	26	23	33	18	6	11	19	2	19

Sources: Author's estimates based on a sample of business leaders.

of business leaders.[1] The chairmen and managing directors of the largest corporations analysed in this study were no exception to the rule (Table 6.1). Throughout the twentieth century, more than 80 per cent came from a middle- or upper middle-class background, with a high proportion of sons of businessmen up to the generation active in the early 1970s. As late as 1930, more than 70 per cent of French and German business leaders were sons of businessmen—a very high figure indeed.

Inevitably, several of the largest companies were still managed by heirs of the founding families. They included Carl Friedrich von Siemens (1872–1941), chairman of the supervisory boards of both Siemens & Halske and Siemens Schuckertwerke from 1919 to his death in 1941, having previously been in command of the executive board; Fritz Thyssen (1873–1950), chairman of the supervisory board of the Vereinigte Stahl-werke;[2] Eugène Schneider (1868–1942), François de Wendel (1871–1949), and Robert Peugeot (1873–1945), all at the head of companies bearing their name; Alfred Mond, later Lord Melchett (1868–1930), chairman of ICI;[3] Walter Samuel, later 2nd Viscount Bearsted (1882–1948), chairman of the Shell Transport and Trading Company founded by his father; and Rupert Edward Guinness, 2nd Earl Iveagh (1874–1967) and Samuel Courtauld (1876–1947), both chairmen of companies bearing their name. The heir to a business dynasty could equally be a son-in-law, such as Gustav Krupp von Bohlen und Halbach (1871–1950) or the baron George Brincard (1871–1953), chairman of the Crédit Lyonnais from 1922 to 1945, who married one of the two daughters of the founder Henri Germain.[4]

These are all evocative names. And yet the image of dynastic perpetuation which they convey is largely misleading. For if the leader of a large corporation in twentieth-century Europe was very likely to be the son of a businessman, he was far less likely to have inherited this position from his father. This can be seen from the figures in Table 6.2, which show that the percentage of *sons of businessmen* was much higher than the percentage of *inheritors*. With the professionalization of business leadership, the fathers of heads of large corporations who were themselves businessmen were either self-employed, or senior executives in another large corporation. This was for example the case with Frederic Goodenough

---

[1] Good comparative analysis, making use of the statistics on social mobility available in most industrialized countries can be found in H. Kaelble, 'Long-Term Changes in the Recruitment of Business Elites: Germany Compared to the U.S., Great Britain and France since the Industrial Revolution', *Journal of Social History*, 13/3 (1980). The most important articles are gathered in Y. Cassis (ed.), *Business Elites* (Aldershot, 1994).

[2] August Thyssen Hütte, founded by Fritz Thyssen's father, played a major role in the merger leading to the creation of the Vereinigte Stahlwerke and held 26% of the new concern's share capital. See W. Treue, *Die Feuer verlöschen nie*, 2 vols. (Düsseldorf, 1966).

[3] The family firm Brunner Mond & Co., founded by his father, was one of two leading protagonists in the merger which led to the formation of ICI in 1926. See W. J. Reader, *Imperial Chemical Industries: A History*, 2 vols. (London, 1970–5).

[4] See J. Rivoire, *Le Crédit Lyonnais: Histoire d'une banque* (Paris, 1989).

Table 6.2. Sons of businessmen and inheritors (%)

	1907		1929			1953			1972			1989		
	GB	F	D	GB	F	D	GB	F	D	GB	F	D	GB	F	D
Sons of businessmen	64	48	65	57	73	73	56	44	44	45	58	32	29	33	44
Inheritors	34	18	17	30	26	34	25	33	11	19	22	12	2	5	8

Sources: Author's estimates based on a sample of business leaders.

(1866–1934), chairman of Barclays Bank from 1916 to 1934, whose father was a merchant in Calcutta; and with Horace Finaly (1871–1945), managing director of the Banque de Paris et des Pays-Bas between 1919 and 1937, whose father was a banker in Budapest before settling in France. Alfred Berliner (1861–1943), managing director of both Siemens & Halske and Siemens Schuckertwerke during the first decade of the twentieth century, was the son of an industrialist from Breslau. The father of Carl Bosch (1874–1930), the first chairman of IG Farben's executive board, owned a plumbing company in Cologne. Geoffrey Heyworth (1894–1974), chairman of Unilever from 1941 to 1959, was the son of a Liverpool corn merchant. In more recent years, Ambroise Roux, chairman of the Compagnie Générale d'Électricité from 1970 to 1986, and André Levy-Lang, chairman of Paribas's board of management from 1990, were both sons of company directors.

Founders of large firms came from the same background. August Thyssen's (1842–1926) father owned a small rolling-mill before setting up as a banker.[5] Eugen Gutman (1840–1925), the son of a Dresden banker, founded the Dresdner Bank in 1872 by convincing his friends Karl and Felix Kuskel to turn their private banking house into a joint-stock company which Gutman headed as managing director from 1872 to 1920. In the French automobile industry, André Citroën (1878–1935) was the son of a diamond merchant,[6] and Louis Renault (1877–1944) of a button manufacturer and clothier.[7] In Britain, two pioneering figures of the aircraft industry had similar business antecedents. Francis Hearle (1886–1935), one of the founders of de Haviland Aircraft in 1920, was the son of an agricultural machinery dealer, while Tom Sopwith (1888–1989), one of the founders and long-term chairman of Hawker Siddeley, was the son of a civil engineer and owner of lead mines.[8]

Nor should a business family background be confused with an upper middle-class background. For most fathers, being in business meant owning or managing a medium-sized company, and their son's accession to the top of a large corporation was an undoubted mark of upward social mobility. Significantly, however, the latter had grown up since their childhood in a business family environment and opted for a business career, either by entering a large corporation which offered prospects of rapid promotion, or by setting up on their own. Leading a large company was an even steeper social climb for businessmen coming from other middle-class backgrounds. It would be tedious to divide the professions into an

[5] See Treue, *Die Feuer verlöschen nie*, vol. i.

[6] See S. Schweitzer, *André Citroën* (Paris, 1992).

[7] See G. Hatry, *Louis Renault: Patron absolu* (Paris, 1982).

[8] See C. M. Sharp, 'Hearle, Francis Trounson (1886–1965), Aircraft Manufacturer', and R. Higham and D. J. Jeremy, 'Sopwith, Sir Thomas Octave Murdoch (1888–), Aircraft Manufacturer', in D. J. Jeremy (ed.), *Dictionary of Business Biography*, 5 vols. (London, 1984–6), vols. iii and v.

infinity of subgroups, but there is no doubt that top lawyers were but a small minority. Most professionals among business leaders' fathers were engineers, clergymen—especially in Britain—or academics. Among the sons of civil servants were many army officers, especially in France. As Maurice Lévy-Leboyer rightly points out, this widening of the recruitment basis of business leaders mostly took place in the new industries, but to a large extent has been concealed by aggregate statistical figures.[9]

On the other hand, the rise from bottom to top in one generation was an exceptional phenomenon. Leading figures with a working-class background included Harry McGowan (1874–1961), chairman of ICI from 1930 to 1950, Frederik Godber (1888–1961), chairman of Shell from 1946 to 1951, and Louis-Joseph Cuvinot (1837–1920), a former senior civil servant and chairman of the Mines d'Anzin. On the whole, the combined proportion of sons of factory workers (whether skilled, semi-skilled, or unskilled), employees, office clerks, etc. rarely reached 10 per cent. The exception that proves the rule, however, was the British business leadership of the late 1980s. Thirty-nine per cent of the chairmen and chief executives of the thirty largest British companies in 1989–90 were sons of manual workers or employees (Table 6.1). This was an astonishingly high percentage, higher than the percentage of businessmen's sons, which stood at 26 per cent. In truth, the result is somewhat distorted by a particularly high percentage of cases with no information. Still, British business leaders with a working- or lower middle-class background accounted for 24 per cent of *all cases*. In the same years, only 9 per cent of the French and 6 per cent of the German top businessmen had a similarly modest background. Did the 'Thatcherite revolution' succeed in so radically reshaping the British business establishment? The answer is not an obvious one, given that these people, whose average age was about 59, were educated, and thus given their first career opportunities, during the period of the Labour governments of 1945 and 1951; on the other hand, one should not underestimate the effects of the cultural changes brought about by Thatcherism and the general environment in which these businessmen reached top position.[10] In any case, the phenomenon is too recent for the historian to evaluate its long-term significance. Comparisons with the generations active in the early to mid-twenty-first century will be able to tell whether this reflected a profound transformation of British society, or whether it should be attributed to erratic statistical results.

To what extent have the social origins of business leaders influenced business performance? In principle, there should be no connection between the two issues. Whether the chairman of an iron and steel

[9] M. Lévy-Leboyer, 'Le Patronat français, 1912–1973', in M. Lévy-Leboyer (ed.), *Le Patronat de la seconde industrialisation* (Paris, 1979).

[10] See for similar conclusions L. Hannah, 'Human Capital Flows and Business Efficiency', in K. Bradley (ed.), *Human Resource Management: People and Performance* (Aldershot, 1992).

company was the son of a grocer, a lawyer, or an industrialist should be irrelevant to his ability to run the company, so far as he proves himself to be the right man for the job—providing of course that the most able person has a genuine opportunity to reach the top position. The most common, though not the only, obstacle to such an outcome is of course family inheritance. This raises the whole issue of the persistence of the family firm, often considered a cause of British industrial decline in the late Victorian and Edwardian ages, and of French economic backwardness until the Second World War.[11]

In Britain, third generation businessmen have been accused of losing not only the founders' innovative and combative spirit, but also the will to enlarge and consolidate the firm which motivated the second generation in business. Brought up since birth in a world of opulence and attracted by a gentlemanly way of life, they allegedly had little time or interest for the rigours of business life and more particularly the unpleasantness of industrial production. Still more gravely, these incompetent, under-motivated businessmen are said to have refused to delegate their powers to professional managers, preferring to retain for themselves an amateurish control over the firm. In France, businessmen have been accused of favouring family interests to the detriment of corporate growth. This behaviour, known as the 'Malthusianism' of the French *patronat*, has been seen as an explanatory factor for slow economic growth in France in the nineteenth and part of the twentieth centuries.[12]

Historical analysis does not take place in a vacuum. It is strongly influenced by the current political and economic climate. French economic performance since 1945, especially during the *Trente Glorieuses* (the thirty years following the Second World War), has dissipated any doubts which might have surrounded the very essence of French entrepreneurship. Conversely, the disappointing performance of the British economy over the same period has had exactly the opposite effect. In France, the so-called 'revisionist' school has become the guardian of the new orthodoxy. The thesis of French economic retardation, put forward in the 1950s above all by American scholars struck by France's apparent state of decay in the immediate aftermath of the Second World War, has been rejected. French economic growth has been judged satisfactory in the long term and firms are considered to have responded adequately to such constraints as technological change, available resources, or internal

---

[11] D. Landes, *The Unbound Prometheus* (Cambridge, 1969); A. D. Chandler, *Scale and Scope* (Cambridge, Mass., 1990); W. Lazonick, *Business Organization and the Myth of the Market Economy* (Cambridge, 1991), are among the forceful exponents of this thesis. For a general discussion of the question, see G. Jones and M. Rose (eds.), *Family Capitalism*, special issue of *Business History*, 34/4 (1993).

[12] See a convincing rejection of this thesis in M. Lévy-Leboyer, 'Le Patronat français a-t-il été malthusien?', *Le Mouvement social*, 3 (1974).

demand.[13] From this standpoint, the size of French enterprises is not regarded as having been a handicap. In Britain, on the other hand, the 'redemption' of the entrepreneur attempted by the 'new' economic history has not met with unanimous agreement.[14] There remains a kind of instinctive reaction that if things went wrong, those at the top should take the blame.

One of the most enduring grievances against businessmen has been the persistence of the family firm. The old thesis was showing signs of obsolescence. But it has more recently been rejuvenated through the work of the doyen of business historians, Alfred Chandler, though British historians have on the whole expressed strong reservations.[15] For Chandler, 'personal capitalism' was the main cause for the late emergence of the 'new industries' in Britain and for the country's ultimate industrial decline; in his view, the failure of family firms is rooted in their inability to create the organizational capabilities required by the modern industrial enterprise.[16] Building on Chandler's work, William Lazonick has suggested that Britain's loss of world economic supremacy derived from her outmoded form of business organization.[17] These analyses obviously go beyond the thesis of the loss of interest in the affairs of the firm by third generation scions of business dynasties. In the final analysis, however, we are still faced with the basic question of how competent inheritors were to manage a large company.

Were inheritors especially numerous among the chairmen and managing directors of the largest British and French companies? Another look at Table 6.2 will show that this was not necessarily the case. The highest percentage of inheritors, 34 per cent, was among British business leaders in 1907; and, more surprisingly, among German business leaders in 1929, that is, in the European country traditionally portrayed as closest to the American model of managerial capitalism, and at the end of a decade marked by a frenzy of rationalization. One could assume most German inheritors to be semi-retired businessmen chairing a supervisory board and content to leave the more demanding managerial duties to salaried managers on the board of management. However, this was far from the

[13] See R. Cameron and C. Freedeman, 'French Economic Growth: A Radical Revision', in *Social Science History*, 7/1 (1983); J. Bouvier, 'Introduction: Libres Propos autour d'une démarche révisionniste', in P. Fridenson and A. Straus (eds.), *Le Capitalisme français, 19e–20e siècles: Blocages et dynamismes d'une croissance* (Paris, 1987).

[14] See D. McCloskey and L. Sandberg, 'From Damnation to Redemption: Judgments on the Late Victorian Entrepreneur', in D. McCloskey (ed.), *Enterprise and Trade in Victorian Britain* (London, 1981).

[15] See R. Church, 'The Limitations of the Personal Capitalism Paradigm', contribution to '*Scale and Scope*: A Review Colloquium', *Business History Review*, 64/4 (1990); L. Hannah, 'Scale and Scope: Towards a European Visible Hand?', *Business History*, 33/2 (1991); B. Supple, 'Scale and Scope: Alfred Chandler and the Dynamics of Industrial Capitalism', *Economic History Review*, 44/3 (1991).

[16] See Chandler, *Scale and Scope*.

[17] See Lazonick, *Business Organization*.

case. Admittedly, 54 per cent chaired a supervisory board, but this group included some of Weimar Germany's most prominent businessmen, who were directly involved in the running of their firms, such as Gustav Krupp, Carl von Siemens, and Paul Silverberg (1876–1959).[18] At executive board level, inheritors included the managing directors of such major firms as the Vereinigte Stahlwerke, Klöckner, Hoesch, and the Disconto-Gesellschaft.

The high percentage of inheritors among British business leaders is less surprising. And in 1907, during the 'classical' period of British economic decline, it was significantly higher than in either France or Germany. Furthermore, half were third generation family members, a stage at which the risks of entrepreneurial failure increase dangerously. Yet family-run large British companies were far from being in decline. On the contrary, many belonged to industries where Britain enjoyed a strong competitive advantage, in particular consumer packaged goods, where the proportion of inheritors was 90 per cent, as against less than 40 per cent in the heavy industries and textiles. Firms such as Cadbury and Fry in the chocolate and confectionery industry, Huntley & Palmers in biscuits, Bass and Guinness in the brewing industry, and Imperial Tobacco were all led by members of the second, sometimes third, or even fourth generation. Family control was also highly successful in the financial sector, including a large commercial bank, Barclays.

In the three countries, the firms more likely to be managed by inheritors belonged to the old industries—iron and steel, textiles, food. With the exception of the heavy industries, Britain had (as we have seen) a greater number of large companies in these industries, hence the higher proportion of inheritors among British business leaders before 1914. In Germany, family control remained strong in the heavy industries which dominated the country's big business. A number of firms, however, were comparatively new and still in the hands of their founders before 1914. The second generation took control only after the First World War, which explains the sharp increase in the proportion of inheritors among German business leaders between 1907 and 1929. They included such figures as Paul Silverberg, chairman of Rheinbraun, Fritz Thyssen, chairman of the Vereinigte Stahlwerke, Fritz Sprigorum (1886–1942), managing director of Hoesch, Ernst Poensgen (1871–1949), member of the executive board of the Vereinigte Stahlwerke, Allan Haarman (1872–1953), managing director of Klöckner-Werke, and Wilhelm and Gerhard Meyer, respectively chairman and managing director of Ilseder Hütte; to whom of course must be added descendants of older dynasties, such as Karl Haniel, chairman of the Gutehoffnungshütte, or Gustav Krupp.

On the face of it the most remarkable result is probably the low

---

[18] Paul Silverberg was chairman of the giant lignite company Rheinische AG für Braunkohlenbergbau (Rheinbraun).

percentage of inheritors at the top of the large French companies during the first half of the twentieth century, a period when French business leadership has been subjected to sharp criticism. This, however, is not really so surprising. For if small and medium-sized enterprises remained, in France as elsewhere, in family hands, large companies called upon the services of outsiders, whether engineers for the post of managing director, or notables from the worlds of politics or high finance for the chairmanship. There were, to be sure, many members of the founding families among the directors of large firms, especially in the heavy industries, but the proportion was smaller among the chairmen, managing directors, and general managers, who were the actual leaders of the firm. At the Aciéries de Longwy, for example, the general manager in 1907 was Alexandre Dreux (1853–1939), a self-made salaried manager, while the chairman was George Rolland (1852–1910), a *polytechnicien* and former senior civil servant who had married into one of the founding families. The chairmanship could, however, return to a member of the founding families, as in 1952 when it was bestowed on Jean Raty (1894–1958), whose family had been represented on the board for three generations.[19]

The competence of inheritors cannot be ascertained on the basis of family origins only. Other variables are necessary. Interestingly, the percentage of university-educated business leaders was more or less the same for inheritors and salaried managers. Inheritors were more likely to have attended university in Britain, less likely in France and Germany. This is an indication of some importance, to the extent of course that one considers higher education as a relevant indicator of a businessman's abilities.

EDUCATION AND TRAINING

Were French businessmen the most competent in Europe? They certainly had the highest level of education. The proportion of business leaders with a university or other type of higher education was already as high as 72 per cent for the generation active before 1914, reached 88 per cent in the 1920s, and continued to increase after the Second World War. This was a very high level indeed, substantially higher than in Germany and even more than in Britain, as can be seen from Table 6.3. Whether French businessmen were better prepared for their profession is of course a more contentious issue. But there were some positive features.

For one thing, French élite education put a strong emphasis on science, more so than in Britain and Germany. This was primarily due to the role played by the *grandes écoles* in the formation of French

[19] See J. M. Moine, *Les Barons du fer: Les Maîtres de forges en Lorraine du milieu du 19ème siècle aux années trente. Histoire sociale d'un patronat sidérurgique* (Nancy, 1989).

Table 6.3. Educational level of business leaders (%)

	1907			1929			1953			1972			1989		
	GB	F	D	GB	F	D	GB	F	D	GB	F	D	GB	F	D
Apprenticeship	18	7	31	11	0	18	10	0	11	3	0	12	0	0	10
Secondary school	47	21	7	39	10	15	33	2	11	28	4	2	17	3	0
Training college	0	0	5	3	2	6	12	2	3	10	6	4	19	2	2
University	35	72	57	47	88	61	45	96	75	59	90	82	64	95	88
Total	100	100	100	100	100	100	100	100	100	100	100	100	100	100	100
No. of Cases	86	46	53	104	56	73	87	77	71	63	55	51	50	57	51
No data	20	17	11	11	15	7	5	12	9	2	4	1	3	0	1

Sources: Author's estimates based on a sample of business leaders.

élites.[20] Several are engineering schools, including the most famous of them, the École Polytechnique, where a fair share of the leaders of France's largest companies has consistently been educated. Graduates from the École Polytechnique usually perfect their education in the various *écoles d'application*, the most prestigious of which are the École des Mines and the École des Ponts et Chaussées, and through them gain access into the famous *grands corps*. Centrale, which has ranked since its foundation in 1829 among the top *grandes écoles*, is also an engineering school, as are the less prestigious *écoles des arts et métiers*, which have mostly catered for middle management. Outside science and engineering, three major institutions have also contributed to business leaders' education: the École Libre des Sciences Politiques (since 1945 the Institut d'Études Politiques) or 'Sciences-Po', the École des Hautes Études Commerciales (HEC), and the École Nationale d'Administration (ENA), established after the Second World War to provide the state with top-level civil servants. Finally, most graduates from the École Normale Supérieure, whether in arts or sciences, did not go into business; but the trend has recently been reversed.

For the generations active until the 1960s, between 60 and 70 per cent of university-educated French business leaders studied science or engineering (Table 6.4), the École Polytechnique alone accounting for some 35 to 45 per cent; French top businessmen were also more likely than their British or German counterparts to have been educated both in science or engineering *and* in law or arts; for example, the École Polytechnique followed by a law degree or, for more recent generations, by the ENA. This was the case of 8 per cent of those active in the early 1950s, and 11 per cent in the late 1980s—a small but by no means negligible percentage. A far greater proportion, on the other hand, amassed diplomas in related disciplines, such as law, the arts, economics, or politics.

One might be surprised that the proportion of university-educated businessmen was not higher in Germany, so ingrained is the belief that Germany's early competitive advantage in the second industrial revolution was due to the quality and diffusion of its scientific and technical education. In fact, until the 1950s about half the university-educated German business leaders had received a scientific or technical training;

---

[20] A good overview of the French educational system in connection with the country's business and economic performance can be found in C. Kindleberger, 'Technical Education and the French Entrepreneur', in E. C. Carter *et al.* (eds.), *Enterprise and Entrepreneurs in Nineteenth and Twentieth Century France* (Baltimore, 1976). Case studies include J. H. Weiss, *The Making of Technological Man: The Social Origins of French Engineering Education* (Cambridge, Mass., 1982); T. Shinn, *Savoir scientifique et pouvoir social: L'École Polytechnique 1794–1914* (Paris, 1980); M. Meuleau, *Histoire d'une grande école (1881–1981)* (Paris, 1981) (HEC) and 'From Inheritors to Managers: The École des Hautes Études Commerciales and Business Firms', in Y. Cassis, F. Crouzet, and T. Gourvish (eds.), *Management and Business in Britain and France: The Age of the Corporate Economy* (Oxford, 1995). For the more recent sociopolitical context, see E. Suleiman, *Elites in French Society: The Politics of Survival* (Princeton, 1978); P. Bourdieu, *La Noblesse d'État: Grandes Écoles et esprit de corps* (Paris, 1989).

Table 6.4. Fields of higher education (%)

	1907			1929			1953			1972			1989		
	GB	F	D	GB	F	D	GB	F	D	GB	F	D	GB	F	D
Dual training[a]	0	0	4	0	0	2	0	8	0	3	4	2	6	11	6
Arts	26	10	4	9	3	0	8	3	0	3	0	0	10	2	0
Economics, business studies	0	5	0	5	3	2	11	3	9	19	4	10	27	15	31
Law, politics	30	14	38	7	28	40	11	18	39	17	35	44	10	22	32
Science, engineering	9	71	50	21	63	52	19	62	48	19	57	37	20	50	25
Others, unspecified	35	0	4	58	3	4	51	6	4	39	0	7	27	0	6
Total	100	100	100	100	100	100	100	100	100	100	100	100	100	100	100
No. of cases	23	21	24	43	36	41	37	63	46	36	46	41	30	54	44

[a] Arts, economics, or law *and* science or engineering.

Sources: Author's estimates based on a sample of business leaders.

the proportion then fell to just over a third in the early 1970s, and to a quarter in the late 1980s (Table 6.4). Law studies were almost as popular, with 40 per cent throughout the period, and represented a much more common path to a top position than in Britain or France. However, the most striking aspect of the educational background of German business leaders is the role played by on-the-job training, through an apprenticeship. The proportion (31 per cent) was particularly high for the generation active before 1914, and included such considerable businessmen as Emil Kirdorf (1847–1938), managing director of the GBAG, Arthur Gwinner (1856–1931), spokesman of the Deutsche Bank's board of management, and Felix Deutsch (1858–1928), managing director of the AEG. The percentage decreased after the First World War, but has remained at around 10 per cent since the 1950s, in sharp contrast to Britain and, especially, France. Businessmen trained on the job have run large companies in all sectors of German industry, and as late as 1990 they could be found at the helm of some of the greatest names in German big business.

The proportion of university-educated business leaders was none the less of the same order of magnitude in France and Germany. Things were different in Britain. Above all, they have been perceived by contemporaries—and by a good many historians—as being radically different, with serious consequences for the British economy. Table 6.3 reveals the extent of these differences. Despite a regular increase, the percentage of university-educated British business leaders has remained persistently lower than in France and Germany. They were hardly more than a third before 1914 and less than 50 per cent from the 1920s to the 1950s. Even in recent years, a university degree has not become, as in France and even Germany, a necessary, though by no means a sufficient, condition to reach the top of the business hierarchy.

This lack of interest in higher education has often been attributed to the attachment of the British to the virtues of the first industrial revolution, when technological breakthroughs were achieved by the practical man, the brilliant inventor. The major innovations of the second industrial revolution, on the other hand, were the result of the systematic application of science to industry. British businessmen, it is often alleged, remained suspicious of university education. The history of British industry is filled with loud proclamations about the uselessness of university degrees. Lord Leverhulme, the founder of Unilever, believed that 'the knowledge of book-trained students was of less value than that of practical craftsmen'; Herbert Austin declared that 'the university mind is a hindrance rather than a help'.[21] Such anecdotal evidence, however, could be misleading, and is certainly contradicted by the very strong record of British firms in industrial research and development before

[21] Quoted in M. Sanderson, *The Universities and British Industry 1850–1970* (London, 1972), 248, 287.

1945.[22] From the inter-war years, large British firms substantially increased their intake of university graduates; and they attracted, through their training schemes and career prospects, graduates not only from the civic but also from the old universities, with more than 40 per cent of Cambridge graduates going to industry and business throughout the 1920s and 1930s.[23]

A more revealing explanation perhaps lies in the conditions of access to higher education which, for all social classes, were more restricted in Britain than in France and Germany.[24] For a long time, education at a major public school was more important, in terms of social prestige, of upper or upper middle-class status, than studying at a university, even Oxford or Cambridge. It is thus not surprising that such a high percentage of British top businessmen began their career at the end of their secondary education: almost half before 1914 and over a quarter as late as the early 1970s. From the 1950s onwards, this low university intake was compensated by professional training, which was more widespread than in France and Germany. This training was provided partly by the self-regulated professions which delivered their own degree, the most important in the business world being the chartered accountants, whose training combined theoretical studies with practical experience under the supervision of the Institute of Chartered Accountants;[25] and partly by technical colleges and engineering schools which did not yet enjoy university status but dispensed a high-quality teaching.[26]

A majority of British business leaders who went on to university attended an élite establishment. Before 1914, 43 per cent went to Oxford or Cambridge; from the 1920s to the 1970s, the percentage was to 65 to 70 per cent. This increase reflects the integration into the upper classes of the leading industrialists, one or two generations later than the financial élite. Could this be the reason for the unpopularity of studying science? From the 1920s onwards, only some 20 per cent chose that option, the proportion having been less than 10 per cent a generation earlier (Table 6.4). These figures might be an underestimate. A British businessman educated at a public school and Oxbridge would as a rule only indicate in *Who's Who* the names of his former school and Oxford or Cambridge college— for example Eton and Trinity College, Cambridge. Though this is a good indicator of social status, it says very little about the type of training he received at Cambridge, unlike the mention of, say, *ancien élève de l'École*

---

[22] D. E. H. Edgerton and S. M. Horrocks, 'British Industrial Research and Development before 1945', *Economic History Review*, 47/2 (1994).

[23] Sanderson, *The Universities and British Industry*.

[24] F. Ringer, *Education and Society in Modern Europe* (Bloomington, Ind., 1979), 230.

[25] See *The History of the Institute of Chartered Accountants in England and Wales 1870–1965* (London, 1966); and E. Jones, *Accountancy and the British Economy 1840–1980: The Evolution of Ernst and Whinney* (London, 1981).

[26] Sanderson, *The Universities and British Industry*.

Polytechnique in the case of a French businessman. As a matter of fact, Oxford and Cambridge had little interest in science, let alone industry, until the 1880s, which was still the formative period of the generation active before 1914, and to a lesser extent in the 1920s. Thereafter— Cambridge from the turn of the century, Oxford a little later—the two ancient universities became centres of excellence in science and many of their graduates, especially from Cambridge, pursued careers in industry.[27] At the same time, however, Oxford and Cambridge have remained highly exclusive universities, continuing to elevate the study of the humanities as best suited for the training of a future élite.

The higher educational path followed by European top businessmen— whether in a law or science faculty, in a *grande école*, or at Oxbridge—was an undoubted mark of social status. But did these studies provide them with an adequate training for the responsibilities of business leadership? One would be inclined to say no, given the actual content of their studies, which remained mostly theoretical and with the most tenuous links to practical business life. In the three countries, one discipline was, until very recently, almost completely missing from top businessmen's training: management and business studies. The first detectable turning-point did not take place before the generation active in the late 1980s, a deferred consequence of the wave of American-type business schools which swept Europe in the 1960s. But its effects remained limited, especially at the highest echelon of the business hierarchy. The way up to the top has remained strongly bound to the educational traditions prevailing in each country, including some fairly recent traditions such as the École Nationale d'Administration (ENA) in France.

The case of Germany is most revealing in this respect. Business economics (*Betriebwirtschaftslehre*) has been taught in specialized colleges, the *Handelshochschulen*, for about a hundred years. The oldest of them was founded in Cologne in 1898, one year before the Harvard Business School. Business economics soon developed into a truly academic discipline and business colleges had already been granted university status before 1914.[28] Their impact on business leaders, however, remained extremely limited. Up to the generation active in the late 1980s, less than 5 per cent of top German businessmen had been trained in one of these colleges. There were about 20 per cent in 1989, a significant change which occurred with the generation who studied in the 1950s. Nevertheless, traditional university education in science, law, economics, or politics remained dominant.

In France, the former *inspecteurs des finances* (controllers of state finance) were for a long time the only leading businessmen who had gone through

---

[27] Sanderson, *The Universities and British Industry*.
[28] See R. Locke, *The End of Practical Man: Entrepreneurship and Higher Education in Germany, France and Great Britain, 1880–1940* (Greenwich, Conn., 1984).

some kind of financial training. This training, needless to say, had not been designed for business purposes. The role of the *inspecteurs des finances* at the head of large corporations, especially banks, was none the less positive, at least before 1914, granted that they handled company finances efficiently.[29] The École des Hautes Commerciales (HEC) was established in 1881, and until recently was the only business-oriented *grande école* in France. Its impact on business leaders' education, however, remained negligible, and only reached some significance (over 10 per cent) with the generation active in the late 1980s. As in Germany, business studies started to take off in France with the generation educated in the 1950s and 1960s. If we include a number of American business schools, such as Harvard, Stanford, or Northwestern, where a handful of subsequently distinguished businessmen put the finishing touches to their education, then 17 per cent of French business leaders active in 1989 had been trained in business and management. The percentage is roughly on a par with Germany, but pales in comparison with the 28 per cent of graduates from the ENA, compared to less than 5 per cent in the early 1970s. This new weight of the ENA has been the major change in the educational pattern of the French business élite since the beginning of the twentieth century, though this pattern has remained rooted in a state-oriented tradition.

A commercial and financial training was more common, and from an earlier stage, among British businessmen. Not, however, that the American influence was especially strong: studies in an American business school were actually more common among French businessmen. By 1989 the London Business School, established in 1963, had not trained more than a small fraction of the country's top managers. Rather, the difference stemmed from the increasing proportion of accountants at the top of the large corporations, as high as 25 per cent in 1989. If one adds another 10 per cent who attended a British or an American business school, then more than a third of the British business leaders of the late 1980s had received a commercial training, as against barely 10 per cent for the generation active fifteen years earlier.

Is there any correlation between types and levels of education and business performance? Generalizations on the subject abound,[30] often seductive in appearance, but superficial or irrelevant when applied to business leadership. Not surprisingly, such generalizations have mostly originated in or about Britain, where explanations of economic decline have been sought in all fields, not least in education. The education of the élite, in other words the public schools, Oxford, and Cambridge, has been in the forefront of these attempts. According to a deeply rooted tradition in

---

[29] See E. Chadeau, *Les Inspecteurs des finances au XIXe siècle (1850–1914): Profil social et rôle économique* (Paris, 1986).

[30] There is a useful survey of the debate in D. H. Aldcroft, *Education, Training and Economic Performance 1944 to 1990* (Manchester, 1992).

British historiography, public schools have caused devastating damage to British industry. The grievances against the public schools are well known: their primary objective was the shaping of a gentleman, whose love of the countryside and distinguished amateurism were the antipodes of the values of modern industrial societies; while their teaching, with its emphasis on classics and neglect of science, was a poor preparation for those who went into business, especially industry, and it diverted many of them into other, more gentlemanly pursuits. As to the two ancient universities, they further reinforced existing prejudices against applied sciences and industry, and thus left a gap in the training of future business leaders.[31]

This interpretation has been rejected by recent historical research.[32] One of its main weaknesses is that it does not stand up to international comparisons. Public schools were highly praised, and even imitated, in France. The École des Roches, one of the most exclusive French private schools, was founded in 1899 by Edmond Demolins, a great admirer of English educational methods, particularly the emphasis on team sport; it remained, however, exceptional and its impact was small. The study of classics was far from being a preserve of the English public schools. Latin, Greek, and literature dominated just as much the curriculum of the French *lycées*. The French *grandes écoles*, on the other hand, have been highly thought of in Britain for turning out a scientifically trained élite of engineers—exactly what Oxford and Cambridge have supposedly been unable to do. Yet the *grandes écoles*, and above all Polytechnique, have been criticized in France for their indifference to the practical application of their teaching, for being too theoretical and being obsessed by mathematics, the pure science *par excellence*. The effects of the selective entrance examination to the *grandes écoles* (the *concours*) have also been judged to be negative, by guaranteeing, to unproven graduates in their early twenties, a place in the country's élite for the rest of their lives, simultaneously barring valuable people for ever from the highest positions. The *grandes écoles* have also been accused of producing administrators and bureaucrats rather than entrepreneurs, and this has been seen as one aspect of the *mal français*.[33]

These criticisms will not surprise those who subscribe to the German model of business education. There have been, admittedly, fewer criticisms directed at the training of German businessmen. Their *technische*

---

[31] The best-known exponent of this thesis is M. Wiener, *English Culture and the Decline of the Industrial Spirit* (Cambridge, 1981).

[32] See in particular H. Berghoff, 'Public Schools and the Decline of the British Economy 1870–1914', *Past and Present*, 129 (1990), and for a convincing rejection of the Wiener thesis, W. D. Rubinstein, *Capitalism, Culture and Decline in Britain, 1750–1990* (London, 1993).

[33] An interesting comparison between Britain and France is provided by C. Shaw, 'Engineers in the Boardroom: Britain and France Compared', in Cassis, Crouzet, and Gourvish (eds.), *Management and Business in Britain and France*.

Hochschulen (technical colleges) have been much admired, especially in the late nineteenth century. First established in the 1860s as a middle course between the theoretical orientation of academic studies and the more practical approach of vocational training, they had gained university status by the turn of the century, reaching a student population of more than 10,000.[34] Their teaching, which included practical experience, was reputedly better adapted to the needs of industry. Whether technical colleges were in practice better in Germany than in France or Britain remains a matter of contention. As a percentage of the population, the number of engineers trained in the various technical high schools was about the same in France and Germany in the second half of the nineteenth century; and according to recent appraisals, the *écoles des arts et métiers* were as good as the *technische Hochschulen*.[35] In any case, the *technische Hochschulen* contributed little to the training of German business leaders: 10 per cent of those active before 1914 were educated there, less than 20 per cent for the late 1920s. Most of them actually studied in a *Gymnasium*, the teaching of which was no less dominated by the classics than a French *lycée* or an English public school. They then went on to a traditional university, the concerns of which were no less theoretical than those of their British and French counterparts. Significantly, the *technische Hochschulen* only started to attract a larger proportion of prospective business leaders when they became indistinguishable from the traditional universities. Finally, one must remember of course that German education in general suffered badly during the Nazi period, both quantitatively and qualitatively, and did not recover until well after the fall of Hitler.

The education of business leaders followed a different pattern in Britain, France, and Germany in the course of the twentieth century. But the main differences did not lie in the actual content of their studies, whether science or business economics. In the three countries, the education and training of the business élite had little relevance to their future business career. What is expected from the chairman or chief executive of a large corporation is not the possession of a specialized or technical knowledge—such expertise is essential at a lower level of the business hierarchy. The point is candidly acknowledged by a quintessential meritocrat, Roger Martin, chairman and managing director of Pont-à-Mousson, the French iron and steel company, between 1964 and 1970, and then of Saint-Gobain, one of the country's largest companies, until his retirement in 1980. In his autobiography, one of the best written by a leading businessman, Martin admits that the technical knowledge he acquired at the École Polytechnique (where he finished fourth in the final

---

[34] A good overview of the movement and penetrating comparisons with Britain can be found in S. Pollard, *Britain's Prime and Britain's Decline: The British Economy 1870–1914* (London, 1989).

[35] Ringer, *Education and Society in Modern Europe*.

examination) and later at the École des Mines was of little use in his subsequent high-flying career.[36] Education at France's most prestigious *grande
école* offered other sorts of advantages: it imbued a strong feeling of
belonging to the élite, and of being recognized as such by the outside
world, and it laid the foundations of a vast network of relationships. The
public schools, Oxford, and Cambridge basically had the same function,
that is, to prepare their students to assume the role of leaders, whether in
business, in politics, or in society. And they performed this function as
efficiently as the French *grandes écoles*. It is true that the French system,
with its selective entrance examination to the *grandes écoles*, was in theory
more meritocratic; in practice, their students' social background has
remained overwhelmingly middle and upper middle class.[37] In Germany
the system was different in that there existed no élite establishments comparable to the *grandes écoles*, the public schools, or Oxbridge; all universities enjoyed more or less the same status. Nevertheless a law degree, very
popular among top businessmen, offered the same type of *general* education well suited to leadership functions. And even specialized training—
such as a doctorate in chemistry, all but compulsory to reach a senior
managerial position in that industry—was valued more for the legitimacy
it conferred within a peer group than the expertise it provided.

The differences in education and training between British, French, and
German top businessmen had little effect on business or economic performance. Rather, they reflect the different traditions which have shaped
the path to élite positions in each of the three countries. In Britain and
France, but not in Germany, this path has required attendance at an exclusive school or university. Membership of the élite has required a university degree in Germany and even more in France, whereas in Britain the
prestige of a public school has for a long time been sufficient. In any case,
prestige and tradition have remained the basic ingredients of the formation of élites, which explains why business schools have been so slow to
establish their hold over the training of European top businessmen. Their
recent success, far from complete, has more to do with their newly
acquired aura of respectability and tradition—which they have long
enjoyed in the United States—than with their direct relevance to the tasks
of business leadership.

CAREER PATTERNS

From this perspective, the professional experience gained before reaching
a senior position must be seen as a determining factor in the acquisition
of business skills. Was this experience acquired in-house? Or was it

---

[36] R. Martin, *Patron de droit divin . . .* (Paris, 1984).
[37] See Bourdieu, *La Noblesse d'État*.

Table 6.5. Hierarchical level at which business leaders entered their firm (with the exception of inheritors) (%)

	1907			1929			1953			1972			1989		
	GB	F	D	GB	F	D	GB	F	D	GB	F	D	GB	F	D
Board of directors, senior management	78	76	84	80	82	78	59	48	73	42	53	52	39	56	43
Junior management	13	12	14	16	15	18	24	52	18	48	47	43	54	44	45
Employee, trainee	9	12	2	4	3	4	17	0	9	10	0	5	7	0	12
Total	100	100	100	100	100	100	100	100	100	100	100	100	100	100	100
No. of cases	61	39	44	76	43	50	66	55	64	52	44	45	49	54	47
No data	15	14	1	21	9	4	12	32	20	2	6	3	5	0	5

Sources: Author's estimates based on a sample of business leaders.

acquired outside—in another company, in self-employment, or in the civil service? We need to consider the hierarchical level at which business leaders entered their firm. In this respect, behaviour was very similar in the three countries. Most businessmen (without taking account of inheritors who entered a family business) joined their company at the highest hierarchical level: as directors—sometimes even chairmen—or general managers (Table 6.5). This was particularly the case in the first part of the century, up to the generation active in the 1950s, when more than 60 per cent, sometimes more than 70 per cent, entered through the front door. The proportion then tended to decrease to about 40 to 50 per cent, but even in 1989 about half the chairmen and managing directors of the largest French and German companies had joined their company at the top.

One way of starting at the top was of course to create one's own company, though it was no simple matter to build it into a large corporation during one's lifetime. Those who achieved such a success found a place in history. They epitomize the very idea of entrepreneurship: risk-taking, audacity, perseverance, but also luck, flair, vision, even creativeness, in short, a genius for business. The entrepreneur is the hero of business history, the one who occasionally gives it a romantic dimension. He has been celebrated, and his contribution to economic growth theorized, by many an economist, beginning with the most famous of them, Joseph Schumpeter.[38]

Does this hero really exist? The concept of entrepreneur is, in truth, of little use to the business historian. Does it apply to a single person—and in that case which one—within a large corporation, or to a team? Can salaried managers be considered as entrepreneurs? Or should this label be reserved to the owners of capital who, in the last analysis, run the risks involved by investment and expansion? In the latter case, the separation between ownership and management rang the knell of entrepreneurs, who could hardly be embodied by a myriad of small shareholders. Should financiers and raiders be seen as a new breed of entrepreneurs, or are only the creators of wealth worthy of the name? While the concept of *entrepreneurship* can be fruitfully used to analyse the innovation process within the large corporation,[39] an effective use of the notion of *entrepreneur* is made the more difficult by the contradictory answers which can be given to these questions.

There can be little doubt, however, that whichever definition is given to entrepreneurs, it will always include the founders of large enterprises.

---

[38] J. Schumpeter, *The Theory of Economic Development* (Cambridge, Mass., 1934). A useful collection of the classical writings on the subject is provided by M. Casson (ed.), *Entrepreneurship* (Aldershot, 1990).

[39] See for example Lazonick, *Business Organization*; R. N. Langlois and P. L. Robertson, *Firms, Markets and Economic Change* (London, 1995).

Before 1914 the highest proportion of founders was in Britain, that aged industrial nation so often condemned for her senescent capitalism and loss of entrepreneurial spirit. The cliché is threadbare. In 1907, 21 per cent of British business leaders had played a decisive part in the foundation of their company, as against 11 per cent in Germany and 10 per cent in France (Table 6.6). These differences mainly reflect the greater business opportunities then existing in Britain, as we have already seen. Some twenty years later, there were still 12 per cent of founders at the head of a major British company, as against 10 per cent in Germany and 8 per cent in France. After the Second World War, only a handful was left in the three countries, though France had the largest number in 1989.

One would expect to find founders of leading firms in the new industries, where there existed possibilities of developing a new technology, reaping monopoly profits, and financing a rapid growth. In 1907 this was the case with two-thirds of the large companies headed by their founder. The most impressive figure was undoubtedly Emil Rathenau (1838–1915), at nearly 70 still the boss of the AEG which he had founded twenty-five years earlier. Rathenau, however, should not completely overshadow another pioneer of the German electrical industry, Siegmund Bergmann (1851–1943), a former collaborator of Thomas Edison who established and managed his own firm, Bergmann Elektrizitäts-Werke. In Britain and France, Hugo Hirst (1863–1943) and Pierre Azaria (1865–1953), the respective (joint) founders of the General Electric Company and of the Compagnie Générale d'Électricité, had not yet reached Rathenau's stature before the war—they were in any case a generation younger—but they definitely approached it in the inter-war years.

In chemicals, the founders were in Britain. John Brunner (1842–1919) and Ludwig Mond (1839–1909), the two founders of Brunner Mond & Co., were still in charge, like William Lever, later Lord Leverhulme (1851–1925), the founder of Lever Brothers, later to become Unilever. Interestingly, the large firms of the German chemical industry had been established some fifty years earlier and were run by members of the second generation in business (such as Gustav von Brüning at Hoechst) or by salaried managers (such as Carl Duisberg at Bayer). In France the only chemical company of any size, Saint-Gobain, had been founded by Colbert nearly 250 years earlier. Likewise in oil and rubber, major companies still had their founder as chairman: Shell, with Marcus Samuel, later Viscount Bearsted (1853–1927); Dunlop, with William Harvey Du Cros (1846–1940); and Michelin, with Édouard Michelin (1859–1940), the real founder of the French firm. Founders also rose to prominence in the new service industries. In mass retailing, there were Théophile Bader (1864–1942), who founded the Galeries Lafayette department store, and on a larger scale Thomas Lipton (1850–1931), founder of the retailing chain bearing his name. Alfred Harmsworth (1865–1922), later Lord Northcliffe,

Table 6.6. Percentage of business leaders who founded their company

	Britain	France	Germany
1907	21	10	11
1929	12	8	9
1953	6	2	2
1972	2	6	2
1989	4	4	0

Source: Author's estimates based on a sample of businessmen.

was the first press baron, heading the Associated Press which comprised the various newspapers he had launched since the 1890s. Colonial enterprises offered wide opportunities for adventurers and serious businessmen alike. There were a few successes but none on such a spectacular scale as Julius Wernher's, the last survivor of the three founders—the two others were Alfred Beit and Cecil Rhodes—of the diamond trust De Beers Consolidated.

By the late 1920s, more than 70 per cent of the companies run by their founder were engaged in one of the new industries. Some were finally rewarded for earlier endeavours. In the German electrical industry, Robert Bosch (1861–1942) managed the firm which he had founded in 1898 but which only reached large proportions in the 1920s with the growth of the motor car industry, supplied by him with electrical accessories.[40] In chemicals, Gerhard Korte (1858–1945) was at 70 chairman of the potash trust Burbach Kaliwerke, which he had started to build at the turn of the century by methodically buying some sixty mines.[41] In synthetic fibres, Max Fremery (1859–1932) was still among the leaders of the Vereinigte Glanzstoff-Fabriken which he had founded thirty years earlier.[42] In the same industry, the rise of Henry Dreyfus (1882–1944) was much quicker: he founded British Celanese in 1916 in Britain after an early career in Switzerland.[43]

The great founder-managers of the period were, however, the pioneers of the motor car industry: Louis Renault (1877–1944), André Citroën (1878–1935), Herbert Austin (1866–1941), William Morris (1878–1963). They ran the four largest European motor companies; in France, they were

[40] See T. Heuss, *Robert Bosch: His Life and Achievements* (New York, 1994).
[41] B. Gerstein, in *Neue deutsche Biographie*, vol. xii (Berlin, 1980).
[42] H. Beau, 'Fremery, Max, Chemiker und Industrieller', *Neue deutsche Biographie*, vol. v (Berlin, 1961).
[43] D. C. Coleman, 'Dreyfus, Henry (1882–1944), Chemical Manufacturer', in Jeremy (ed.), *Dictionary of Business Biography*, vol. ii.

probably the country's two largest firms. Individual success of such magnitude has not been equalled since then. Nevertheless there have been some serious contenders. The first one is the aircraft manufacturer Marcel Dassault (1892–1986), in the 1950s and 1960s an almost mythical figure, symbol of France's economic and technological recovery after the Second World War.[44] The second is Jules Thorn (1899–1980), an Austrian immigrant to Britain who set up on his own in the 1920s. His company, Thorn Electrical Industries, specialized in household electrical goods, radio, and television, for which demand soared after the Second World War, and became a multinational empire in the 1960s.[45] The third one is Francis Bouygues (1922–1993), the 'concrete king', probably the most impressive figure among the founders still active in the late 1980s: his small firm established in 1951 had become thirty years later the world's number one in the building industry and one of the ten largest French industrial companies.[46] The service industries have presented the best opportunities for entrepreneurs in the last three decades. French supermarket and hypermarket chains, such as Leclerc, Intermarché, and Promodès, grew extremely fast in one generation and were still run by their founders in the late 1980s.[47] In Britain the advertising agency founded in 1970 by the brothers Charles and Maurice Saatchi had expanded world-wide to become one of the country's twenty largest companies by 1989, before falling on harder times.[48]

Among the founders of large companies, the creators can be distinguished from the predators. The former mostly relied for their expansion on internal growth, and vastly extended their own scale of operations. The latter relied on external growth and made a far greater, if not exclusive, use of mergers and acquisitions. Predators have been so far a much smaller group, possibly because their main weapon, the takeover bid, is fairly recent. It had hardly been used before the 1950s in Britain, before the 1980s in France, and has remained to this day a rarity in Germany. In addition, takeover bids, whether friendly or hostile, were most often made by already large and well-established companies in order to expand or diversify their activities. They were rarely the means of creating from scratch a giant company. This, however, has not proved impossible, at least for James, later Lord Hanson (born 1922): the conglomerate he had built since the 1960s had become the seventh largest British industrial

[44] See E. Chadeau, *L'Économie du risque: Les Entrepreneurs* (Paris, 1988); C. Carlier, *Marcel Dassault: La Légende d'un siècle* (Paris, 1992).

[45] S. Bowden, 'Thorn, Sir Jules (1899–1980), Electrical Appliance Manufacturer and Distributor', in Jeremy (ed.), *Dictionary of Business Biography*, vol. v.

[46] See D. Barjot, 'Francis Bouygues: L'Ascension d'un entrepreneur (1952–1989)', *Vingtième Siècle, revue d'histoire*, 35 (1992).

[47] See E. Chadeau, 'Mass Retailing: A Last Chance for the Family Firm in France, 1945–1990?', in Cassis, Crouzet, and Gourvish (eds.), *Management and Business in Britain and France*.

[48] See I. Fallon, *The Brothers: The Rise and Rise of Saatchi and Saatchi* (London, 1988).

company by 1989—it did not rank among the top 100 in 1976—by taking over and reorganizing ever larger companies, such as Imperial Group in 1986 and Consolidated Goldfields in 1988, before failing to capture the ultimate prey, ICI, in 1991.[49] Predators did not neglect the traditional industries. Here the prize must surely be awarded to the four Willot brothers. They belonged to a family of small textile manufacturers established in the north of France since the beginning of this century. The Agache-Willot group, which they built through a series of bold amalgamations, was the thirtieth largest French industrial company in 1972, before being wound up in 1981.[50]

In recent years, predators have been more commonly associated with the 'Anglo-Saxon', market-oriented form of capitalism, and creators with its German version. But this has not always been the case. In absolute terms, more predators have been running large companies in Germany than in Britain throughout the century. Their golden age was in the inflationary 1920s, which were propitious for such initiatives. Hugo Stinnes and Peter Klöckner built their empires through bold acquisitions and amalgamations. So did Friedrich Flick and Otto Wolff in the heavy industries, and Gunther Quandt in electrical engineering.

The early career of the founder of what was to become a large firm was, not surprisingly, in self-employment: more than 80 per cent had set up on their own before the age of 30. However, the vast majority of business leaders who did not found their own company gained practical experience in a different environment. Until the 1960s, top businessmen who entered their company at board or senior management level held, prior to their appointment, one of the three following positions: partner in a private firm; senior civil servant; director or senior manager of a medium-sized, or occasionally a large, company. Only a small minority came from the world of politics, the military, or the professions. These three types of professional background coexisted, of course, in the three countries, but only up to a point. What is more striking is the fact that one particular type was predominant in each country: the partnership in Britain; the civil service in France; the corporate ladder in Germany.

It is often assumed that a partner in a private firm and a chairman or chief executive of a large corporation are two diametrically opposed types of businessmen. But are they? Especially in the first age of big business, in the early twentieth century? For the best example of the osmosis existing between the two, take the top management of General Motors, the largest American industrial company and a textbook case for the study of managerial capitalism. Its president from 1923 to 1937, Alfred Sloan, is

[49] See A. Brummer and R. Cowe, *Hanson: A Biography* (London, 1994).
[50] See M. Battiau, *Les Industries textiles de la région Nord Pas-de-Calais: Étude d'une concentration géographique d'entreprises et de sa remise en cause* (Lille, 1976); B. Boussemart and J.-C. Rabier, *Le Dossier Agache-Willot: Un capitalisme à contre-courant* (Paris, 1983).

rightly considered (including by Chandler) as the archetype of the professional salaried manager. But Sloan reached his position following the takeover by General Motors of the roller-bearings manufacturing firm which he was running and in which he held, jointly with his father, a majority stake.[51]

This passage from private firm to large joint-stock company was very frequent from the late nineteenth century to the 1930s, though the outcome was not necessarily a thorough professionalization. In pre-1914 Britain, such transitions were often the result of a merger between a number of old-established private firms which kept a high degree of autonomy within the new concern. For people such as Henry William Wills, the first chairman of Imperial Tobacco in 1901, Henry Shepherd Cross, the first chairman of the Bleachers' Association in 1898, or Francis Augustus Bevan, the first chairman of Barclays Bank in 1896, their new position at the head of a giant company did not involve much change in their professional status. The links between private firms and joint-stock companies could take other forms, such as the presence of business *notables*—private bankers, merchants, company directors, and others—on the boards of clearing banks, insurance, shipping, or even industrial companies. John Trotter (1854–1913), a merchant in the City of London, was chairman of the Commercial Union Assurance Company; William Forwood, a Liverpool merchant, was chairman of the Cunard Steamship Company from 1888 to 1922; Fortescue Flannery, a consulting engineer, was chairman of the Callenders Cable and Construction Company from 1912 to 1943; and Walter Gibbs (1888–1969), a partner in the famous City merchant bank Antony Gibbs & Sons, was chairman of the Westminster Bank from 1939 to 1965.

Professionalization *à la* Sloan became more frequent from the 1920s onwards. William Milligan Fraser (1888–1970), for example, chairman of Anglo-Persian Oil from 1941 to 1956, was in charge of the Scottish Oil Company, founded by his father, until its takeover by Anglo-Persian Oil in 1923.[52] The private bankers who lost their independence in the amalgamation movement preceding the First World War were quick to adapt to the joint-stock banks and the increasing demands on a chairman's time in the inter-war years. Lloyds Bank's chairman from 1922 to 1945 was John William Beaumont Pease (1869–1950), later Lord Wardington, a former private banker who had joined the bank as a director nearly twenty years earlier in 1903.[53] Professionalization could also mean leaving a privately owned firm to join a large corporation. Such moves were often made by

---

[51] A. Sloan, *My Years with General Motors* (New York, 1963).

[52] R. W. Ferrier, 'Fraser, William Milligan, 1st Lord Strathalmond of Pumpherston (1888–1970), Petroleum Entrepreneur', in Jeremy (ed.), *Dictionary of Business Biography*, vol. ii.

[53] J. R. Winton, 'Pease, John William Beaumont, 1st Lord Wardington in the County of Northumberland (1869–1950), Clearing Banker', in Jeremy (ed.), *Dictionary of Business Biog-*

chartered accountants, most famously by Francis D'Arcy Cooper (1882–1941), senior partner of Cooper Brothers, one of the oldest accountancy firms in the City. Lever Brothers was one of their largest customers and Cooper had the confidence of Lord Leverhulme, who invited him to join the policy-making 'inner cabinet' he had set up in 1921 to sort out the company's financial difficulties. Cooper was to stay with Lever Brothers. He resigned from Cooper Brothers in 1923 on his appointment as vice-chairman and was chairman from 1925 until his death in 1941.[54] Ellis Hunter (1892–1961) followed a similar path. A partner in Peat Marwick & Mitchell, another old-established City firm of chartered accountants, he joined the iron and steel company Dorman Long in 1935, as chairman of the bondholders' association, becoming deputy chairman and managing director in 1938, and finally chairman from 1948 to 1961.[55] Hugh Beaver (1890–1967), a partner in the firm of consulting engineers Alexander Gibb & Co. after serving ten years with the Indian police, was responsible for the construction of the new Guinness brewery in Park Royal in London between 1932 and 1936. After the war, he was invited to join Guinness, at the express wish of Lord Iveagh, as assistant managing director and took over as managing director from 1946 to 1960.[56]

German business offered less flexibility for transitions from private firms to public companies. Before 1914 a fair proportion of business leaders entering their firm at the highest level came from a private firm. But they were business *notables*, merchants, bankers, and industrialists who chaired the supervisory boards of the large companies. Wilhelm Herz (1823–1914), one of Berlin's most prominent merchants, was chairman of the Deutsche Bank's supervisory board from 1876 to 1914.[57] Albert von Oppenheim, a Cologne private banker, was chairman of the supervisory board of Phoenix, the iron and steel concern in which his bank, Sal. Oppenheim Jr. & Cie, had been involved since the mid-nineteenth century.[58] Gustav Hartmann (1842–1910), owner of an engineering firm in the Ruhr, chaired the supervisory board of Krupp in the interim separat-

raphy, vol. iv; on the integration of private bankers to the joint-stock banks, see Y. Cassis, *City Bankers, 1890–1914* (Cambridge, 1994).

[54] J. R. Edwards, 'Cooper, Sir Francis D'Arcy (1882–1941), Accountant and Industrial Manager', in Jeremy (ed.), *Dictionary of Business Biography*, vol. i; C. Wilson, *The History of Unilever: A Study in Economic Growth and Social Change*, 2 vols. (London, 1954).

[55] C. Wilson, 'Hunter, Sir Ellis (1892–1961), Steel Company Chairman', in Jeremy (ed.), *Dictionary of Business Biography*, vol. iii; see also S. Tolliday, *Business, Banking, and Politics: The Case of British Steel, 1918–1939* (Cambridge, Mass., 1987), 78–9.

[56] T. Corran, 'Beaver, Sir Hugh Eyre Campbell (1890–1967), Brewer and Civil Engineer', in Jeremy (ed.), *Dictionary of Business Biography*, vol. i.

[57] See E. Achterberg, *Berliner Hochfinanz: Kaiser, Fürsten, Millionäre um 1900* (Frankfurt am Main, 1963); E. W. Schmidt, *Männer der Deutschen Bank und des Disconto-Gesellschaft* (Düsseldorf, 1957).

[58] See M. Stürmer, G. Teichmann, and W. Treue, *Wägen und Wagen: Sal. Oppenheim jr. & Cie. Geschichte einer Bank und einer Familie* (Munich, 1989), 292–5.

ing the death of his friend Friedrich Alfred Krupp in 1902 and the advent of Gustav Krupp von Bohlen und Halbach in 1910.[59]

From the 1920s, experience of senior managerial responsibilities was gained within the corporate sector. Nearly 60 per cent of the leading German businessmen who joined their company at the top had previously held an equally senior position in another, usually smaller company. In the age of consolidation of big business, many a German leader cut his teeth on the management of a medium-sized company before operating on a larger scale. Paul Reusch (1868–1956) was on the executive board of the Friedrich-Wilhelmhütte when in 1905 he accepted, at the age of 37, the post of managing director of the Gutehoffnungshütte, one of the oldest and largest iron and steel concerns in the Ruhr.[60] Max Steinthal (1850–1940) after a banking apprenticeship joined in 1871, aged only 21, the executive board of the Padersteinsche Bank in Berlin. Two years later he was offered a seat on the Deutsche Bank's executive board in charge of foreign exchanges, where he remained until 1906; he went on to become chairman of the supervisory board from 1914 to 1933.[61]

Mergers played a major part in the shaping of this career pattern. Albert Vögler (1877–1945), for example, the first chairman of the Vereinigte Stahlwerke's executive board, had been managing director of Deutsch-Luxemburg from 1915 to 1926 and Hugo Stinnes's right-hand man; his colleague and successor in 1935, Ernst Poensgen (1871–1940), had been a managing director of Phoenix between 1911 and 1926. More modest takeovers could also open doors. To give but one instance, Heinrich Kamp (1841–1927) became managing director of Phoenix in 1898 (until 1908), following the takeover in 1897 of the Westfälische Union, a medium-sized iron and steel concern of which he was managing director. Mergers, however, should not conceal the progressive nature of many business careers in Germany. Modern career structures were set up earlier than in Britain and France, consisting of rungs leading to the very top, and of strategic moves from one firm to another at a key stage. Albert Vögler started his career as an engineer with the Union AG, in Dortmund, joined the executive board in 1906, and moved to Deutsch-Luxemburg in 1910 as the result of the merger between the two firms. Carl Bosch (1874–1940) entered IG Farben on its foundation in 1925 as chairman of the executive board. He was granted the top job in his capacity as managing director of BASF, the largest of the amalgamating companies; but he had joined BASF in 1899 as a chemist, becoming managing director twenty years later.

In France the route to the top rarely included a stage with a large company, unlike Germany and also Britain. Since the beginning of the

[59] S. Haubold, 'Hartmann, Gustav, Fabrikant, Wirtschaftsberater', in *Neue deutsche Biographie*, vol. vii (Berlin, 1966).
[60] See E. Maschke, *Es ensteht ein Konzern: Paul Reusch und die GHH* (Tübingen, 1969).
[61] Schmidt, *Männer der Deutschen Bank*.

Table 6.7. Previous career of business leaders who joined their firm at top hierarchical level (with the exception of inheritors) (%)

	1907			1929			1953			1972			1989		
	GB	F	D	GB	F	D	GB	F	D	GB	F	D	GB	F	D
Civil service	3	38	14	5	43	6	0	55	16	14	50	14	6	57	17
Private firm	58	32	46	55	18	30	41	0	25	24	15	18	12	0	0
Senior management	8	5	31	33	14	55	38	36	50	48	25	64	58	37	78
Junior management	13	10	3	0	0	3	3	0	3	4	5	0	6	6	0
Professions	6	0	6	0	0	6	6	0	0	0	0	0	6	0	0
Other	12	15	0	7	25	0	12	9	6	10	5	4	12	0	5
Total	100	100	100	100	100	100	100	100	100	100	100	100	100	100	100
No. of cases	36	19	36	44	28	36	32	11	32	21	20	22	17	30	18

Sources: Author's estimates based on a sample of business leaders.

century, more than half the business leaders who had joined their company at the highest hierarchical level came directly from the civil service (Table 6.7).[62] Some were *notables* whose profile was well suited to the chairmanship of a large company. For example the baron Hély d'Oissel, *maître de requêtes* at the Conseil d'État, one of the French *grands corps*, and member of Parliament, was chairman of the Société Générale. Charles Laurent (1856–1939), chairman of the Cour des Comptes, another *grand corps*, was French ambassador in Berlin from 1920 to 1928 before his appointment as chairman of Thomson-Houston. Most of them, however, were engineers (in industry) or *inspecteurs des finances* (in banking) and were directly involved in the running of the firm, as general managers or managing directors. Léon Lévy (1851–1925), a *polytechnicien*, left the civil service in 1891, where he had reached the post of chief mining engineer after fifteen years' service, to become general manager of the Forges de Châtillon-Commentry et Neuves-Maisons, an iron and steel company.[63] Louis Champy (1870–1955), also a *polytechnicien* and mining engineer in the state administration from 1895 to 1904, joined the Mines d'Anzin as assistant general manager and was general manager from 1910 to 1936. As for the business leaders coming from private partnerships, they were all business *notables*, such as the private banker Jean de Neuflize (1850–1928), chairman of the Assurances Générales, or the textile industrialist Anatole Descamps (1833–?), chairman of the Mines de Lens.[64] In any case, their number fell dramatically after the First World War.

Modern professional careers developed earlier in Germany because of the firms' internal structure. The largest among them were the first in Europe to set up a centralized and hierarchical organization, often inspired by the Prussian State bureaucracy.[65] This type of corporate career has become the norm in European big business since the 1950s. The main novelty in the last thirty years has been the higher proportion of business leaders who joined their company at an intermediary level—as engineers, junior executives in the commercial or financial services, and so on—rather than at the highest level, and who have consequently spent their entire career in the same company (Table 6.8).

Despite this apparent convergence, the recruitment of top businessmen has continued to follow a specific course in France. Admittedly in the last thirty years the percentage of business leaders joining their company in a

[62] For a general discussion of the passage from the civil service to the private sector, a phenomenon known as *pantouflage*, see C. Charle, 'Le Pantouflage en France (vers 1880–vers 1980)', *Annales ESC* (1987), 5: 1115–37.

[63] Archives Nationales, Paris, LH 1629 d.53.

[64] On the links between the Compagnie des Mines de Lens and the textile dynasties of the north of France, see M. Gillet, *Les Charbonnages du Nord de la France au XIXe siècle* (Paris, 1973).

[65] See J. Kocka, 'The Rise of the Modern Industrial Enterprise in Germany', in A. D. Chandler and H. Daems (eds.), *Managerial Hierarchies: Comparative Perspectives on the Rise of the Modern Industrial Enterprise* (Cambridge, Mass., 1980); Chandler, *Scale and Scope*.

Table 6.8. Previous career of business leaders who joined their firm at junior managerial level (with the exception of inheritors) (%)

	1972			1989		
	GB	F	D	GB	F	D
No previous career	46	22	55	50	38	53
Civil service	0	33	6	8	30	0
Junior management	33	17	27	30	25	16
Professions	4	6	0	4	0	10
Other	17	22	12	8	7	21
Total	100	100	100	100	100	100
No. of cases	24	18	18	24	24	19

Sources: Author's estimates based on a sample of business leaders.

middle-ranking position was roughly the same in three countries (Table 6.5). However, these figures conceal two important differences. First, the vast majority of French business leaders joining their company at this level (61 per cent for the generation active in 1972, 75 per cent in 1989) were *managing directors*, not chairmen; and very few of them ever reached the chairmanship. French company chairmen (the PDGs) have thus continued to be recruited from outside. The second difference concerns previous professional experience. While Britain has drawn nearer to the German model of corporate recruitment, business leaders in France have continued to come from the higher ranks of the civil service. Their percentage has even increased in the last forty years, rising from 38 per cent for the generation active in the early 1950s to 42 per cent twenty years later and 59 per cent in the late 1980s. This recruitment pattern, which 'parachutes' a senior civil servant to the top of a large company, has been seen as a less effective method of finding an outstanding leader than an internal selection process. In particular, it has been accused of causing personal relationships within the firm to deteriorate and of demoralizing junior and senior executives.[66]

Competence is also a matter of age. Not surprisingly, business leaders throughout the century have not been young people. The professionalization of business careers led to a rise of the average age at which they reached a top position—whether chairman, general manager, or director: from 44 before 1914 to 52 in 1989. There were of course some differences

[66] M. Bauer and B. Bertin-Mourot, *'Les 200' en France et en Allemagne: Deux modèles de détection-sélection-formation de dirigeants de grandes entreprises* (Paris, n.d. [1992]).

between types of businessmen: heirs tended to reach the highest echelon at a younger age than outside managers; it took longer to become chairman than managing director. In Germany since the 1950s most chairmen of supervisory boards have been the just-retired chairman of the executive board; they occupy this post from the ages of 65 to 70, thus remaining involved in the company's affairs without retaining managerial responsibilities.

As a corollary, the number of years spent at the top has been greatly reduced. The changes have been even more striking here, with average time spent at the helm falling from nearly twenty-five years before 1914 to barely ten by the early 1970s. The average age of business leaders has remained fairly constant throughout the century, between 57 and 59 for the five benchmark years. However, age differences within the business world have narrowed. Until the 1950s there were more 'young' but also more 'old' business leaders than today or twenty years ago. In the three countries there were more business leaders over 65 than under 45; and more over 75 than under 35. What is the optimum age to lead a large company? The answer is not easy. But the age at which some of the chairmen were still active leaves one pondering. The oldest in the 1907 sample was Wilhelm Herz, chairman of the supervisory board of the Deutsche Bank at 84. In 1952 Ernest Carnot was chairman of the Viscose Française at 86. Nor were these isolated cases.

Put another way, a leading businessman rarely quit for reasons of age. Usually he died in harness. For the generations active before the Second World War, death was by far the most common cause of ceasing working: this was the case with 59 per cent of British and 56 per cent of German top businessmen active in 1907, and in the three countries of more than 40 per cent of those active in 1929. Some died at a very old age. James Reckitt (1833–1924), chairman of the chemical company Reckitt & Sons, was 91 years old, like Herz. Average retirement age was 70 plus until the 1950s. William Forwood stepped down as chairman of Cunard in 1922 aged 82, Alexandre Dreux as chairman of Longwy in 1933 aged 80, and Emil Kirdorf as managing director of GBAG in 1926 aged 79. Dismissals and forced resignations, though rare, did occur as a sanction against poor performance or outright failure. In 1922, Philip Arthur Du Cros was replaced as Dunlop's chairmanship by Eric Geddes in the wake of the firm's near bankruptcy. The depression of the 1930s took its toll: in 1931, Philip Nash, AEI's managing director, was sacked by the board; Alphonse Gérard, Saint-Gobain's chairman, resigned following criticism of his tenure; while Karl Lahusen and Hermann Rodewald, respectively chairmen of Nordwolle's executive and supervisory boards, had to leave after their firm had collapsed. But resignations could also be caused by political motives. The advent of Nazism in Germany led several leading Jewish businessmen, such as Paul Silverberg, head of Rheinbraun, and Georg

Solmssen of the Disconto-Gesellschaft, to give up their functions in 1933; other, non Jewish businessmen—such as Fritz Thyssen, Ernst Poensgen, and Paul Reusch—became disenchanted with the regime at a later stage and also had to resign and leave the country.

Circumstances have changed in the last thirty years. Only an insignificant number of business leaders have died in office, before normal retirement age, such as Michel Paul-Cavallier (1909–64), managing director of Pont-à-Mousson, who died at 55; or Ulrich Haberland (1900–61), chairman of Bayer's executive board, who died at 61. Terrorism, on the other hand, claimed the lives of the leaders of Germany's two leading banks: Jürgen Ponto, of Dresdner Bank, assassinated in 1977, aged 54, and Alfred Herrhausen, of Deutsche Bank, assassinated in 1989, aged 59. Few have continued after the age of 70: in 1972 the oldest in the sample was Jules Thorn, chairman of Thorn Electrical Companies, aged 73; in 1990 it was Konrad Henkel, chairman of the supervisory board of Degussa, aged 74. Retirement and promotion from managing director to chairman have become the main reasons for leaving a job, with dismissals becoming a more frequent possibility, including from the top of the very largest companies.

To what extent companies have been handicapped by the loss of a leader remains to be analysed in a historical perspective—though a definite answer is unlikely ever to be provided. Individuals do of course matter. However, throughout the century and across Europe, business leaders have displayed many common features—in their social, family, and educational backgrounds, in the way they built their career, the age at which they reached the top and retired—which tend to surpass their singularity. The more so as their decisions have had to be made within restricted parameters.

7

Decision-Making

In the last analysis, business leadership comes down to decision-making. The success or even the survival of a company depends on the strategic choices made by its leaders, as far as investment, innovation, internal organization, networks of relationships, and many others are concerned. How were these decisions made? This is one of the most important questions confronting the business historian; yet much as we would like to know how bosses have actually worked, the decision-making process—consultations, deliberations, conflicts, outside influences—remains largely enshrined in secrecy, not even always disclosed by companies' internal records.

However, at least four structural factors affecting this process can be analysed and compared. The first two are endogenous. The functioning of a company has in part been shaped by the legal framework; whether a company was run by a unitary or by a two-tier board could, for example, affect the way decisions were made. Equally important is the organizational structure of the firm, set up by business leaders themselves in order to implement their strategic decisons and seize new opportunities. The last two factors are exogenous. One concerns the network of relationships within which business leaders operate, as reflected in interlocking directorships. Another is the relationships between banks, financial markets, and industry.

COMPANY BOARDS

The origins of the single and two-tier boards go back to the company laws of the 1860s—1856–62 in Britain, 1863–7 in France, 1870 in Germany—which freed the way for the growth of joint-stock companies. They assigned the responsibility for their running to a single body in Britain and France, the board of directors (*conseil d'administration* in French); but to two in Germany: a management or executive board (*Vorstand*) and a supervisory board (*Aufsichtsrat*). The legislators' intention was to separate by law the day-to-day running of the firm from strategic decision-making.[1] However, despite these legal conditions, the differences between

---

[1] Good comparisons, from both a legal and historical standpoint, in N. Horn, 'Aktienrechtliche Unternehmensorganisation in der Hochindustrialisierung (1860–1920):

Britain and France on the one hand, and Germany on the other, can be seen as purely formal. After all, up to the Second World War and even beyond, British and French board members tended to delegate the daily routine of managing the firm to salaried managers, confining themselves to supervisory tasks. This was the case in most large companies with a long-standing separation between ownership and management, such as joint-stock banks, insurance companies, railway companies, and public utilities.[2] Separation between management and control thus potentially existed in all three countries—*de facto* in Britain and France, *de jure* in Germany.

In practice, however, this would only have been the case if German company law had achieved its objective. In the event, it entirely missed it. Far from limiting itself to daily managerial tasks, the *Vorstand* soon seized upon the responsibility of designing the firm's long-term strategy.[3] The supervisory board's control became increasingly remote, its authority being felt only in times of serious crisis; and the chairman alone kept in touch with the running of the firm. The executive board members of a German company were thus in no way comparable to the general managers of a British or French company. Their position was rather that of executive directors or, as they were often called at the time, managing directors—in French *administrateurs délégués*. In fact, during the first part of the twentieth century, separation between management and control occurred more often in British and French than in German companies.

As a result, it is easier to locate the seat of power in the large German corporations. In the overwhelming majority of cases, it lay with the *Vorstand*, the executive board, and especially with its chairman who often held the title of *Generaldirektor*. Whatever the emphasis sometimes given to the collegiate nature of German top management, in reality executive board chairmen overshadowed their fellow members, not only in the large coal, iron, and steel concerns that tended to be associated with one dominant figure, such as Emil Kirdorf at the Gelsenkirchener Bergwerks or Paul Reusch at the Gutehoffnungshütte,[4] but also in the new industries, with such leading personalities as Emil Rathenau at the AEG and Paul Duisberg at Bayer. The formation of huge conglomerates in the 1920s led to an increase in the number of members of the *Vorstand*, comprising as

---

Deutschland, England, Frankreich und die USA im Vergleich', in N. Horn and J. Kocka (eds.), *Recht und Entwicklung der Grossunternehmen im 19. und frühen 20. Jahrhundert* (Göttingen, 1979).

[2] See Y. Cassis, *City Bankers, 1890–1914* (Cambridge, 1994); T. Gourvish, 'A British Business Elite: The Chief Executive Managers of the Railway Industry 1850–1922', *Business History Review*, 47/3 (1973).

[3] Horn, 'Aktienrechtliche Unternehmensorganisation'.

[4] See for example E. G. Spencer, 'Rulers of the Ruhr: Leadership and Authority in German Big Business before 1914', *Business History Review*, 53/1 (1979); G. D. Feldman, *Iron and Steel in German Inflation, 1916–1923* (Princeton, 1977).

Table 7.1. Supervisory board chairmen of the leading German companies (%)

	1907	1929	1953	1972	1989
Family interests	45	43	7	20	8
Business world	25	14	21	28	20
Banks	20	17	34	12	20
Former executive board chairmen	0	20	21	36	44
Others	10	6	17	4	8
Total	100	100	100	100	100
No. of cases	20	35	29	25	25

Sources: Author's estimates based on a sample of business leaders.

many as thirty-four members at IG Farben. The real power there, however, was in the hands of a smaller central committee of eight members set up in 1930 by the executive board's chairman Carl Bosch, with Carl Duisberg, the supervisory board chairman, as adviser.[5]

The influence of the supervisory boards' chairmen should not be underestimated, especially before the Second World War. Four types of businessmen usually held this position (Table 7.1). The first were the representatives of family interests; some enjoyed considerable power, such as Carl Friedrich von Siemens or Gustav Krupp von Bohlen und Halbach in the inter-war years, though others adopted a more withdrawn attitude. Within this group, even greater power was exercised by representatives of private interests who actually ruled a single company, or more often a group of companies, from the supervisory rather than from the executive board. Businessmen such as Hugo Stinnes, Peter Klöckner, and Friedrich Flick, who had set up powerful groups, were in the position of quasi-'executive' chairmen. The percentage of family representatives decreased considerably after the Second World War. They have been replaced, as it were, by a group whose importance has consistently grown since then: the former executive board chairmen, granted the chairmanship of the supervisory board on their retirement. A third group consisted of banks' representatives. Though highly influential, it was by no means the largest group and remained confined to a number of companies traditionally linked to a particular bank, for example the iron and steel concern Phoenix and the Cologne private bank Oppenheim, or Daimler-Benz and the Deutsche Bank. The fourth group was made up of people of high pres-

[5] G. Plumpe, *Die IG Farbenindustrie AG: Wirtschaft, Technik und Politik 1904–1945* (Berlin, 1990).

tige and influence in the business community, such as merchants, company directors, and leaders of large industrial corporations.

If German business leaders can be fairly easily identified as the respective chairmen of the two boards, the same cannot be said of their British and French counterparts. Before 1914 some company chairmen were no more involved in the running of their firm than the supervisory board chairman of a German company, for example in British banking,[6] as well as in a number of industrial companies, including the then largest British firm, Imperial Tobacco.[7] On the other hand, executive chairmen were far from being uncommon, especially in Britain; their number increased after the First World War and included the chairmen of most leading companies.[8] The power to devise and implement a strategy was sometimes in the hands of a dominant managing director, such as Otto Ernest Philippi at J. & P. Coats before 1914.[9] Managing directors in French heavy industry were often in this position, for example Alexandre Dreux at Longwy and Henry Darcy at Châtillon-Commentry, both of whom eventually made it to the chairmanship.[10] There were of course a number of straightforward cases where the chairman and a managing director were obviously in charge. Very often, however, the locus of power can be identified only on a case-by-case basis.

In France, company directors (the *administrateurs*) tended to devolve a greater part of their reponsibilities to managers *outside* the board. Interestingly, these managers enjoyed a higher degree of autonomy than their British counterparts. This may be surprising, as inconsistent with the widespread view of the persistence of family control in French business. Such a view, however, applies to the vast majority of French firms—small and medium-sized enterprises—but not to the large corporations, with which we are primarily concerned here. The board of directors of these companies included a high proportion of *notables*, who devoted but a fraction of their time to business matters. Even in the iron and steel industry, a traditional family stronghold, the distance separating the works from the head office, often located in Paris, further alienated the directors from the day-to-day running of the firm. The status of French senior managers was further enhanced by their level of education, which was much higher than that of their British counterparts and brought them closer to the country's social élite. Though obviously less rich, and of a more recent

    [6] Cassis, *City Bankers*.
    [7] B. W. E. Alford, *W. D. & H. O. Wills and the Development of the UK Tobacco Industry, 1786–1965* (London, 1973), 182, 327.
    [8] Harry McGowan at ICI, Francis D'Arcy Cooper at Unilever, Hugo Hirst at GEC, Herbert Lawrence at Vickers, Eric Geddes at Dunlop, John Cadman at Anglo-Persian Oil, Frederic Goodenough at Barclays Bank, to name but the most famous. See their entries in D. Jeremy (ed.), *Dictionary of Business Biography*, 5 vols. (London, 1984–6).
    [9] J. B. K. Hunter, 'Otto Ernest Philippi', in A. Slaven and S. Checkland (eds.), *Dictionary of Scottish Business Biography 1860–1960*, i. *The Staple Industries* (Aberdeen, 1986), 389–92.
    [10] J. M. Moine, *Les Barons du fer: Les Maîtres de forges en Lorraine du milieu du 19ème siècle aux années trente. Histoire sociale d'un patronat sidérurgique* (Nancy, 1989).

bourgeois ascent, they were none the less likely to have been educated at the same *grande école*, most often the École Polytechnique, as members of the board. In Britain, on the other hand, the separation between gentlemen and players was deeply rooted in the educational system.[11] Salaried managers, including general managers, were recruited at around 15 or 16 years old, were trained on the job, and had to climb every step of the ladder. Even those who received a further education did not follow the noble path through a public school followed by Oxford or Cambridge.

In the end, the main difference between the three countries was not so much a matter of company legislation or whether there existed a two-tier or a single board. Before the Second World War, the real—and often overlooked—difference concerned the socio-professional status of the emerging professional businessman. The early power gained by the *Vorstand* meant that salaried managers were earlier in command in Germany than in Britain and France, where they remained in a somewhat subordinate position. In this respect, an obvious convergence has taken place in the last fifty years. Professional managers have now become the real, and only, decision-makers in European big business. This has required more important changes in company legislation in France than in Britain or Germany.[12]

In Germany, management has remained firmly in the hands of the *Vorstand*, under the loose monitoring of the supervisory board. A 1937 law, enacted by the Nazis, reinforced its authority, and especially that of its chairman, thus undermining the collegiate principle which had officially prevailed so far, and which was restored in 1970. Nevertheless, although the title of *Generaldirektor* has fallen into disuse since the war, there can be no question about the existence of a 'number one' in all major German companies, whether he carries the title of chairman (*Vorstandvorsitzender*) or the more discreet appellation of spokesman (*Sprecher*).[13] Likewise in Britain, power has remained in the hands of the board of directors, the composition of which, however, underwent a profound transformation. Professionalization has proceeded slowly, starting in the 1920s in the most forward-looking large companies—ICI, for example, soon adopted a policy of recruiting young graduates, offering them prospects of promotion up to board level[14]—and spreading since the 1960s.

The professionalization of the board of directors has in fact brought Britain closer to the German model. The implementation of strategic decisions, previously often performed by senior managers under the board's supervision, has been undertaken by executive directors who are full

---

[11] See D. C. Coleman, 'Gentlemen and Players', *Economic History Review*, 26 (1973).

[12] For a useful survey of current company legislation and related issues in the three countries, as well as in the United States and Japan, see J. Charkham, *Keeping Good Company: A Study of Corporate Governance in Five Countries* (Oxford, 1994).

[13] See H. Joly, 'L'Élite industrielle allemande: Métier, pouvoir et politiques 1933–1989', unpublished Ph.D. thesis (École des Hautes Études en Sciences Sociales Paris, 1993), 21–2.

[14] See W. J. Reader, *Imperial Chemical Industries: A History*, 2 vols. (Oxford, 1970–5).

members of the country's business élite. This has opened the question of
the control of management. The practical answer has been to entrust non-
executive directors with this task. Their representation on the boards of
the large companies has substantially increased, reaching an average of
44 per cent by 1993.[15] British non-executive directors do not appear to
perform their duty either more or less efficiently than their German counterparts on the supervisory board. None the less important differences
from Germany subsist, especially in terms of the composition of the two
groups.

As is well known, membership of the supervisory boards of German
companies includes workers' representatives, alongside shareholders'
representatives, in accordance with the principle of *Mitbestimmung*, or co-
determination. Co-determination was first introduced in 1951 in the coal,
iron, and steel industry (the *Montanindustrie*), which still formed the bulk
of German big business. Their supervisory boards had to include an equal
number of representatives of workers and shareholders, and both sides
had to agree on a neutral chairman. In addition, workers had a say in the
appointment of the member of the executive board responsible for labour
matters (the *Arbeitdirektor*). Such conditions did not apply to the rest of
German industries, where workers' representation (introduced in 1952)
was restricted to only a third of the supervisory board. However, the
number of companies with extensive workers' representation diminished
in the following decades, as a result of the decline of heavy industry, its
increased concentration, and the diversification into other activities of
some of its largest groups, such as Thyssen or Mannesmann. Trade union
pressure to extend the coal and iron regulations to the entire German
industry was naturally opposed by employers. A compromise was
reached in 1976. Workers gained equal representation on supervisory
boards; however, one of their representatives had to be of managerial
status, and the chairman, who has a casting vote, is in practice normally
a representative of the shareholders. On the other hand, candidates to the
executive board must be elected by a two-thirds majority, which requires
the agreement of at least part of the employees' representatives.[16]

Admittedly the effects of co-determination on business leadership have
been rather limited, though not entirely negligible. Workers' representatives can hardly be seen as part of the country's business élite. Their part
in choosing the leaders of the largest companies has also been minimal,
even in the heavy industries where they were in a position to influence
events. On some occasions, however, they successfully opposed the shareholders' choice for membership of the *Vorstand*. In the heavy industries,

[15] G. Owen, *The Future of Britain's Boards of Directors: Two Tiers or One?* (London, The Institute of Chartered Accountants, 1995).
[16] See C. Lane, *Management and Labour in Europe: The Industrial Enterprise in Germany,
Britain and France* (Aldershot, 1989).

co-determination has also ensured that, even without formal opposition on the part of employees' representatives, a traditionally autocratic business leadership has entered into a permanent dialogue with representatives of the workforce.[17]

Another difference concerns the concentration of power in the hands of a single person, through the combination of the functions of chairman and managing director. This has become widespread in large British companies, though the practice was recently criticized by the Cadbury report on corporate governance, published in 1992.[18] Whatever the powers of the executive board chairman of a German company, they do not extend thus far. But they certainly do in France, where the identification of the company with a single 'number one', which has become a common feature of European big business in the last two decades, has been pushed to its limit.

This was a result of the 1940 company law, which rendered mandatory the merger of the functions of chairman and general manager, thus creating a new all-powerful executive, the *PDG*, or *président directeur général*. The new law was clearly inspired by the German example, set up by the Nazis a few years earlier, which the Vichy government was keen to emulate. But the French legislation was more than mere plagiarism in its exaltation of the leader. It was also the result of the professionalization of business leadership that had been taking place throughout Europe. The new *PDG* was a more professional executive than the *notables* who traditionally chaired French companies, yet he retained the social and professional status of board membership. The *président directeur général* has been rightly described as an absolute monarch with no real check to his powers, apart from the political authority over nationalized companies. The question of the control of management remains open in France, even though an answer has been available since 1973 with the creation of a new company law, once again inspired by the German model. This adopted the two-tier board, though without requiring employee representation.[19] However, companies have been left free to choose their favoured type of corporate governance. By the late 1980s, less than 10 per cent had opted for the new two-tier system, and hardly any among the large corporations. A notable exception is the banking group Paribas, which modified its statutes in 1990.

Business leadership is partly shaped by the requirements of company legislation prevailing in each country. But the differences between Britain, France, and Germany have been more a matter of form than content. In the course of the twentieth century, the three countries have moved in the same direction, though not at the same time or at the same rhythm.

---

[17] See Joly, 'L'Élite industrielle allemande'.

[18] *Report of the Committee on the Financial Aspects of Corporate Governance* (1992).

[19] B. Opetit and A. Sayag, *Les Structures juridiques de l'entreprise* (Paris, 1983).

Business leaders have gradually become full-time professionals. In the process, they have strengthened executive power within the large corporation without, however, eradicating the recurring demand for control over management.

ORGANIZATIONAL STRUCTURES

Have differences in business organization proved more significant? For a generation of business historians, this has been *the* most relevant question in the discipline. And behind it lies Alfred Chandler's monumental work. The structure of the firm is at the very core of his analysis, not only of the rise of big business but of the whole development of industrial capitalism. Business enterprises have advanced through a number of stages: from the personal firm, managed by its owners; to the entrepreneurial, or family-controlled enterprise; and finally to the managerial enterprise, where ownership and management have become totally separate. Chandler's work provides powerful tools for a comparison of business organizations. One is the concept of 'organizational capabilities', which successful firms have developed by investing in production, marketing, and management. Another is the organizational structure of the firm. Chandler has described in great detail the advent, first of the multiunit, multifunctional enterprise; and then, as firms became more diversified, of the multidivisional enterprise.[20] Centralization and division by function (production, sales, finance, research and development, etc.) prevail in the former; decentralization and division by product feature in the latter, with each of the firm's divisions—for example explosives, dyes, paints, pharmaceuticals, etc. in a chemical company—being itself divided into a number of functional units. The development of complex organizational structures has obviously affected the decision-making process, especially as far as business leaders are concerned: top managers have been able to delegate an increasing number of tasks to a hierarchy of managers and to concentrate on the company's long-term strategy.

Not only does Chandler's work provide powerful analytical tools, but these tools have already been put to extensive use. The historical relevance of the 'Chandler thesis' (which originated from the study of American business) for European business has been assessed by eminent national specialists;[21] while Chandler set himself the formidable task of comparing the American and European experiences (though France had

[20] A good overview in A. Chandler, *Scale and Scope* (Cambridge, Mass., 1990), 14–46.
[21] See especially L. Hannah, 'Visible and Invisible Hands in Great Britain', J. Kocka, 'The Rise of the Modern Industrial Enterprise in Germany', and M. Lévy-Leboyer, 'The Large Corporation in Modern France', in A. Chandler and H. Daems (eds.), *Managerial Hierarchies: Comparative Perspectives on the Rise of the Modern Industrial Enterprise* (Cambridge, Mass., 1980).

to be left out in the event), resulting in 1990 in *Scale and Scope*. The results, however, are mixed. Large parts of Chandler's analysis are of course irrefutable, to the point of having reached the status of common knowledge. One cannot seriously doubt, for example, that the firms which made the first investments in production, marketing, and management gained a powerful competitive advantage; or that managerial hierarchies are essential for running large and complex business organizations. Chandler's combination of empirical historical evidence with bold generalizations has also aroused much interest among economists dissatisfied with the neo-classical theory, or rather absence of theory, of the firm.[22] Such generalizations, however, pose more problems to the historian than to the economist, and it is at this level that Chandler's conclusions are least convincing.

In a European comparative perspective, the question is whether analytical concepts designed for the study of individual companies can be applied to assess the performance of entire economies. The problem is Chandler's explicit reference to the superiority of the American model of business organization, characterized by a high degree of integration and diversification, the early advent of managerial capitalism, and the predominance of the multidivisional form of organization. Within the European context, Chandler is in no doubt about the superiority of the German system, by virtue of its assumed closeness to the American model. *Scale and Scope*, admittedly, only compares the American, British, and German experiences; but France, though not included in the book, is on the whole likened to Britain.[23] However, such a superiority has not been conspicuous so far in our analysis, whether in terms of size, performance, or forms of ownership.

Does a closer look at organizational structures reveal more significant differences between the three countries? The truth is that we still know very little about the internal organization of the vast majority of large European corporations before 1914 or even 1945. A quantitative analysis of the level of vertical integration and product diversification in the 100 largest German industrial companies in 1887, 1907, and 1927 was carried out by Jürgen Kocka and Hannes Siegrist in the early days of the Chandler debate,[24] but no similar studies were undertaken for Britain and France. German companies are assumed to have reached a significantly

---

[22] See for example O. Williamson, *Markets and Hierarchies: Analysis and Antitrust Implications* (New York, 1975); R. Nelson and S. Winter, *An Evolutionary Theory of Economic Change* (Cambridge, Mass., 1982); W. Lazonick, *Business Organization and the Myth of the Market Economy* (Cambridge, 1991); R. Langlois and P. Robertson, *Firms, Markets and Economic Change* (London, 1995).

[23] Chandler, *Scale and Scope*, 596.

[24] J. Kocka and H. Siegrist, 'Die 100 grössten deutschen Industrieunternehmen im späten 19. und frühen 20. Jahrhundert', in Horn and Kocka (eds.), *Recht und Entwicklung*; H. Siegrist, 'Deutsche Grossunternehmen vom späten 19. Jahrhundert bis zur Weimarer Republik', *Geschichte und Gesellschaft*, 6/1 (1980).

higher level of integration and diversification than their British counterparts before 1914; in fact, they were even more diversified than the largest American companies. However, this was not seen by the authors as indicative of a more advanced stage of development, rather as a reflection of Germany's relative economic backwardness, especially its absence of a well-developed industrial and commercial tradition, its rudimentary and unpredictable markets, and its lack of a competitive business environment.

In any case, levels of integration and diversification are only a very rough indicator of managerial structures. A qualitative approach would no doubt prove more revealing. However, apart from a few famous cases (such as Siemens, Bayer, the Vereinigte Stahlwerke, IG Farben, Unilever, Anglo-Persian Oil, ICI, or Saint-Gobain), we do not know which decisions were taken at top management level, whether they were related to day-to-day runnning or to long-term strategic planning. We know very little about the administrative and technical support given by middle managers, or in Chandlerian terminology the depth of managerial hierarchies. Exploratory inquiries in this field have revealed that throughout the twentieth century the ratio of white collars to blue collars was probably not higher in Germany than in British or French manufacturing industry.[25] Comparative research on engineers, and more generally on middle management, *within* business enterprises is still in its infancy.[26] This is a promising field, which goes far beyond the scope of this study centred on business élites. However, new research suggests that the superiority of German firms in that matter has been widely exaggerated by the Chandlerian school. This can be seen, for example, in the strong record of British industrial research and development in the inter-war years.[27]

Some authors, especially in Germany, have been rather circumspect about the quality of German management before 1914. Kocka, for example, describes it as 'an intricate mixture of system and improvisation, bureaucratic and personal methods, fixed order and flexibility'.[28]

[25] See L. Hannah, 'Delusions of Durable Dominance or The Invisible Hand Strikes Back: A Critique of the New Orthodoxy in Internationally Comparative Business History, 1980s' (Centre for Economic Performance, London School of Economics, 1995), 57.

[26] For the United States, see Olivier Zunz's innovative book *Making America Corporate 1870–1920* (Chicago, 1990).

[27] See D. E. H. Edgerton and S. M. Horrocks, 'British Industrial Research and Development before 1945', *Economic History Review*, 47/2 (1994); see also Arno Mietschke's promising study of engineers in the German and English electrical industries in the inter-war years, especially his comparison of BTH's works at Rugby, and AEG's works at Hennigsdorf: 'Ingenieure in der deutschen und englischen Elektroindustrie der Zwischenkriegszeit', unpub. paper (Arbeitsstelle für vergleichende Gesellschaftsgeschichte, Freie Universität Berlin, Apr. 1994).

[28] J. Kocka, 'Entrepreneurs and Managers in German Industrialization', in P. Mathias and N. M. Postan (eds.), *The Cambridge Economic History of Europe*, vii. *The Industrial Economies: Capital, Labour, and Enterprise*, part 1: *Britain, France, Germany, and Scandinavia* (Cambridge, 1978), 575.

Chandler's far greater enthusiasm rests on the indisputable superiority of the German electrical and chemical industries before 1914; and on the respective performances of the British and German economies since the late nineteenth century. However, the comparative evidence on the organizational structures of British and German enterprises gathered in *Scale and Scope* is extremely thin. German superiority is often taken for granted, leading to dangerous generalizations bordering on prejudice. And even Alfred Chandler is not entirely immune to it. His comparison between the chocolate-makers Cadbury and Stollwerck, which in his view 'effectively illustrate the differences between the personal ways of British management and the more impersonal, systematic and professional ways of German management',[29] is revealing in that respect.

Cadbury and Stollwerck were founded within a few years of each other, respectively in 1831 and 1839. They strongly expanded in the last quarter of the nineteenth century following the construction of a large modern works, in Birmingham for Cadbury, in Cologne for Stollwerck. Early this century they were of a similar size, with a share capital of around £1 million and a 4,000- to 5,000-strong workforce. In Chandler's description, Stollwerck appears very much as the more dynamic firm, especially in marketing, where it pioneered dispensing machines, and in multinational development through its opening of a factory in Hungary in 1886 and, more importantly, in the United States in 1900. Chandler attributes this dynamism to the building of managerial hierarchies, though the family remained in control at the top: before 1914, the entire executive board was made up of members of the Stollwerck family. By contrast, Cadbury is described as much more conservative, with less-developed distribution facilities before 1914, no direct foreign investments, and its markets restricted to the British empire. According to Chandler, Cadbury only employed a limited number of salaried managers, though the assertion is not supported by much detail.[30] Whatever these early differences, their impact on the two firms' later development is far from clear. By 1929, Cadbury had become a truly large company, with £3.2 million capital and employing nearly 12,000 people. Stollwerck had remained a medium-sized company, with little more than £800,000 capital and 3,300 employees. Even more tellingly, Cadbury's market capitalization exceeded £10 million as against a mere £1.5 million for Stollwerck. As to their longer-term development, Cadbury is today one of the global players in the food and drink industry and a household name across the world through some of its brand products, while few have heard of Stollwerck.

[29] Chandler, *Scale and Scope*, 399.
[30] Ibid. 399–402. In fact, Robert Fitzgerald has shown that 'by 1900, Cadbury already had a basic multifunctional organization, and, in the following years, the number of managers and white-collar staff was greatly expanded', *Rowntree and the Marketing Revolution 1862–1969* (Cambridge, 1995), 204.

Rather than the basic differences between British and German management, the comparison between Cadbury and Stollwerck highlights the limitations of the Chandlerian concepts for the comparative analysis of European big business.[31] These concepts are invaluable for the study of single firms, provided they are applied with flexibility. Adequate managerial structures, for example, can be perfectly compatible with the family firm, as shown by innumerable historical cases. Similarly, in given circumstances, networks of relationships could be preferable to vertical integration and managerial hierarchies. Such flexibility can be found in John Kay's notion of 'architecture', which he defines as 'a network of relational contracts within, or around, the firm'.[32] Applied to entire economies, Chandler's analysis becomes totally ineffective, being either based on insufficient or incorrect information, or unable to explain business performance. Failures to set up an appropriate organizational structure have occurred in British, French, and German companies. Explanations have to be found at the level of individual firms rather than in national characteristics.

MULTIPLE DIRECTORSHIPS

Walther Rathenau claimed in 1912 that 300 men, each of whom knew each other, guided the economic fortunes of Europe.[33] The son of Emil Rathenau, the founder of the giant electrical concern AEG, he was himself a banker, an industrialist, and a politician—eventually assassinated in 1922 while foreign minister of the Weimar Republic. His claim might have been excessive, but it was certainly telling. To this day multiple directorships continue to fascinate observers of the business world, for they represent the most obvious evidence of the concentration of economic power in the hands of a few individuals.

Historians and social scientists have long made ample use of overlapping directorships to detect links between two or several companies and to identify business groups. The 'power of the banks', especially the German banks, has often been measured by the number of seats held by bankers on the boards of other companies.[34] In 1913 the Deutsche Bank held 78 seats on the supervisory boards of 73 companies, and the

---

[31] As has also been observed, Chandler's model does not allow for other forms of economic development, in particular for the role of small and medium-sized entreprises which have played a crucial role, not only in the 19th century, but also in recent decades, especially in Germany, where the *Mittelstand* has been seen as forming the backbone of the country's economic strength.

[32] J. Kay, *Foundations of Corporate Success* (Oxford, 1993), 66–86.

[33] Quoted in W. Mosse, *Jews in the German Economy: The German-Jewish Economic Elite 1820–1935* (Oxford, 1987), 7.

[34] The classical work is Rudolf Hilferding's *Das Finanzkapital* (Vienna, 1910).

Disconto-Gesellschaft 67 seats in 47 companies. As is well known, however, the method is rather problematic. The significance of a directorship, whether in terms of actual participation in the decision-making process or simply of control, can be overestimated, and other forms of intervention underestimated.

More sophisticated approaches have been developed, especially by sociologists, in the last two decades.[35] The possibility of handling huge databases, including virtually the entire corporate leadership, has reactivated the analysis of interlocking directorships as a way of tracing networks of relationships, and more generally of studying the internal structure of the business world. Although the value of these approaches should not be dismissed,[36] they run the risk either of demonstrating the obvious, or of reproducing similar clichés to those prevailing in other approaches to business history, for example the 'centrality' of the German big banks, or the 'atomistic structure' of British business. A few lessons can none the less be learnt from an analysis of the directorships held by the chairmen and managing directors of Europe's major companies. Of particular interest is whether Britain, France, and Germany have displayed significant differences in the extent of their business élites' economic power; and the effect that this might have had on the decision-making process of their leading companies.

Should business leaders be defined as much by their outside directorships as by their position at the top of one company? The number of seats held by some of the most prominent members of the business community, especially in Imperial and Weimar Germany, was indeed impressive. In 1908 Carl Fürstenberg, managing director of the Berliner Handelsgesellschaft, one of the big Berlin banks, sat on the supervisory board of 44 companies; Louis Hagen, a partner in the Cologne private banking house Sal. Oppenheim & Cie, was not far behind with 42 seats. In the late 1920s Jakob Goldschmidt, one of the managing directors of the Danat Bank, held more than 100 directorships! In Britain and France, the maximum then was a more modest 30–40 seats.

Number, however, should not be equated with power or even influence. It is doubtful if any businessman can have a serious impact on the policies of more than half a dozen companies. More importantly, all directorships do not have the same significance. There is a great deal of difference

---

[35] See for example F. N. Stokman, R. Ziegler, and J. Scott (eds.), *Networks of Corporate Power: An Analysis of Ten Countries* (Cambridge, 1985); M. S. Mizruchi and M. Schwartz (eds.), *Intercorporate Relations: The Structural Analysis of Business* (Cambridge, 1987); J. Scott, *Social Network Analysis: A Handbook* (London, 1991).

[36] There have recently been a few serious attempts to apply the social network analysis to the study of business history. See in particular J. Ottosson, 'Stability and Change in Personal Networks: Interlocking Directorates in Banks and Industry 1903–1939', unpub. Ph.D. thesis (University of Uppsala, 1993) (with a summary in English); and Peter Eigner's forthcoming doctoral thesis on interlocking directorships in inter-war Austria.

between the directorship of a *large* company and that, even it is the chair-manship, of a second-rank firm or of a subsidiary company. The election to the board of a major company is an undeniable mark of prestige and weight within the business community, and is much sought after by the most prominent business leaders. Such mandates offer wide opportunities for useful contacts and access to information as well as direct interven-tion in various fields of business activity. Holding the chairmanship of more than one major company has been a rare, and indeed a highly prized, occurrence.

It is therefore to the directorships, and chairmanships, of large compa-nies that we must turn our attention. It must be stated at the outset that only a minority of Europe's business leaders had a seat on the board of more than one other large company (Table 7.2). With the exception of Germany in the late 1920s and early 1970s, this never applied to more than a third. In fact it was fairly common not to hold any major outside direc-torship at all, especially before 1914 and after the 1960s. Before 1914 this was the case with such major businessmen as Archibald Coats, chairman of the giant textile company, Edward Cecil Guinness, later Lord Iveagh, chairman of the famous brewery, and Thomas Edward Vickers, chairman of the shipbuilding and armament concern; elsewhere, Charles Schneider, head of the iron, steel, and armaments manufacturer, and Emile Béthenod, chairman of the Crédit Lyonnais, were in the same position, as were Alfred Berliner, managing director of Siemens, Carl Duisberg of Bayer, and Paul Reusch of the Gutehoffnungshütte.

The list is no less impressive in the following decades, with in the 1920s bankers such as Evelyn Beckett, chairman of the Westminster, and Beau-mont Pease, chairman of Lloyds, or industrialists such as Alphonse Gérard, chairman of Saint-Gobain, Gustav Krupp, and Ernst Poensgen, member of the executive board of the Vereinigte Stahlwerke; as well as the pioneers of the motor industry Herbert Austin, William Morris, André Citroën, Louis Renault, and Fritz von Opel. More recently, in the early 1970s, Antony Tuke, chairman of Barclays Bank, Ernest Woodroofe, chairman of Unilever, Jacques de Fouchier, chairman of the Banque de Paris et des Pays-Bas, Pierre Jouven, chairman of Pechiney-Ugine-Kuhlmann, and Kurt Lotz, member of the *Vorstand* of Volkswagen, did not sit on the board of any other *major* company; no more than did, in 1989, Lord Hanson, chairman of Hanson Trust, Peter Holmes, chairman of Shell, Alain Gomez, chairman of Thomson, or Wolfgang Hilger, member of the *Vorstand* of Hoechst. There is no need to add to the list to be convinced that, throughout the twentieth century, leading businessmen have primarily been the leaders of one large company. At the other extreme, the magnates—those who sat on the board of five major companies or more—were a small minority; again with the exception of Germany in the 1920s and 1970s, they were no more than 10

Table 7.2. Business leaders with a seat on the board of another major company (%)

	1907			1929			1953			1972			1990		
	GB	F	D	GB	F	D	GB	F	D	GB	F	D	GB	F	D
None	75	61	60	54	48	34	46	44	55	65	45	22	56	61	47
One seat	7	11	17	16	18	12	30	36	24	15	22	8	14	16	21
Two seats	12	13	9	11	9	16	12	7	10	11	13	24	14	11	10
Three seats	5	11	4	6	11	6	9	9	5	3	14	5	10	7	8
Four seats	0	2	2	5	7	8	3	4	3	3	2	16	2	2	6
Five seats or more	1	2	8	8	7	24	0	0	3	3	4	25	4	3	8
Total	100	100	100	100	100	100	100	100	100	100	100	100	100	100	100
No. of cases	86	46	53	104	56	74	87	77	71	63	55	51	50	57	51

Sources: Author's estimates based on a sample of business leaders.

per cent, and most often less then 5 per cent, especially in Britain and France (Table 7.2).

Business leaders with a seat on the board of another company can be grouped in three broad categories: the *notables*, the bankers, and the professionals. All types of directors were to be found in the three countries, especially the professionals; *notables*, however, were more common in Britain and France, while bankers as company directors were primarily a German species.

Notables owed their seat on the board of a large company to their prestige in the world of business or politics. Unless they were among the company's large shareholders or major customers, such directors were recruited for their wide network of relationships, their sound business judgement, their business experience, which could all be of some benefit to the company; or simply for the added prestige which could be brought through the close association with a renowned personality. In any case, they were not expected to take much part in the company's actual management, or even in the elaboration of its strategy. Such directors were mostly present in the British and French railway companies before 1914, in the large banks and insurance companies, as well as in public utility companies. William Houldsworth, chairman of the Fine Cotton Spinners from 1898 to 1908, was also director of the London and North Eastern Railway Company, the National Bank of Scotland, and the Manchester Ship Canal Company; William Henry Wills, later Lord Winterstoke and first chairman of Imperial Tobacco from 1901 to 1911, was also a director of the Great Western Railway Company and of Phoenix Assurance. In France, Ernest Dejardin, chairman of the Mines d'Aniche, was also a director of the railway company Paris-Lyon-Méditerranée, of the Société Générale, and of the Compagnie Générale Transatlantique, as well as of two industrial companies, the iron and steel concern Denain-Anzin and the sugar refinery Say.

Unlike the *notable*, who was an independent director, the 'professional' represented his firm's interests on the board of another company. This meant that particular links existed between the two companies, whether through cross-shareholding or through a significant stake—including full ownership—held by one company in the other. Business groups, holding companies, parent and subsidiary companies, and joint ventures were some of the most common forms taken by these links. The 'professional' director was more involved than the *notable* in the management of the company: if not in its day-to-day running, at least in designing its strategy and monitoring its execution, especially if he was a representative of a parent company.

In their vast majority, subsidiaries were small or medium-sized companies. Membership of their boards was not a particular mark of prestige within the business community, nor did it significantly widen the holders' network of relationships. It was rather an extension of the responsibilities of running the parent company. Consequently, the *total* number of directorships or chairmanships in subsidiary companies held by a member of the main board are of no particular interest in a study of business leadership. Take Henry Railing, managing director of the General Electric Company. In 1929 he held twenty-four directorships, one of the highest numbers among British top businessmen, yet they all consisted of GEC subsidiaries, mostly abroad: GEC India, GEC China, GEC France, Anglo-Argentine General Electric Company, and so on.

Some subsidiaries, however, could be large companies and enjoy a certain degree of autonomy, particularly when they were jointly controlled by several companies, or were self-contained units within a holding company. The role of the 'professional' director would vary according to the size and status of the companies on which he served. Francis D'Arcy Cooper, for example, the chairman of Unilever, was in 1929 chairman of three other large companies (apart from the sister company in the Netherlands Unilever NV): Candles, a lubricant manufacturer; the Niger Company, an African trading firm; and McFisheries, a chain of retail food shops. They were all large companies linked to Unilever: Candles's capital stood at £8,510,000, the Niger Company's at £4,750,000, McFisheries' at £2,500,000. Candles was jointly owned with the Shell Oil Group, while the Niger Company enjoyed a large degree of autonomy from Unilever's central management.[37]

Business groups were a more common feature in France. Rather than fully owning large subsidiaries at home or abroad, companies were linked to one another through a subtly hierarchical network of cross-shareholdings. Business groups were not only composed of a constellation of small and medium-sized companies revolving around one large firm. The structure was usually more complex, as several large firms often joined forces to establish one or several joint subsidiaries in order to increase their borrowing capacity.[38] This was for example the case in the electrical industry in the 1920s.[39] Multiple directorships played a major role in these arrangements. The so-called 'groupe de la rue de Messine', led by Albert Petsche and Ernest Mercier, is one among many instances:[40] Albert Petsche, the chairman of the Union d'Électricité, was also a director of the major companies belonging to the group, in particular the Com-

[37] C. Wilson, *The History of Unilever: A Study in Economic Growth and Social Change*, 2 vols. (London, 1954), i. 274; D. K. Fieldhouse, *Unilever Overseas: The Anatomy of a Multinational 1895–1965* (London, 1978), 61.

[38] See Lévy-Leboyer, 'Large Corporation in Modern France', 142–6.

[39] See H. Morsel, 'Les Groupes dans les industries électriques en France avant la nationalisation', *Cahiers d'histoire*, 26/4 (1981), 365–76.

[40] See R. F. Kuisel, *Ernest Mercier: French Technocrat* (Berkeley and Los Angeles, 1967).

pagnie Parisienne de Distribution d'Électricité, the Énergie Électrique du Littoral Méditerranéen, the Lyonnaise des Eaux, as well as the Société Alsacienne de Constructions Mécaniques.

It must be stressed that the difference between the *notable* and the 'professional' derived from the *type of company* in which a directorship was held, rather than from the *type of businessman* to which the holder might correspond. A self-made full-time managing director of an electrical engineering company, who could be seen as typifying the modern professional businessman, would be but a *notable* on the board of a large commercial bank. In other words, the same leading businessman could be, and often was, a *notable* on the boards of some companies, and a 'professional' on others. This was the case, among many others, of Lord Pirrie, chairman of the shipbuilding company Harland & Wolff, where he made his entire career and of which he was the undisputed head from 1895 until his death in 1924; he was also chairman of the African Steamship Company, a platform from which he built his huge shipping interests. Pirrie in 1907 was chairman or director of more than thirty companies. In most of them, which were shipping companies belonging to the Royal Mail Group, he was a 'professional'. In others, such as the Midland Bank, the South Western Railway, or the Eastern Telegraph Company, he was a *notable*. But he was a business *notable*. This notion should not be limited to the nineteenth-century world of private banking and industrial dynasties. A better definition would be the most prominent members of the business community, whose prestige, activities, and responsibilities extended beyond the running of their own firm. In the course of the twentieth century this role came to be assumed by the professional leaders of the largest companies.

It is significant in this respect that, since the Second World War, the *notable* has not been superseded, as an outside company director, by the 'professional'. Both have continued to coexist, the former in the large independent companies, the latter in subsidiary companies, or in those affiliated in some degree to a parent company. It is as a *notable* that the chairman of a top industrial company sits on the board of another major industrial company, or on the board of a large bank or insurance company. In 1973 Arnold Hall, the chairman of Hawker Siddeley, was also a director of ICI, Lloyds Bank, and Phoenix Assurance; while Wilfrid Baumgartner, the chairman of Rhône-Poulenc, was also a director of Peugeot, Pechiney-Ugine-Kuhlmann, the Compagnie Française des Pétroles, and the Denain-Nord-Est-Longwy group, as well as on the supervisory board of the Deutsche Bank. In 1989 Peter Walters, the chairman of BP, was deputy chairman of Thorn-EMI and the National Westminster Bank and a director of Smithkline Beecham; while Jean Gandois, chairman of Pechiney, was also a director of BSN, Peugeot, the Lyonnaise des Eaux, Vallourec, and Paribas.

The proportion of leading businessmen with a seat on the board of one or several other major companies has remained fairly constant in the course of the twentieth century. What has changed in the last thirty years is the size of the largest companies, and the concentration on their boards of several members of the business leadership, a group appropriately labelled the 'inner circle' by Michael Useem.[41] The widespread influence of these new *notables*, in the worlds of both business and politics, and their capacity to act as leaders of the business community as a whole, are of course far more important than whatever managerial duties they may contribute.

The pattern of multiple directorships was broadly similar between Britain and France. This was primarily due to the fact that in both countries the responsibility for running the company was entrusted to a single board. Differences might have been expected to arise as a result of the slower development of big business in France before 1945. Business leadership, however, displayed a number of common features, especially the existence in London and Paris of a financial aristocracy traditionally represented on the boards of the large banks, insurance companies, railway companies, and others such as utilities or colonial companies.

There were, apparently, more differences from Germany. First, leading businessmen there tended to hold a higher number of outside directorships of large companies than their British and French counterparts. This was especially the case in the 1920s, when 24 per cent sat on the boards of five or more other *large* companies: the record, seventeen seats, was jointly held by Jakob Goldschmidt and Carl Fürstenberg, the latter at the age of 78. And secondly, the big holders of multiple directorships were mainly bankers.

The first difference derives partly from the two-tier system prevailing in Germany. Virtually all outside directorships consisted of seats on *supervisory* boards, which ususally met on a quarterly basis and did not require any involvement in the management of the firm. The duties were thus less than on a British or even a French board and the plurality easier. This undoubtedly reduces the significance of multiple directorships in German big business. In addition, the phenomenon was by far at its strongest in the 1920s. This was the decade when 'organized capitalism' was intensified by the effects of war and inflation. Rationalization, mergers, ententes, cartels, 'communities of interests' all reached new heights, reflected in the number of overlapping directorships between major companies. The 'Americanization' of German industry after 1945 led to a dismantling of these structures, which is visible in the sharp decrease of the number of pluralities in the early 1950s, though they were to increase again in the 1970s.

[41] M. Useem, *The Inner Circle: Large Corporations and the Rise of Business Political Activity in the U.S. and the U.K.* (New York, 1984).

As in Britain and France, 'professional' directors represented their firm on the board of another company and were mostly, though not exclusively, members of their company's executive board. A seat on a German supervisory board offered fewer possibilities of intervention than a seat on a British or French board of directors. The chairman, however, who was the only really influential member of the supervisory board, was often a representative of outside interests, even in autonomous and independent companies, and most of them were bankers. Should bankers on the supervisory board of a German company be considered as *notables* or as 'professionals'? The answer is usually assumed to be straightforward: they undoubtedly were 'professionals', and clearly represented their bank's long-term involvement in the company concerned. There were, undoubtedly, a number of such obvious cases, including Max Steinthal of the Deutsche Bank who took an active part in the reorganization of Mannesmann in the 1890s and chaired its supervisory board from 1896 to 1932. Most cases, however, were much less clear. Rather than a question of status, which fell between that of a *notable* and that of a professional, the presence of bankers on the supervisory boards of industrial companies raises the more fundamental—and more complex—question of the relationships between banks, finance, and industry.

BANKS AND INDUSTRY

Large banks have formed an integral part of the world of big business ever since their emergence in the mid-nineteenth century. As leaders of large companies, top bankers have continually had to make strategic decisions on which depended the success of their enterprise. And yet banks and bankers have often been perceived as different, partly because they deal with an abstract commodity, partly because of the central role played by banks in the economy. Through their innumerable customers from all economic sectors, they acquire a particularly close knowledge of the entire industrial and commercial spectrum. Rightly or wrongly, banks are considered as carrying a special responsibility for economic growth, a responsibility they are expected to meet by providing adequate support to industry. The role played by the banks in the 'real economy' has been one of the most heated issues relating to big business. And also one of the most politicized. Take for example the idea of the 'superiority' of the German banking system, of its alleged greater ability to foster industrial investment. It is firmly ingrained in British opinion, especially the media, and even permeates the historical profession. And yet in the last decade or so, specialists have come to the conclusion that differences between the two countries have been far less significant than is conventionally assumed. Of course, as in all domains of historical knowledge, divergences remain, though they are probably smaller in this field than in many others.

Two major questions are at the centre of the debate: the extent to which banks and financial markets have provided adequate funds to industry; and the extent to which banks have 'controlled' or even 'dominated' industry. The more recent contrasts between 'bank-based' and 'market-based' systems are but variations on the same themes. Significantly, the two questions have not aroused the same amount of interest and controversy in the three countries. Britain and France have been mainly, though not entirely, concerned by the first, Germany by the second. These differences derive from a different *conception* of what banks should do; and from a different *perception* of the way banks have performed their duties, by contemporaries and historians alike.

The conception of the role of the banks has been different in Britain, France, and Germany ever since the birth of modern banking. In Britain, banking has basically meant deposit banking. The golden rule of bankers has been not to tie up in long-term investments the money deposited with them on a short-term basis. Assets must thus be as liquid as possible. Before 1914, for example, self-liquidating bills of exchange bought in the open market were especially popular; investments were in Consols or other highly liquid securities, not in industrial securities; advances were granted on a short-term basis, whether in the form of loans (granted for a fixed sum and for a given period) or of overdrafts (which customers could use as they required up to a limit agreed beforehand with the bank).[42] Moreover, according to the British banking orthodoxy which developed in the second half of the nineteenth century, the bank should not provide industrial firms with working capital, but only give them temporary accommodation to tide them over short periods, when they are short of money and payments fall due.[43] For their long-term requirements, industrialists could raise money on the capital markets, traditionally more developed than in continental Europe. However, because of the specialization of the English banking system, clearing banks did not issue securities on behalf of industrial customers; this task was undertaken by independent financiers, such as company promoters, and increasingly since the 1920s by the merchant banks.

The role of the banks has been seen in a different light in Germany, where from the start the emphasis has been on *credit* rather than on

---

[42] See C. A. E. Goodhart, *The Business of Banking 1891–1914* (London, 1972).

[43] See for example the evidence given by Felix Schuster, governor of the Union Bank of London, and one of the guardians of British banking orthodoxy, to the National Monetary Commission, *Interviews on the Banking and Currency Systems of England, France, Germany, Switzerland and Italy* (Washington, NMC, 61st Congress, 2nd Session, Senate Doc. No 405, 1910), 78.

deposits.[44] Industrial finance was thus considered as perfectly natural. Whereas British banks specialized in a number of well-defined functions, German universal banks undertook all types of operations: they collected deposits, granted short-term commercial credit as well as medium and long-term industrial credit, discounted bills of exchange, and acted as brokers and as issuing houses. The current account was considered as the cornerstone of the long-term relationship between a banker and his customer, with renewable credits usable for investment purposes. The issue of securities on behalf of customers was seen as strengthening links between bankers and clients, especially as banks held shares in the company on a temporary or even on a permanent basis. The bank was thus assumed to be interested in that company's long-term success, and was represented on its supervisory board.[45]

The French banking system is usually seen as standing roughly halfway between the British and German models. It was probably closer to the former, though there undoubtedly existed specific French characteristics. In fact, the German universal banks which emerged in the 1850s were partly modelled on the Crédit Mobilier, a French bank founded in 1852 by the brothers Émile and Isaac Péreire. The Darmstädter Bank, in particular, was founded in 1853 under the auspices of the Crédit Mobilier. Influenced by Saint-Simonian ideas, its objective was to mobilize savings for industrial development, but it failed in 1867, having tied itself up in too many ventures.[46] In the first phase of their existence, in the 1860s and 1870s, the big French deposit banks (Crédit Lyonnais, Société Générale, Comptoir d'Escompte) were firmly engaged in industrial finance, but they got their fingers burnt and pulled out in the 1880s.[47] During the next eighty years, they closely followed the principles of the English joint-stock banks. This came to be known as the 'doctrine Henri Germain', from the name of the founder of the Crédit Lyonnais and its chairman until 1905, who laid down the unwritten rule of maintaining liquid assets. More risky industrial financing was left to another type of bank, the *banques d'affaires* (investment banks), the objective of which was not only to make long-term investments, but to control the industrial, financial, and other companies in which they held a significant stake. The most famous of them has been, ever since its foundation in 1871, the Banque de Paris et des Pays-Bas. However, the separation between deposit banks and investment banks has never been clear-cut. It was enacted by the Banking Law of

[44] See D. Ziegler, 'The Origins of the "Macmillan Gap": Comparing Britain and Germany in the Early Twentieth Century', paper presented at the Conference on 'Banks and Customers: Institutional Theory and Banking Practices', Business History Unit, London School of Economics, Sept. 1991.

[45] See J. Riesser, *The German Great Banks and their Concentration* (Washington, 1911).

[46] See J. Autin, *Les Frères Péreire: Le Bonheur d'entreprendre* (Paris, 1984).

[47] See J. Bouvier, *Le Crédit Lyonnais de 1863 à 1882: Les Années de formation d'une banque de dépôts*, 2 vols. (Paris, 1961).

1945, but the banking system was to a large extent despecialized by a decree of the Ministry of Finance of 1966, opening up the way for French universal banking, with sometimes unhappy results.

Given these national characteristics, it is not surprising that the debate on the relationships between banks and industry has taken a different turn in each of the three countries. In Germany, the question of the 'power of the banks' has been foremost. Rudolf Hilferding's thesis, famously set out in *Das Finanzkapital* (1910), has given rise to much controversy. In Hilferding's view, banks played a central role in the evolution of capitalism in the late nineteenth and early twentieth centuries. Relying mostly on the experiences of universal banking in Germany and Austria, Hilferding reached the conclusion that banking capital and industrial capital had merged by the turn of the century, to form what he termed 'finance capital', in which banks clearly held the upper hand. In the process the banks were able, according to Hilferding, to exert their control over the entire economy. In the last decades, a similar analysis has underlain the left's criticism of the excessive power wielded by the big three banks (Deutsche Bank, Dresdner Bank, Commerzbank), while the neoliberal right has been alarmed by the distorting effects of banking concentration on the working of a market economy.[48]

The criticisms faced by the British banks have been just the opposite.[49] Far from dominating industry, they have been accused of keeping it at arm's length. This is part of an old historiographical tradition holding that the financial sector has contributed to Britain's economic decline.[50] Commercial banks have been criticized for their reluctance to provide long-term finance and to assume industrial leadership, for example in the rationalization of the old industries in the inter-war years. Merchant banks have been criticized for their lack of interest in domestic industry, especially before 1914. The capital markets have been equally blamed for their excessive segmentation and imperfect information, resulting in a bias towards foreign investment to the detriment of domestic industrial securities.[51] For all these critics, the German model has served as an implicit or explicit reference. Financial power has also been denounced in

[48] See H. Wixforth and D. Ziegler, '*Bankenmacht*: Universal Banking and German Industry in Historical Perspective', in Y. Cassis, G. D. Feldman, and U. Olsson (eds.), *The Evolution of Financial Institutions and Markets in Twentieth Century Europe* (Aldershot, 1995).

[49] For a survey of the debate, see Y. Cassis, 'British Finance: Success and Controversy', in J. J. Van Helten and Y. Cassis (eds.), *Capitalism in a Mature Economy: Financial Institutions, Capital Exports and British Industry, 1870–1939* (Aldershot, 1990); M. Collins, *Banks and Industrial Finance in Britain 1800–1939* (Basingstoke, 1991).

[50] See for example P. Anderson, 'The Figures of Descent', *New Left Review*, 161 (1987); G. Ingham, *Capitalism Divided? The City and Industry in British Social Development* (London, 1984); S. Newton and D. Porter, *Modernization Frustrated: The Politics of Industrial Decline in Britain since 1900* (London, 1988).

[51] Cf. W. P. Kennedy, *Industrial Structure, Capital Markets and the Origins of British Industrial Decline* (Cambridge, 1987).

Britain, from Hobson to Hutton, but in terms differing from Germany: the concern has mainly centred around the City's pervasive influence at the economic, social, and political levels, and its ability to promote its interests, if necessary to the detriment of manufacturing industry.

French banks have for a long time been subjected to the same criticisms as their British counterparts: a lack of interest in domestic industry and a strong preference for foreign investments, which Lysis was already denouncing early in the century in his pamphlet *Contre l'oligarchie financière*. Controversies surrounding the banks have continued throughout the century, though with much less intensity than in Britain—a mutedness reflecting partly the sustained growth of the French economy during the thirty years following the Second World War, and partly the fact that French commercial banks have tended, especially in the last thirty years, to act also as universal banks. Instead, with the nationalization of the deposit banks in 1946, the debate has shifted towards the increased grip of the state on the French banking system, which had started during the depression of the 1930s with the growth of the savings banks and other state institutions.[52] The question of the 'power of the banks' has also been debated in France, though in a context reminiscent of Germany rather than Britain. The *banques d'affaires*, Paribas and Indosuez, have been in the front line, being seen as in a position to influence the policies of major industrial groups through their complex network of cross-shareholdings.[53]

Historical evidence reveals a picture often at odds with these heated polemics. In the first place, in any discussion of banks and industrial finance, a distinction must be made between the large corporations on the one hand, and small and medium-sized firms on the other. The preference of the large banks for large industrial customers was made clear in a number of official inquiries: in France with the 'Commission Chargée d'Étudier l'Organisation du Crédit Bancaire en France', which led to the 1917 Act and opened the way for the creation of popular banks; in Germany with the Enquête-Ausschuss of the late 1920s; and in Britain with the Macmillan Committee of the early 1930s. Financial support for small and medium-sized companies was mostly provided at the local level, and significant differences existed in this respect between the banking systems of the three countries. By the turn of the century, the few regional banks of any significance left in England—Scotland was a separate case—were in Lancashire, the centre of the cotton industry, whereas powerful regional banks were still active in the industrial areas of France

---

[52] See A. Gueslin and M. Lescure, 'Les Banques publiques, parapubliques et coopératives françaises (vers 1920–vers 1960)', in M. Lévy-Leboyer (ed.), *Les Banques en Europe de l'Ouest de 1920 à nos jours* (Paris, 1995).
[53] See for example F. Morin, *La Structure financière du capitalisme français* (Paris, 1974); P. Allard *et al.*, *Dictionnaire des groupes industriels et financiers en France* (Paris, 1978).

and Germany, such as the Crédit du Nord in the north of France, the Société Nancéenne de Crédit in Lorraine, and the Schaafhausenscher Bankverein in the Ruhr. There remained only 41 deposit banks in England and Wales in 1913. The number of *private* banks in Germany in 1902 may have been as high as 2,500, or 1,400 according to more conservative estimates; there were still 60 regional banks and 1,100 private banks by 1929, though the latter's number decreased considerably during the Nazi period, falling to 492 in 1942. The figures are less reliable for France, but local banks remained solidly entrenched in France until 1914.[54] Their gradual elimination after the war benefited the regional banks rather than the large Parisian deposit banks, but they were mostly supplanted by public and parapublic institutions which borrowed their banking practices to a large extent. Historical research into local and regional banks, including savings banks, is only in its infancy, and a much clearer picture should emerge in the next decade or so. As for the large banks and industrial companies, with which we are primarily concerned here, differences between the three countries were far less significant.

The other key point concerns the decisive role played by self-finance. In each country since the beginning of industrialization, it has been by far the major source of industrial finance. In Germany between 1896 and 1911 it contributed to more than 50 per cent for 86 per cent of all firms, and to more than 75 per cent for a fifth of them—this in the country and the period when the banks' contribution is considered by many as decisive. In inter-war Britain, gross business savings were sufficient to support investment activity.[55] In France in the mid-1950s, ploughed-back profits were responsible for more than 50 per cent of financial requirements in all industrial sectors, and for more than 75 per cent in the extractive industries, textiles, food, wood, and paper.[56] The contribution of the banks must thus be put in perspective.

In France, banks on the whole have been absolved from the sin of 'failing' industry. Industrial disengagement from the 1880s did not mean disaffection. Banks remained interested in industrial firms, their most important customers. They granted them ample and cheap commercial credit, mostly in the form of bills of exchange. For long-term finance, French banks were much more active than their English counterparts in the role of intermediary between industrial customer and capital market. Between 1911 and 1914, for example, the Crédit Lyonnais floated thirty-two issues on behalf of industrial clients.[57] The *banques d'affaires*, for their

[54] See L. Bergeron, *Les Capitalistes en France, 1780–1914* (Paris, 1978), 105–14.

[55] W. A. Thomas, *The Finance of British Industry 1918–1976* (London, 1978), 13.

[56] A. Straus, 'Structures financières et performances des entreprises industrielles en France dans la seconde moitié du XXe siècle', *Entreprises et histoire*, 2 (1992), 23.

[57] See A. Plessis, 'Les Banques, le crédit et l'économie', in M. Lévy-Leboyer and J.-C. Casanova (eds.), *Entre l'État et le marché: L'Économie française des années 1880 à nos jours* (Paris, 1991).

part, played a more active role in industrial finance. The Banque de Paris et des Pays-Bas was actively involved in the steel industry (Forges et Aciéries du Nord et de l'Est) and in the electrical and electrical engineering industries in the late nineteenth and early twentieth centuries; however, its attempts at reorganizing the French electricity industry in the 1920s were too ambitious, leading to partial withdrawal, and concentration on its banking and financial activities.[58] Nor should one forget the regional banks, which played a crucial role in the financing of small and medium-sized companies.[59]

French banks, admittedly, were seriously weakened in the inter-war years, and much of their funds was diverted from private to public use. Nevertheless, in the few years between the stabilization of the franc in 1928 and the deepening of the depression in 1933, they drew nearer to their industrial customers through their advances and their operations on the capital markets as well as through a number of innovations, in particular the creation of subsidiary companies specializing in medium-term credit. One such was the Société Anonyme de Crédit à l'Industrie Française, jointly set up in 1928 by the Société Générale, the Crédit Commercial de France, and the Banque Nationale de Crédit. Banks, however, remained inactive on the stock market and used a significant part of their liquid assets on foreign financial markets.[60] Finally, banks' credit to industry ceased to be an issue during the thirty years which followed the Second World War, for far from being insufficient, the use of bank credit as a source of industrial financing has, on the contrary, been considered as excessive.[61]

The belief that banks did not fulfil their duties towards industry is more deeply rooted in Britain, though British finance has always attracted a large circle of admirers. During the first half of the nineteenth century, local bankers were linked at both a personal and a business level to industrialists, with permanent overdrafts and rolled-over short-term loans being equivalent to a long-term commitment in industrial finance.[62] The amalgamation movement which gathered pace in the 1880s and 1890s undoubtedly affected banking industrial policy, as general managers in London, in their endeavour to harmonize practices within their bank, put an end to what they considered to be over-commitments. However, commercial banks rarely refused industrial clients' explicit requests for new

[58] See E. Bussière, *Paribas: Europe and the World, 1872–1992* (Antwerp, 1992), 70–91, and 'Paribas and the Rationalization of the French Electricity Industry, 1900–1930', in Y. Cassis, F. Crouzet, and T. Gourvish (eds.), *Management and Business in Britain and France* (Oxford, 1995), 204–13.

[59] See M. Lescure, 'Banks and Small Enterprises in France', in Cassis, Feldman, and Olsson (eds.), *Evolution of Financial Institutions and Markets*, 315–27.

[60] See Plessis, 'Les Banques, le crédit et l'économie'.

[61] Straus, 'Structures financières et performances des entreprises', 20.

[62] See P. L. Cottrell, *Industrial Finance, 1830–1914: The Finance and Organization of English Manufacturing Industry* (London, 1980), 200–36.

loans.[63] The heart of the matter is that, up to 1914, there appears to have been little such demand from industry, especially from the staple industries, which were able to rely on the capital markets.

The situation changed during the inter-war years. During the 1919–20 boom, the clearing banks abandoned much of their past conservatism and prudence and granted large overdrafts, particularly to the heavy industries, which with the downturn of the 1920s often had to be converted into frozen loans and nursed for the remainder of the period. This new long-term involvement in industrial finance was, however, in essence forced upon the banks by the prevailing circumstances rather than deliberately chosen as a new policy. Nevertheless, commercial banks adopted on the whole a positive attitude towards industry, which was dictated not only by security motives and short-term expediency.[64] In fact, British banks established long-term relationships with their customers, and undoubtedly possessed detailed and intimate knowledge of their affairs; overdrafts, in particular, were a form of lending which provided banks with essential information, especially as they were renewed in relationships which often lasted for decades.[65]

Large industrial companies were also able to make effective use of the flexibility of the capital markets. There was, for example, no scarcity of capital in two of the most important pre-1914 industries: brewing and iron and steel. However, each industry adopted a capital structure appropriate to its specific conditions: the buoyant brewing industry was highly geared, the public houses purchased in the 'scramble for property' providing adequate security for the issue of debentures; while the more cyclical iron and steel industry was not prepared to accept the risks associated with high capital gearing.[66] The functioning of the markets is unlikely to have been affected by unscrupulous company promoters who probably remained peripheral to the issuing business before 1914. Merchant banks, as well as stockbrokers, entered the domestic issuing business after the First World War, partly to compensate for the declining opportunities for foreign issues, but also because of the vastly increased capital requirements of domestic industrial companies.[67] The role of the Stock Exchange

[63] See F. Capie and M. Collins, 'Industrial Lending by English Commercial Banks, 1860s–1914: Why Did Banks Refuse Loans?', *Business History*, 38/1 (1996).

[64] See D. Ross, 'The Clearing Banks and Industry: New Perspectives on the Inter-war Years', in Van Helten and Cassis (eds.), *Capitalism in a Mature Economy*, 52–70.

[65] D. Ross, 'Information, Collateral and British Bank Lending in the 1930s', in Cassis, Feldman, and Olsson (eds.), *Evolution of Financial Institutions and Markets*, 273–94. The high proportion of industrial overdrafts which were unsecured also testifies to the banks' close knowledge of their customers; see Capie and Collins, 'Industrial Lending by English Commercial Banks', 34–5.

[66] K. Watson, 'The New Issue Market as a Source of Finance for the UK Brewing and Iron, and Steel Industries, 1870–1913', in Cassis, Feldman, and Olsson (eds.), *Evolution of Financial Institutions and Markets*, 209–48.

[67] See S. Diaper, 'Merchant Banking in the Inter-war Period: The Case of Kleinwort, Sons, & Co.', *Business History*, 28 (1986); K. Burk, *Morgan Grenfell, 1838–1988: The Biography of a Merchant Bank* (Oxford, 1989); D. Kynaston, *Cazenove & Co: A History* (London, 1991).

in industrial finance also grew considerably during that period, acting as a useful intermediary between lenders as borrowers: banks could not lend long-term, but they could lend short-term against industrial securities representing long-term debt, thus avoiding the risks of direct investment in industry incurred by their German counterparts.[68]

There remains the question of banking leadership, of the entrepreneurial role which banks might have played, for example by underwriting the initial risks, or those incurred by a later expansion; of their regulatory role, for example in implementing the restructuring of an industry through mergers, or in forcing the replacement of an inadequate management. German universal banks are often believed to have been best equipped for this task, by virtue of their close relationship with their customers, cemented by a presence on the supervisory boards of industrial companies. But were they really in a position to influence the policy of the large industrial enterprises? Not according to one of the leaders of the Ruhr heavy industry, Emil Kirdorf, who declared in 1905 that 'the influence of large banks on the industry of the Rhineland and Westphalia has never been so limited as it is now' and that 'the large banks seek the favours of industry, not the reverse'.[69] Many recent studies have provided corroboration. In particular Hilferding's thesis of the domination of industry by the banks has been subjected to close scrutiny and shown to be far removed from the actual relationship between the big banks and their large industrial customers.

Two major factors stood in the way of banking dominance over German industry.[70] The first was the high level of self-finance, which meant that large industrial companies did not rely on long-term banking credit to finance their expansion. Firms which required outside finance turned to the capital market for new issues of equity capital or debentures. The second factor was that large industrial companies dealt simultaneously with several banks in competition with each other, competition intensified in the inter-war years as the suppliers of capital widened to include foreign banks. The iron and steel concern Phoenix kept an account with forty-three banks, thirty-one of which were foreign. As a rule, the supervisory boards of the major industrial companies included representatives of several, if not all, of the great Berlin banks, plus a number of regional banks and private banks: the possibilities of a dominant influence by a single bank were thus greatly reduced. Relationships between bankers and customers varied according to the type of company (family firms, such as Krupp or Siemens, were less susceptible to outside influence) and

---

[68] R. Michie, 'The Stock Exchange and the British Economy, 1870–1939', in Van Helten and Cassis (eds.), *Capitalism in a Mature Economy*, 95–114.

[69] Quoted by Kocka, 'Entrepreneurs and Managers', 570.

[70] The arguments which follow are borrowed from V. Wellhöner, *Grossbanken und Grossindustrie im Kaiserreich* (Göttingen, 1989), and H. Wixforth, *Banken und Schwerindustrie in der Weimarer Republik* (Cologue, 1995).

to its performances (high profits further reduced the banks' influence). Nor should personality be underestimated: Hugo Stinnes was not the type of man to tolerate the banks' interference in his affairs, even though he had to rely on vast amounts of outside capital to finance the meteoric rise of his company, Deutsch-Luxemburg, in the decade preceding the First World War.

In the end, the only position from which a bank could influence the policy of a large industrial company was that of a major shareholder, as was the case of the Deutsche Bank with Mannesmann. But Mannesmann was the exception rather than the rule. In these circumstances, the German universal banks could hardly take on the leadership role with which they are sometimes credited. Significantly, bankers themselves did not see their role on a supervisory board as that of 'leaders of industry', but more prosaically as a way of ensuring interest payment on their investment, and more generally as a way of maintaining good business relationships with valued customers. They could also act as advisers, and mediators in cases of conflicts. Decisions were made by industrialists, including those with global strategic implications such as the restructuring of an entire industry. Bankers played only a marginal role in the great merger of the iron and steel industry leading to the foundation of the Vereinigte Stahlwerke in 1926; and even though they favoured such a consolidation, in no way did they initiate it.

All this is not to deny the positive role played by universal banks in German economic growth.[71] It is rather to underline three points. First, significant differences existed between the British, French, and German banking systems. Secondly, the effects of these differences on the relationships between banks and industry, at least as far as large companies were concerned, were less marked than is often assumed. And thirdly, there is no evidence to suggest that industrial success or failure in any of the three countries had much to do with the role played by the banks. It is probably too early to reach similar conclusions about the more recent decades, but one cannot help being struck by the permanence of the terms of the debate, whether it relates to the remoteness of the British banks from industry, the power of the German banks, the entrenched belief in the superiority of the 'bank-based' over the 'market-based' system, and the paucity of empirical evidence.[72]

Such an emphasis put on the role of banks in the German economy is surprising. Historically, finance has always held a stronger position in

[71] Richard Tilly's contributions are particularly important in this respect. For an overview, see R. Tilly, 'An Overview of the Role of the Large German Banks up to 1914', in Y. Cassis (ed.), *Finance and Financiers in European History, 1880–1960* (Cambridge, 1992), 93–112.

[72] A good discussion of the question, which refutes the commonly held view of the superiority of the German system, is J. Edwards and K. Fischer, *Banks, Finance and Investment in Germany* (Cambridge, 1994). On the power of the German banks, see J. Esser, 'Bank Power in Germany Revisited', *West European Politics*, 13/4 (1990).

Britain than in either France or Germany. The prestige and power of German banks derived from the support they were prepared to give to industry, which for most of the century has been the dominant partner.[73] The prestige of British banking was not subordinate to industry. It derived above all from the international position of the City of London, which itself depended on world trade rather than domestic industry. For all their involvement in industry, German bankers never enjoyed the same social prestige or political influence as the Ruhr industrialists. In Britain, by contrast, City bankers have from an early stage been integrated into the upper classes and moved in the same circles as the political élite. Whether these differences have directly affected the relationships between banks and industrial companies is difficult to assess. But they underline the importance of the socio-political dimension of big business.

[73] See G. Feldman, 'Banks and Banking in Germany after the First World War: Strategies of Defence', in Cassis (ed.), *Finance and Financiers in European History*, 257–9.

PART IV

BUSINESS, SOCIETY, AND POLITICS

The position of business élites at the top of the social hierarchy is ensured by the possession of three main assets: economic power, social prestige, and political influence. The combination of these three assets at their zenith was, for example, a characteristic feature of the financial aristocracy in Britain and France in the second half of the nineteenth century: Lords Rothschild and Revelstoke in the City of London, or Alphonse de Rothschild and Rodolphe Hottinguer in Paris, were certainly in this position, with their immense wealth, involvement in the biggest financial operations of the day, network of relationships in the highest society, and personal closeness to political power. Such a potent combination has become rarer in the course of the twentieth century, the strength of one asset tending to compensate for the weakness of another. A high social status, for example, associated with ancient lineage, has often made up for a declining economic position and vice versa.

Business history has become increasingly fragmented in the last two or three decades, developing along three quite separate lines of approach: economic (with questions of business strategy and business performance, etc.), social (businessmen's social origins and education, networks of relationships, etc.), and political (business interest groups, state intervention, etc.). Some studies have made use of more than one line of approach, and this is surely the way forward. However, integrating the three levels and taking account of the interaction between them is an essential, though extremely difficult, task. The last part of this book is a modest attempt in this direction.

So far we have been concerned with economic power: large and successful companies constitute its very source. The nature of this power, however, has been altered by increased separation between ownership and control—top businessmen might well have gained in global economic influence (through leading a giant oligopoly) what they have lost in absolute control over their firm (which ultimately can only be guaranteed by majority ownership). We now turn to the social prestige and political influence brought about by economic power. Some social aspects of big business have already been discussed, in particular social origins and education, whose relevance to the analysis of business performance is more readily perceived. In the next two chapters, closer attention will be paid to wealth, social integration into the upper classes, and forms of political intervention. These are parts of what has become known as 'business culture': the type of relationships existing between the business élite and other élite groups, whether at the social or political level, is revealing of the degree of social acceptance of business values, and this can be related to the broad theme of economic and business performance. More importantly, however, in all three countries wealth, status, and power have been a permanent motivation for business activity and a patent manifestation of business success—cultural differences in this respect can be too easily exaggerated. This is an essential dimension of big business whose power—real and mythical—has provoked fascination and outcry over the last hundred years.

8

Wealth, Status, and Power before 1914

The pre-1914 years were the formative years, the years of big business social and political apprenticeship, the period during which accumulated wealth was progressively translated into social status and political influence. The extent of this formative period cannot be precisely delimited. It varied not only between the three countries, but between the various groups making up each country's business élite, starting in the late eighteenth century for the oldest British banking dynasties, in the late nineteenth century for most German heavy industrialists. This chapter compares the socio-political position reached by the British, French, and German business leaderships at the beginning of the twentieth century. A specific configuration had already emerged in each country, though it was still to evolve in the course of the century.

BUSINESS FORTUNES

The major cause behind the rise of businessmen to the top of the social hierarchy has been the accumulation of wealth. Wealth might not be a sufficient condition for acceptability into the higher social circles, at least for the first generation, but it certainly is a necessary one. By the end of the nineteenth century, in all European countries, businessmen had become the richest socio-professional group. In Britain, landowners remained the wealthiest group until the 1870s. According to William Rubinstein, they accounted for 80 per cent of the millionaires deceased between 1858 and 1879. For the period 1900–19 their percentage fell to 27 per cent.[1] By 1912 the situation was not very different in Germany, where 25 per cent of the millionaires were landowners and 68 per cent businessmen.[2] Three are no equivalent statistics available for France. However, it is worth noting that in 1911 the average estate of a Paris businessman was 1,450,773 francs (£58,031), as against 334,650 francs (£13,386) for landowners and *rentiers*.[3]

British, French, and German businessmen thus held a similar position in the wealth hierarchies of their respective countries. But how did they compare with one another? Had top German industrialists become the

---

[1] W. D. Rubinstein, *Men of Property: The Very Wealthy in Britain since the Industrial Revolution* (London, 1981).

[2] D. Augustine, *Patricians and Parvenus: Wealth and High Society in Wilhelmine Germany* (Oxford, 1994).

[3] A. Daumard, *Les Fortunes françaises au XIXe siècle* (Paris, 1973).

wealthiest business group in Europe before 1914? What was the level of fortune of the leaders of the large companies? Answering these questions would help us to understand better the socio-cultural context in which big business operated in the three countries. One must be aware, however, of the difficulties of studying business wealth, and even more of comparing it between various countries. One problem is the paucity of available data; this applies especially to France before 1914. Another problem is that data, when available, are not readily compatible. For Britain, for example, we know the fortune left at their death by all businessmen included in the sample. It should be remembered, however, that a businessman active in, say, 1911 could well have died as late as the 1940s or even the 1950s, and that such a time lag is likely to create distortions. For Germany there exists a reliable estimate by a retired tax inspector of the fortunes held by all German millionaires in the years 1911 and 1912.[4] As 1 million marks was worth £50,000 before 1914, there is a good chance that a fair proportion of the leaders of German top companies were included in these compilations. Are these two sets of data compatible? Only as far as rough estimates and global orders of magnitude are concerned—but they can be useful.

In all three countries the greatest business fortunes achieved a comparable level before 1914, at around £10 million.[5] This was the case with people such as the merchant and merchant banker Charles Morrison, or the diamond magnate Julius Wernher in Britain; Bertha Krupp von Bohlen und Halbach, or Max von Goldschmidt-Rothschild in Germany; Alphonse and Gustave de Rothschild in Paris. The only exception appears to be the British shipping magnate and financier John Ellerman whose fortune, according to Rubinstein, may have reached £55 million in 1916, and who left more than £36 million at his death in 1933.[6] The distribution between economic sectors is also strikingly similar. The tertiary sector accounted for about half the businessmen leaving £500,000 or more in Britain, and those with 6 million marks (£300,000) or more in Germany.[7] In both countries, bankers were the largest single group (27 per cent in Germany, 22 per cent in Britain); the percentage of heavy industrialists was also very close (12.4 per cent in Germany, 13.5 per cent in Britain). There are unfortunately no equivalent figures for France. However, considering the concentration of millionaires in Paris and the huge fortunes of some of the régents of the Banque de France,[8] mostly bankers, there is a clear indica-

[4] R. Martin, *Das Jahrbuch der Milionäre Deutschlands*, 19 vols. (Berlin, 1911–14).

[5] W. Rubinstein (ed.), *Wealth and the Wealthy in the Modern World* (London, 1980), 19.

[6] W. D. Rubinstein, 'Ellerman, Sir John Reeves (1862–1933), Shipping Magnate and Financier', in D. Jeremy (ed.), *Dictionary of Business Biography*, 5 vols. (London, 1984–6), vol. ii.

[7] Rubinstein, *Men of Property*, 61–5; Augustine, *Patricians and Parvenus*, 29.

[8] A. Plessis, *Régents et gouverneurs de la Banque de France sous le Second Empire* (Geneva, 1985), and 'Bankers in French Society, 1880s–1960s', in Y. Cassis (ed.), *Finance and Financiers in European History, 1880–1960* (Cambridge, 1992).

tion that banking and finance accounted for a fair proportion of France's largest fortunes.

The main difference between the three countries lay in the number of wealthy businessmen. There can be little doubt that this number was substantially higher in Britain before 1914. Britain was an older industrialized country, and Germany's faster economic growth between 1880 and 1914 was not enough to make up the deficit in that respect. Moreover, Britain's dominant position in the world economy before the First World War, her empire, and the role of the City of London as the world's financial centre were sources of highly profitable business activities.

The number of businessmen worth £500,000 or more must have been at least twice as high in Britain as in Germany and France in the early twentieth century. There were 230 German businessmen worth that amount in 1911: Rudolf Martin's estimates, carefully analysed by Dolores Augustine, can be taken as a relatively reliable point of departure.[9] There is no comparable figure for Britain. However, according to Rubinstein's compilations, 362 British businessmen left a fortune of such magnitude between 1900 and 1919, and another 502 between 1920 and 1939, making a total of 864.[10] Even allowing for the businessmen who died during the first ten years of the century, for the depreciation of the pound, and for the fortunes made during the First World War (but without counterbalancing it by donations *inter vivos* to avoid death duties, or for money lost during the depression of the 1930s), we can reasonably assume that at least 460 of them (i.e. twice as many as the 230 in Germany) were worth half a million pounds in 1911. Estimates are even less reliable for France. Adeline Daumard gives a figure of 500 estates valued at 5 million francs (£200,000) between 1902 and 1913.[11] We can assume that two-thirds of them were businessmen, say between 300 and 350, though it is impossible to know how many of them left £500,000 or more (12.5 million francs). On the other hand, we must take into account the number of wealthy businessmen who died in the following three decades. It would be extremely hazardous to suggest any figure, but in all likelihood the number of German and French businessmen who were half-millionaires (in pounds sterling) in 1911 was fairly close.

How many were at the helm of the largest industrial and financial companies of the day? Not surprisingly, only a minority. Salaried managers were growing in importance, while many inheritors of great business wealth had stopped playing—or had never played—any significant part in the business. The most extreme example is that of Bertha Krupp, who inherited her father's company, the largest in Germany, in 1902. Other

---

[9] Augustine, *Patricians and Parvenus*.
[10] Rubinstein, *Men of Property*.
[11] A. Daumard, 'Wealth and Affluence in France since the Beginning of the Nineteenth Century', in Rubinstein (ed.), *Wealth and the Wealthy*, 104.

millionaires could be involved in business activities, though not as chairmen or directors of a major company: Ernest Cassel became as rich as Bertha Krupp through his financial dealings without even being a partner in a private firm.[12] In the world of trade and finance in particular, huge profits could still be generated by firms whose size had become comparatively modest—with a capital of around £500,000—by the standards of the twentieth century. This largely explains the high proportion of merchants and bankers among the richest businessmen not only in Britain, but also in Germany.

Great wealth was nevertheless present on the boards of the large companies, above all in Britain. Twenty-one per cent of the chairmen and managing directors of the largest companies were millionaires, as against 10 per cent in Germany and 8 per cent in France. The proportion rises to 34 per cent in Britain and 26 per cent in Germany if we consider those worth half a million pounds or more. Looking at the phenomenon from a different angle, Table 8.1 lists a selection of major British, French, and German companies whose chairman or managing director was at least a half-millionaire in pounds sterling. In both Britain and Germany, they were among the largest and most successful companies. The high number of British companies—double that in Germany—is once again striking, though not surprising. As we have seen, the proportion of owners, whether founders or inheritors, who were running their company was higher in Britain; and these companies, as we have also seen, were highly profitable.

Below this group of very rich businessmen, the leaders of the major British, French, and German companies were unquestionably men of ample means. Ninety-two per cent of them in Britain and 84 per cent in Germany were worth £100,000 or more, a very substantial amount before 1914 (some £4 million to £5 million in today's money). We lack information about the level of fortune of France's top businessmen, but a sample, established on a different basis for the year 1901, reveals that 57.2 per cent of company chairmen and deputy chairmen left an estate of 2 million francs (£80,000) or more.[13]

ARISTOCRACY AND BOURGEOISIE

Wealth never meant automatic admission into the upper classes, and in this respect differences were more pronounced between the three countries. Before 1914, whatever the advance of industrial society in Europe,

[12] See P. Thane, 'Cassel, Sir Ernest Joseph (1852–1921), Merchant Banker and International Financier', in Jeremy (ed.), *Dictionary of Business Biography*, vol. i.
[13] C. Charle, *Les Élites de la République* (Paris, 1987). The sample was established on the basis of businessmen with an entry in the French *Who's Who*.

Table 8.1. Large companies whose chairman or managing director was worth £500,000 or more, 1907–1912

	Britain	France	Germany
Banking	Rothschild Schröder (Midland)	Rothschild	Deutsche Bank Dresdner Bank Berliner Handelsgesellschaft

Heavy
    industry
	Armstrong
	Vickers
	GKN
	Harland &
	    Wolff
	Palmers
	    Shipbuilding
		Schneider
		De Wendel
			Thyssen
			GBAG
			Deutsch-Luxemburg
			(Phoenix)
			(Eschweiler Bergwerks)
			(Laurahütte)
			(Hohenlohe Werke)

Electrical engineering			Siemens Felten & Guilleaume

Mechanical
    engineering
	Metropolitan
	    Carriage
	Howard &
	    Bullough		

Chemicals	Brunner Mond Lever Brothers Reckitts		Hoechst Bayer
Textiles	J. & P. Coats		

Food, drink,
    and tobacco
	Imperial Tobacco
	Guinness
	Bass
	Watneys
	Fry
	Huntley &
	    Palmers		

Shipping	P. & O. British India Ellerman Lines		
Miscellaneous	Shell De Beers Associated Newspapers		

Note: Parentheses indicate a company whose chairman's fortune was made in another sector.

the degree of integration into the upper classes must still be measured with reference to the landed aristocracy. This poses two problems. First, the position of the old aristocracy differed markedly in Britain, France, and Germany;[14] in none of the three countries, however, should it be dismissed as anachronistic, whether at the economic, social, political, or symbolic level. The second problem is how to interpret the integration of the business élites and the landed aristocracy. From an economic point of view, should it be seen as a mark of business success? Or as the seeds of entrepreneurial failure? And from a socio-political point of view, should it be seen as evidence of the strength or weakness of the middle class? The former question has been mostly debated in Britain, the latter in Germany. The argument here is that a high degree of integration was an undoubted mark of success, whether for an individual businessman or for the business classes as a whole. The 'entrepreneurial spirit' of a nation has never been affected by the social pursuits of its most succesful entrepreneurs, while social recognition of business success can hardly be seen as reflecting a national culture adverse to bourgeois values.

The British aristocracy remained the grandest in Europe, despite an accelerated decline which left it much weaker than it had been at its apogee only a generation earlier.[15] Nevertheless, aristocrats, especially at the highest ranks (dukes, marquesses, earls), were still rich, and though no longer the single largest occupational group among the country's wealthholders they still included more than a handful of huge fortunes. Landed fortunes were also being converted, mainly through the City of London, into stocks and shares. Nor had the aristocracy lost all its political power: in the House of Lords, despite its diminished influence after 1910; in the House of Commons where, even in 1906, about 20 per cent of the members were linked to the landed establishment; and most importantly, in the cabinet, which it completely dominated until 1905 and where, although in a minority, it retained a weighty presence in the following decades. There were also the aristocracy's traditional strongholds such as the diplomatic service and the army, despite the decline in the proportion of high-ranking officers of noble origins by the eve of the First World War. But it was at the social level that the aristocracy's predominance remained the strongest. An aristocratic life-style, in particular the possession of a country seat—though not necessarily of a landed estate—became a pre-condition of social acceptability, while 'society' remained very much the old aristocracy's preserve.

The Prussian aristocracy, unquestionably the dominant component of

---

[14] For a recent comparative survey, see *Les Noblesses européennes au XIXème siècle*, Actes du colloque organisé par l'École Française de Rome (Milan–Rome, Università di Milano–École Française de Rome, 1988).

[15] See F. M. L. Thompson, *English Landed Society in the Nineteenth Century* (London, 1963); D. Cannadine, *The Decline and Fall of the British Aristocracy* (New Haven, 1990).

the German aristocracy, was never as rich as its British counterpart.[16] Many impoverished or landless *Junkers*, who had inherited a title but no land, had to rely on state employment to secure an income. There were, however, a few extremely wealthy magnates: Prince Henckel von Donnersmarck, the richest Prussian aristocrat whose wealth mostly derived from his mining and industrial interests in Upper Silesia, was almost as rich as the Duke of Westminster, whose wealth mostly derived from urban property. In addition, thanks to protective tariffs and also to agricultural progress, many landowners were able to improve their position in the three decades preceding the First World War. Furthermore, the aristocracy retained more political power in a German empire under Prussian hegemony than was the case in Britain. This was primarily due to its control over both Prussia's Upper and Lower Chambers—the *Herrenhaus* and the *Landrat*. The latter was elected through a complex three-class voting system which ensured that two-thirds of the deputies were elected by the wealthiest groups. Moreover, the aristocracy was ubiquitous in the upper echelons of the state bureaucracy, which had enormous political weight. Social life, however, never took off in united Germany. The vast majority of the *Junkers* were too poor to enjoy the life-style of the English gentry, let alone the aristocratic grandees. And Berlin's rise from provincial city to metropolis in the last quarter of the nineteenth century was not matched by a social life as hectic as in London or indeed Paris.

For exactly the opposite was true of France, where the aristocracy's credentials were of an almost exclusively social nature. Unlike her neighbours, France was a bourgeois republic. And if the aristocracy had not disappeared in the course of the nineteenth century, its existence did not rest on the same constitutional foundations as in Britain and Germany.[17] The use of titles was permitted by law, but there was no monarchy and no House of Lords, and there was much abuse of false titles. There were, to be sure, a few very wealthy French noblemen, whether with *ancien régime* or more recent imperial titles, but as a consequence of the land lost during the Revolution there were far fewer great landowners than in either Britain or Germany. Divided between Legitimists, Orleanists, and Bonapartists, French aristocrats had lost all political influence by the end of the nineteenth century, although they remained powerful in the diplomatic service and in the army. Above all, they still enjoyed social prestige, not only in the more traditional Catholic areas such as the west, but also, most importantly, in Parisian high society, whose brilliance equalled

---

[16] See W. Mosse, 'Nobility and Middle Classes in Nineteenth-Century Europe: A Comparative Study', in J. Kocka and A. Mitchell (eds.), *Bourgeois Society in Nineteenth Century Europe* (Oxford, 1993).

[17] See C. Charle, *Histoire sociale de la France au XIXème siècle* (Paris, 1991); T. Zeldin, *France, 1848–1945*, i. *Ambition, Love and Politics* (Oxford, 1973).

London. In their *salons*, immortalized by Proust, the French grandees of the *belle époque* could still show the distance which separated them from the mere bourgeoisie.

In the three countries, businessmen formed the very core of this bourgeoisie. Indeed, a narrow definition of the bourgeoisie would only consider as bourgeois the owners of the means of production. Even taking a broader view, it is significant that other social categories, such as the professions, are usually *added* to businessmen in order to draw a complete picture of the bourgeoisie, thereby emphasizing their key position.[18] The importance of businessmen increases when one considers the *grande bourgeoisie*, the upper middle class. In France, the *dynasties bourgeoises* of Emmanuel Beau de Loménie and the mythical *deux-cent familles* are made up of the great banking and industrial families and their connections in the social and political spheres.

Were these two worlds so far apart in the decade preceding the First World War? Were the upper classes of industrialized European societies still divided between aristocracy and bourgeoisie? Or were they formed by a constellation of élite groups including great landowners, top businessmen, senior politicians, senior civil servants, and the most prominent among professional men and, possibly, intellectuals? Had the most succesful businessmen been absorbed, pure and simple, into the ranks of the nobility, or had a merger between the two taken place, leading to the formation of a renewed upper class? And finally, did the structure of each country's upper class have any effect on its business and economic performance?

The social status enjoyed by business leaders was not the same in Britain, France, and Germany, nor was it the same between the various components of each country's business élites. They all had, however, a few common features, the most important being a similar social background. Businessmen, as we have seen, were in their vast majority sons of businessmen. This is not in itself an indication of social status, and this high degree of self-recruitment did not increase top businessmen's networks of relationships. The extent to which other élite groups were recruited from the ranks of businessmen can be indicative, though the figures can only suggest a general trend. Take politicians: in Britain only 7.7 per cent of Conservative cabinet ministers between 1900 and 1919 were sons of businessmen, landowners still providing the bulk of the political élite (50 per cent); while in France 26 per cent of the ministers of the Third Republic before 1914 were sons of businessmen, as against 11.4 per cent in Germany.[19] As for senior civil servants, 11 to 24 per cent—depending

[18] See Y. Cassis, 'Businessmen and the Bourgeoisie in Western Europe', in Kocka and Mitchell (eds.), *Bourgeois Society in Nineteenth Century Europe*.

[19] H. Kaelble, *Historical Research on Social Mobility* (London, 1982); J. Estèbe, *Les Ministres de la République, 1871–1914* (Paris, 1982).

on the *Corps*—were sons of big businessmen in France, the proportion rising to 20 to 36 per cent if medium-sized enterprises are taken into account. The corresponding figures for Germany are 1.2 and 20.5 per cent.[20] There are unfortunately no comparable data for Britain. The recruitment of other élite groups was therefore more diverse than that of businessmen, with a more bourgeois character and greater circulation between élite groups in France.

Other indications are given by education. This is mainly the case with Britain, where education at a major public school (above all Eton, but also Harrow, Rugby, Winchester, and a few others) and one of the ancient universities (Oxford and Cambridge) may be seen as a criterion of absorption into the upper classes. Taken as a single group, a higher proportion of the leaders of major companies in 1907 were educated at a public school (27.3 per cent) than of provincial businessmen from Birmingham, Bristol, and Manchester (19.6 per cent) or of businessmen of the same generation selected for inclusion in the *Dictionary of Business Biography* (12.7 per cent for those born between 1840 and 1869, and 17.2 per cent for those born between 1870 and 1899).[21] This indicates a higher degree of integration into the upper classes, which seems consistent with their position at the top of the business hierarchy. However, this group of business leaders was far from being homogeneous: 72 per cent of those educated at a public school belonged to two sectors: banking and finance, and drink and tobacco, thus confirming the early integration of bankers and brewers into the upper classes. Only two heavy industrialists and one cottonmaster followed a similar educational path. This is also in line with previous analyses of wider samples of bankers and industrialists: 74 per cent of the members of the banking community between 1890 and 1914 attended a public school, compared with 31 per cent of the steel industrialists active between 1905 and 1925.[22]

Such indicators do not exist for France and Germany. Education at a German *Gymnasium* or a French *lycée* can hardly be considered as a sign of integration into the upper classes, even though some great Parisian *lycées* were certainly very exclusive, as were some private Catholic colleges. University education cannot be considered as a status symbol in any of the three countries. However, an important social aspect of education, whether at secondary or university level, should not be overlooked: namely, the *esprit de corps* which some establishments instilled in their students and which persisted long after their schooldays. The

[20] Charle, *Les Élites de la République*; H. Henning, *Die deutsche Beamtenschaf im 19. Jahrhundert* (Stuttgart, 1984).

[21] H. Berghoff, 'Public Schools and the Decline of the British Economy 1870–1914', *Past and Present*, 129 (1990); C. Shaw, 'Characteristics of British Business Leaders: Findings from the DBB', unpub. paper (Business History Unit, London School of Economics, 1986).

[22] See Y. Cassis, *City Bankers, 1890–1914* (Cambridge, 1994); C. Erikson, *British Industrialists: Steel and Hosiery 1850–1950* (Cambridge, 1959).

English public schools are famous in that respect, and so are the French *grandes écoles*, though they did not exactly operate in the same way. The public schools had a predominantly social function, the *grandes écoles* a professional one. In the more meritocratic French system, the *grandes écoles* did offer the possibility of reaching the top to people starting with a relative handicap, but they were quite superfluous for scions of banking and industrial dynasties. This was exactly the opposite of the role played by the English public schools which educated the sons of the already established landed and business élites. However, prominent members of the French business élite went to a *grande école* in order to acquire professional qualifications. François de Wendel, for example, head of the famous iron and steel family firm, had been to the École des Mines between 1894 and 1898. Members of the Peugeot dynasty traditionally attended the engineering school Centrale. The *grandes écoles* were also important in linking together the political and the business élites, in particular through the *polytechniciens* and the *inspecteurs des finances*, who were present in both the state administration and the private sector with, as we have seen, frequent transfers from the former to the latter. Nothing similar existed in Germany, apart from the student associations, the *Korps* and the *Burschenschaften*, which provided students from the same university with a national network of relationships that included *alumni*. However, the absence of élite educational establishments necessarily reduced the scope of such networks. In addition, the presence of future businessmen in these associations, which were mostly famous for promoting the practice of duelling among their members, has not been clearly assessed.[23]

To what extent did top businessmen lead an aristocratic way of life? An essential pre-condition was to live in the right place, and the difference between capital and region was crucial in that respect. Not surprisingly, given the concentration of the country's big business in the capital, French business leaders resided in their overwhelming majority in Paris: 89 per cent had an address there, including most steelmasters from the Lorraine region; not only the chairmen, usually members of the founding dynasties or *notables*, but also salaried managers directly responsible for the running of the firm. Léon Lévy, for example, general manager of Châtillon-Commentry, or Adrien de Montgolfier, managing director of Marine-Homécourt, both resided in Paris. Only the Nord kept, up to a point, a separate identity. The two leaders of the largest French coal-mining company (the Mines de Lens), its chairman Anatole Descamps and its general manager Louis Mercier, lived in the region. But the Nord, with its dense network of family relationships dominated by the textile industrialists, was not wholly integrated into the upper strata of French business, despite being home to some of the largest coal, iron, and steel companies.

---

[23] See K. Jarausch, *Students, Society and Politics in Imperial Germany: The Rise of Academic Illiberalism* (Princeton, 1982).

London, like Paris, was the centre of British political, business, and social life. Yet only 53 per cent of British business leaders had an address in the capital. Two main factors explain this paradoxical difference from France. First, business life was less concentrated in Britain than in France. Several major industrial companies did not move their head office to London until after the First World War. Large provincial cities such as Manchester, Birmingham, and Glasgow still retained a strong municipal identity. A region like Lancashire was able to resist the wave of banking amalgamation and remain financially 'autonomous'—i.e. retain a few independent medium-sized to large banks—until the 1920s. Top industrialists such as William Houldsworth, chairman of the Fine Cotton Spinners, or William Cruddas, director of Armstrong Whitworth, continued to live in the north of England, the former in Manchester, the latter in Newcastle, though both were, or had been, Conservative MPs. All industrialists, however, did not live in a provincial city. Although the division between capital and region still reflected a separation between finance and industry, the attractions of the capital were becoming very strong for successful industrialists and several had a residence in London: brewers, not surprisingly (Lord Burton, of Bass; Lord Iveagh, of Guinness; Cosmo Orbe Bonsor, of Watneys); but also heavy industrialists (Albert Vickers; Andrew Noble, of Armstrong; Lord Pirrie, of Harland & Wolff) and others. Secondly, London has always had less significance for the British upper class than Paris for the French *aristocratie* and *grande bourgeoisie*. Living in the country with an occasional visit to the capital was perfectly compatible with, and even characteristic of, an aristocratic way of life. This was the case with a good third of the British business leaders, who only had a country address.

The distinction between a national and a provincial bourgeoisie does not apply in the same way to Germany. Despite the weight of Prussia in the German empire and the increasing importance of Berlin, the country remained far less centralized than either France or Britain. And even though 43 per cent of the leaders of the largest companies lived in Berlin, this was a result less of the political importance or the social appeal of the capital of the Reich than of the role of Berlin as a business centre, especially for banking and electrical engineering. Indeed, 30 per cent of German business leaders lived in the Ruhr, in the neighbouring cities of Bochum, Essen, Dortmund, Duisburg, Mühlheim, Düsseldorf, and Cologne. The most striking difference between Germany and her two western neighbours was the regular coincidence between place of work and place of residence—the latter being of course understood in the wide sense of the word, as top industrialists had by then ceased to live next to their smoky plants. The only exceptions were the Berlin bankers who chaired the supervisory board of an industrial company. The German business élite, and indeed the German upper class as a whole, were thus

scattered, as a consequence not only of the country's business organization, but of its educational system, and more generally of its political
structure.

Life-styles varied among businessmen. The most conspicuous group
were the millionaires, or plutocrats, who were part of London society in
the Edwardian age, people like the merchant banker Lord Rothschild, the
financier Ernest Cassel, the South African diamond magnate Julius
Wernher, the 'grocer' Thomas Lipton, and the 'brewer' Lord Iveagh.[24]
They formed, however, but a small minority of the leaders of the largest
companies. Many of the so-called plutocrats had either entirely retired
from business, for example Lord Wimborne, heir of the Guest family of
ironmasters; or they were only partly active in firms which had lost much
of their past grandeur, for example Lords Wandsworth and Michelham,
of the Stern family of merchant bankers. Most top businessmen did not
have the time, or the desire, or simply the financial means to lead such a
life. The same was true of Paris and Berlin. An aristocratic life-style should
not be confused with being involved in all society events. One of its characteristics was an address in the capital coupled with a seat in the country.
This was the case with 51 per cent of the top French businessmen. In
Britain, 69 per cent had a country seat, and among them 37 per cent also
had a London address. They lived in their majority in the two capitals'
most aristocratic areas: the 8th and 16th *arrondissements* in Paris, Mayfair
and Belgravia in London. Similarly in Berlin rich businessmen and the
aristocracy lived in the distinguished western areas near the Tiergarten;
owning a country house had also become quite common at this level.

Clubs formed part of this social life, above all in London, where membership of one of the gentlemen's clubs (Carlton, Brooks, Athenaeum,
Travellers, White's, etc.) was a mark of upper-class status. Needless to say,
only the most prominent of the provincial industrialists were members of
a London club, whereas it was common practice for the financial élite.
Paris also had its clubs, with subtle divisions between the old clubs
(Jockey Club, Cercle de la rue Royale, Cercle de l'Union, etc.), attended
by the aristocracy and the *haute bourgeoisie*, and the more bourgeois clubs
(Automobile Club de France, Bois de Boulogne, etc.) attended by newer
businessmen. There were no such clubs in Berlin. However, the financial
aristocracy did entertain on a grand scale during the season and mix with
the old aristocracy. Social life was much more restricted, and had a distinctly provincial flavour, in Rhineland-Westphalia; leading industrialists,
even the most prominent of them (people such as Paul Reusch, August
Thyssen, Emil Kirdorf, and Carl Duisberg), socialized almost exclusively
within bourgeois circles, and especially with other businessmen.[25]

---

[24] For a lively description of this group, see J. Camplin, *The Rise of the Plutocrats* (London,
1976).
[25] See Augustine, *Patricians and Parvenus*, 226–33.

Titles were another mark of social status, although their nature differed in the three countries. There were no ennoblements in France, where the *légion d'honneur*, despite its prestige, was fairly commonly conferred on top businessemen and cannot be compared with a hereditary peerage in Britain and Germany. Such titles remained a rare honour despite their proliferation—246 granted in Britain between 1886 and 1914, and 836 in Germany between 1890 and 1918—and increasing venality in the late nineteenth and early twentieth centuries. Other titles had a specific function, for example the title of *Kommerzienrat*—commercial councillor—in Germany, which was specifically designed for businessmen and had no equivalent in Britain and France.

In France 75 per cent of top businessmen were decorated with the *légion d'honneur*. In fact only political reasons could prevent a successful businessman from receiving that honour. It was for example considered that conferring the *légion d'honneur* on Louis Mercier, general manager of the Mines de Lens, would have a bad effect on the advanced Republicans and in particular on the working population of the Pas-de-Calais coal-mines, given that Louis Mercier had always shown an open hostility to the miners' union. Anatole Descamps, a textile industrialist and chairman of the same Mines de Lens, was also rejected because of his conservative political opinions.[26] Ennoblement was more frequent among British than among German top businessmen. In Britain 19 per cent were peers, including four viscounts (Northcliffe, Leverhulme, Pirrie, and Bearsted) and two earls (Iveagh and Inchcape), as against 12 per cent in Germany, with only two barons (the bankers Albert and Eduard von Oppenheim), the others having to be content with a mere *von*. Twenty-three per cent of British business leaders had the title of baronet (none had inherited it) and another 12 per cent had been granted a knighthood.

The total percentage of titled businessmen was about the same (56 per cent) in Germany if to the few ennobled businessmen are added those who were granted the title of councillor—*Kommerzienrat*, and *Bergrat* for those engaged in the mining industry. There were in fact two classes of councillors: a majority of 28 per cent belonged to a first class of privy councillors (*Geheimer Rat*), while the remaining 14 per cent were simple councillors. The title rewarded men who had not only been successful in business, but who were also seen as having acted to the public good through their belonging to chambers of commerce, business associations, charitable organizations, and so on. The title of *Kommerzienrat* carried enormous prestige in the business community, not only because it was a sign of high economic and social standing, but also because the suffix *Rat* suggested equality with the highly esteemed Prussian bureaucracy. However, it might well have lost some of its appeal by the early

---

[26] Archives Nationales, F12/5209 (Louis Mercier), F12/8572 (Anatole Descamps).

twentieth century. While it has been suggested that 'people would rather be called Herr Commercial Councillor than Herr Baron',[27] it also appears that a good many businessmen felt that a commercial title could add little to their status and influence: if they could pay for the honour, they would have preferred ennoblement. For whatever its prestige, the title of councillor set the business community apart from the rest of the social élite.

It is this relative isolation which mainly differentiated the German business élite from its British and French counterparts. The phenomenon is even more visible in the way that top German businessmen contracted their matrimonial alliances, a most revealing aspect of the type of relationships existing between various élite groups. It has not been possible to analyse the marriages of the chairmen and managing directors included in the sample. Unlike other indicators, such as social origins, education, careers, outside directorships, titles, and so on, data on fathers-in-law are extremely difficult to collect, especially in three different countries. However, precious indications can be gathered from the handful of good social studies of business groups existing in each of the three countries.

In Britain the most striking feature was the high degree of integration of the City aristocracy and of the landed aristocracy: 35 per cent of the members of the London banking community married daughters of the aristocracy or gentry; the percentage rises to 60 per cent if one adds other groups traditionally bound to the landed interests, such as army and navy officers, senior clergymen, politicians, and civil servants. More important than these percentages, it can be observed that a succession of marriages and intermarriages between banking families and families from the landed aristocracy led to a more complete merger and the formation of a renewed élite.[28] Industrialists were on the whole excluded from this network of relationships.

In France, according to Christophe Charle's figures, 54.5 per cent of big businessmen married into the *fractions possédantes* (i.e. mostly into business), 21.8 per cent married the daughters of senior civil servants, and 10.9 per cent the daughters of professionals. Interestingly, 38.4 per cent of civil servants and 39 per cent of ministers married into business, thus confirming the greater circulation of élites in France. However, the most interesting point made by Charle is that, in addition to the well-known strategies of social promotion through marriage for the upwardly mobile, and of social and business consolidation through intermarriages for the old-established families, there existed a third strategy of diversification into other socio-professional élite groups. At the highest echelon of this

[27] K. Kodelka-Hanisch, 'The Titled Businessman: Prussian Commercial Councillors in the Rhineland and Westphalia during the Nineteenth Century', in D. Blackbourn and R. Evans (eds.), *The German Bourgeoisie: Essays on the Social History of the German Middle Classes from the Late Eighteenth to the Early Twentieth Century* (London, 1991), 107.

[28] See Cassis, *City Bankers.*

strategy of diversification, marriages took place in one and the same world. As Charle puts it: 'Professional classifications became meaningless as the people involved were part of society, indeed "high society".'[29]

In Germany, according to Dolores Augustine's figures on the wealthiest businessmen, 17 per cent married daughters of the aristocracy, 62 per cent the daughter of a fellow businessman, and 17 per cent daughters of members of the *Bildungsbürgertum* (the educated middle classes).[30] The proportion of alliances with business families was therefore significantly higher than in the French business élite or the British financial community. But these figures are still lower than those obtained by H. Henning for the most prominent businessmen in Westphalia (those with the title of *Kommerzienrat*): 85 per cent married into business families (66 per cent into big business, 19 per cent into medium-sized and small business).[31] German big businessmen were therefore more isolated, whether from the landed aristocracy or from other bourgeois groups, than their British and French counterparts.

Beyond the 10 to 15 per cent difference, statistically not very significant, it is the position of top businessmen within the dominating élite of their respective country which was different. In Britain and France the upper echelons of the business classes merged with other groups to form a dominating élite. In Britain, the merger of the City aristocracy with the landed aristocracy formed the embryo of what would become known as the Establishment. In France, the Parisian *aristocratie financière* merged with the *grande bourgeoisie de robe* to form the *classe dominante*, from which the old aristocracy was not absent, even though it was more in the position of 'junior partner' than in Britain.[32] What characterized these two groups was their deep social unity: their members belonged to the same world and were sometimes related to one another.

No such group existed in Germany. In particular, there was no German equivalent of the British or French financial aristocracy. In Britain and France bankers were the first group to be integrated into the upper classes, whereas in Germany the banking community was largely Jewish and so could not be absorbed fully into the dominating élite. Such a complete merger leading to the formation of a social single group did not take place in Imperial Germany—even though the aristocracy was increasingly sharing its power with *Grossbürgertum*, and they shared the same way of life, met socially, and intermarriages were becoming more frequent. On

[29] See Charle, *Les Élites de la République*.
[30] Augustine, *Patricians and Parvenus*, 80.
[31] H. Henning, 'Soziale Verflechtungen der Unternehmer in Westfalen 1860–1914', *Zeitschrift für Unternehmensgeschichte*, 23 (1978), 13.
[32] Significantly, endogamy was still high within the French aristocracy in the early 20th cent.; see C. Grange, 'Noblesse et bourgeoisie dans la France du XXe siècle: Les "Gens du Bottin mondain"', unpub. doctoral thesis (École des Hautes Études en Sciences Sociales, Paris, 1992), 167–82.

the other hand, links between German leading businessmen and the other bourgeois élite groups were not as close as in France; and in any case, given the strength, both social and political, of the German aristocracy, closer links would not have been sufficient to form a single dominating élite.

POLITICAL INFLUENCE

A top businessman was by necessity involved in politics. The very size of his firm, his economic weight both as a producer and as an employer, put him in the public sphere. Business activities could influence the course of policy-making, and be in turn affected by political decisions. Yet only a few businessmen got directly involved in political activities, whether out of personal convictions, or as part of the collective action of an interest group. Most preferred to entrust representatives with a task requiring both time and professional skills. Take Parliament, in many respects the most obvious arena of political intervention, providing as it were an immediate measure of the degree of interrelationships between business and politics. By the early twentieth century, very few business leaders had embarked on a parliamentary career. For by then it had become a career, obeying different rules from those prevailing in business, and with which businessmen were not spontaneously at ease. Businessmen, for example, have never been the most talented orators or public debaters. With the introduction of universal suffrage, they had to face an electorate which could be hostile, for example in constituencies with a high density of working-class voters. By the early twentieth century, France and Germany's foremost industrialists, Krupp and Schneider, could no longer secure election for themselves or for their representatives against left-wing opponents in their respectives constituencies of Essen and Le Creusot.[33]

The increased professionalization of both business and political careers could also lead to conflicting interests: Edward Holden, managing director of the Midland Bank and Liberal MP between 1906 and 1910, not only found the extra amount of work overwhelming, but also thought that speaking in Parliament carried the risk of antagonizing those of his customers who belonged to the other main political party.[34] Direct involvement in parliamentary activities also ran counter to one of businessmen's golden rules of political intervention: discretion. François de Wendel, the steel magnate, was elected a deputy in 1914, aged 40, against the will of the rest of his family who thought that the firm would suffer rather than

[33] H. Jaeger, *Unternehmer in der deutschen Politik, 1890–1918* (Bonn, 1967), 91–2; J. A. Roy, *Histoire de la famille Schneider et du Creusot* (Paris, 1962), 87.
[34] Cassis, *City Bankers*, 273–4.

benefit from his political ambitions.[35] Similarly, his colleagues at the Comité des Forges, the pressure group of French heavy industrialists, would rather have had him outside than inside Parliament.

Nevertheless, Parliament has recurrently appealed to businessmen, especially in Britain. In 1907, 22 per cent of the leaders of the country's major companies were, or had been at some stage, members of Parliament. This compares with 17 per cent in France and 4 per cent in Germany. These figures should in no way be seen as percentages of business representation in Parliament, which could be measured either through the number of MPs on the board of public companies, or through the number of MPs representing business interests in Parliament. The percentages resulting from such calculations would no doubt be higher, but they would include politicians linked to the world of business, as opposed to businessmen engaged in politics. Differentiating between the two, however, is not always easy, especially in France where the passage from the world of politics—including the civil service—to the world of business has been more frequent than elsewhere in Europe. Florent Guillain (1844–1915), chairman of the electrical concern Thomson-Houston, is a case in point. A *polytechnicien* and former civil servant, he left the state service in 1896, aged 52, to enter the world of business and politics. As a politician he was a deputy, and soon (1898–9) minister for the colonies. But he was also a leading figure in French big business, not only as chairman of one of the country's largest industrial companies, but also as a director of several other major companies, including the Mines d'Anzin and the iron and steel concern Marine-Homécourt,[36] and as chairman of the Comité des Forges, France's most powerful business interest group. On the other hand, the two mythical figures of French industry in the *belle époque*, the ironmasters Charles Schneider and François de Wendel, still symbolized through their presence in Parliament the more traditional links between business and politics, though they were never to sit together, the former ending his political career in 1910, the latter starting his in 1914.

These traditional links lasted longer in Britain, where all the MPs among the chairmen and managing directors of the leading companies came from the world of business, though some had given up daily attendance at their firm. For example William Henry Wills, later Lord Winterstoke, the chairman of Imperial Tobacco, who retired from active management in 1880 at the age of 50; or John Brunner, chairman of the chemical company Brunner Mond & Co., who allowed himself more time

[35] J.-N. Jeanneney, *François de Wendel en République: L'Argent et le pouvoir, 1914–1940* (Paris, 1976), 17–19.

[36] Florent Guillain was also a director of the Ateliers et Chantiers de France, the railway company Paris-Lyon-Méditerranée, the Suez Canal Company, and the Banque de France.

for politics after the incorporation of his firm as a public company in 1881. This must have been the case with most top businessmen engaged in politics, and it is little surprise that, in both Britain and France, the overwhelming majority of top businessmen members of Parliament were chairmen of their company. Only two in Britain, and a single one in France, were managing directors. In Britain, Holden of the Midland Bank was the only genuine salaried manager. Arthur Philip Du Cros, managing director of Dunlop, was the son of the company's founder and chairman, William Henry Du Cros, and he succeeded his father as MP for Hastings in 1908. In France, Adrien de Montgolfier, managing director of the iron and steel concern Marine-Homécourt, had a less conventional career. Born in 1831, he entered the civil service after Polytechnique and the Ponts et Chaussées before joining Marine-Homécourt in 1879. More unusually, he had been deputy of the Loire constituency between 1871 and 1876, and senator between 1876 and 1879. Although his parliamentary career had ended by the time he joined the company, this was a unique step in a managing director's career at the time.

The contrast is striking with Germany, where only two of the major companies' leaders were, or had previously been, involved in parliamentary politics. One was Walther vom Rath, chairman of the supervisory board of the chemical company Hoechst, formerly known as Meister, Lucius & Brüning. He was the archetypal business *notable* engaged in politics: the son of a merchant in Amsterdam and Cologne, and himself a lawyer in the state administration, he married Maximiliane Meister and replaced his father-in-law on Hoechst's supervisory board on the latter's retirement. The other, Carl Knupe, a managing director of Deutsch-Luxemburg, the iron and steel concern, belonged to that rare species of professional salaried managers who embarked on a political career. The contrast with Britain and France was due to two main factors, of the same kind as those discussed in connection with businessmen's social status in Imperial Germany. First, there was the question of the powers of the German Parliament. Whatever its importance, which had been steadily growing in the decades preceding the First World War, the Reich Chancellor and his ministers were ultimately not responsible to the Reichstag. As a result, businessmen lost interest in parliamentary politics.[37] It must be said, however, that this phenomenon was not confined to Germany. The same feeling can be observed in all European countries, including those with parliamentary government. Everywhere the number of businessmen sitting in Parliament sharply declined in the last quarter of the nineteenth century. Secondly, as we have seen, German top businessmen were more isolated from the country's other élite groups—landowners, politicians, civil servants, professionals—than their British and French

---

[37] Jaeger, *Unternehmer in der deutschen Politik*, 91–4.

counterparts, and their feeble presence in Parliament was another reflection of this relative isolation.

Was this compensated by the strength of their pressure groups? For there is little doubt that big business interests were better organized in Germany than in Britain and France, both at central and sectoral levels. One must not forget that before the First World War no peak association existed in either Britain or France: the Federation of British Industries (FBI) was founded in 1916, the Confédération Générale de la Production Française (CGPF) in 1919. In German, by contrast, the Central Verband Deutscher Industrieller (CVDI) was established as early as 1876 in order to strengthen the campaign in favour of protectionism. However, despite its claims to central and national representation, the CVDI was created and dominated by the Ruhr heavy industrialists.[38] So much so that the representatives of the chemical industries, who had joined in 1882, left for that very reason in 1889; and they founded in 1895, with other representatives from the light and export industries, a rival central organization, the Bund der Industrieller (BDI). However, the BDI turned out to be the mouthpiece of the small and medium-sized enterprises which, with a few exceptions, were dominant in these sectors.[39]

The same balance of power existed between industrial sectors.[40] Heavy industry was the most strongly and efficiently organized. In the first place, its associations were the oldest in the country. The Mining Association— a short name for the Association of the Mining Interests in the Dortmund Mining Jurisdiction—was created in 1858, making it one of the earliest trade associations in Germany. The Langnamverein—or Long Name Association—followed in 1871 (its full name, the Association for the Maintenance of Common Interests of the Rhineland and Westphalia, was totally impractical): it was at first concerned with the inadequacy of the railway system, which could not transport enough coal during the boom of the early 1870s, but soon turned its attention and energy to the introduction of a protective tariff. In 1874, the Association of Iron and Steel Industrialists—Verein Deutschen Eisen und Stahl Industrieller (VDESI)— was established to strengthen the pro-tariff camp. The heavy industry could thus rely on four interest groups: a central association (the CVDI), two branch associations (the Mining Association and the VDESI), and a regional one (the Langnamverein). These associations were active not only

---

[38] See H. Kaelble, *Industrielle Interessenpolitik in der wilhelminischen Gesellschaft* (Berlin, 1967).

[39] See H.-P. Ullmann, *Der Bund der Industriellen: Organisation, Einfluss und Politik klein- und mittelbetrieblicher Industrieller im deutschen Kaiserreich* (Göttingen, 1976).

[40] See T. Pierenkemper, 'Trade Associations in Germany in the Late Nineteenth and Early Twentieth Century', unpub. paper; F. Blaich, *Staat und Verbände in Deutschland zwischen 1871 and 1945* (Wiesbaden, 1979); W. Fischer, 'Staatsverwaltung und Interessenverbände in Deutschland 1871–1914', in H. J. Varain (ed.), *Interessenverbände in Deutschland* (Cologne, 1973).

in Rhineland-Westphalia, but also in the capital, Berlin. In addition, they were closely linked together, in particular sharing the same senior executives. The key figure was Axel Bueck, a salaried executive recruited outside the industry, who was secretary-general of the Langnamverein, of the CVDI, and of the north-west section (i.e. Rhineland-Westphalia) of the VDESI. The increasing power of this type of salaried business representative went hand in hand with a transformation of the role of the interest groups, in particular in heavy industry. In the last decade of the nineteenth century, the CVDI turned itself into a 'private ministry' for industry, and strove to change its role from that of an adviser to that of a joint decision-maker.[41]

Business organizations remained much weaker in other industrial sectors. Apart from the chemical industry, trade associations were not formed before the very end of the century: the Association of Machine Builders—Verein Deutscher Maschinenbau Anstalten (VDMA)—in 1892 and the Association for the Maintenance of the Common Economic Interests of the German Electro-technical Industry in 1902. The VDMA had been founded under the auspices of heavy industry and did not start to win some independence until 1913, when it moved its headquarters from Düsseldorf to Berlin.[42] These associations' main problem, however, was the difficulty they had in organizing themselves. They lacked a strong regional basis, their products were not as homogeneous as those of heavy industry, and their members, mostly small and medium-sized enterprises, were too numerous, with interests far more difficult to conciliate than those of the integrated giant coal, iron, and steel concerns.

The German model of early 'organized capitalism' has often been contrasted with the British and French 'liberal' models, which persisted until the First World War and beyond. Such characterization, however, tends to portray British and French businessmen as divided and on the defensive, thus underestimating their real political strength. In fact, different forms of intervention prevailed in each country; furthermore, they had already started to converge by the early twentieth century, especially in Germany and France.

The organization of heavy industry was hardly less impressive in France than in Germany. The Comité des Forges was founded in 1864, ten years before its German counterpart, the VDESI.[43] However, for much of the rest of the century it remained rather ineffectual, a club of *notables* marred by internal divisions. Its weakness was conspicuous during the

[41] Kaelble, *Industrielle Interessenpolitik*.

[42] See G. D. Feldman and U. Nocken, 'Trade Associations and Economic Power: Interest Group Development in the German Iron and Steel and Machine Building Industries, 1900–1933', *Business History Review*, 49/4 (1975).

[43] On the Comité des Forges, see M. Rust, 'Business and Politics in the Third Republic: The Comité des Forges and the French Steel Industry, 1896–1914', unpub. Ph.D. thesis (Princeton University, 1973).

battle over tariff reform in the 1880s, the outcome of which was the Méline Tariff of 1892. Although marking the end of France's commitment to free trade, it was a moderate tariff which managed to accommodate conflicting industrial, commercial, and agricultural interests.[44] In the end the iron and steel industry from the Lorraine and the Nord did secure the tariff protection they demanded, and the French market became *de facto* reserved to French producers. Thereafter, the Comité des Forges underwent a profound reorganization, which turned it into a modern, efficient pressure group, run by full-time salaried managers and with direct access to senior politicians and civil servants in the relevant ministerial departments. It was capable not only of lobbying a department when a bill came up for reading, but of being integrated into the decision-making process through prior consultation or even direct participation in the drafting of the bill. Between 1906 and 1910 the Comité des Forges actively participated in the legislation establishing a weekly day of rest, and subsequently in implementing the administrative regulation. It was thus able to incorporate all its wishes into the final Act, in particular special regulations concerning workers in blast-furnaces running twenty-four hours a day and seven days a week.

Like its German counterpart, French heavy industry could rely on a network of closely interrelated associations. A series of them were created at the turn of the century. The Union des Industries Métallurgiques et Minières (UIMM) was founded in 1900 to defend the interests of the coal-mining, iron and steel, and heavy engineering employers, mainly in matters of labour legislation and social unrest. The others were linked to specific industries: the Railways Material Association (Chambre Syndicale du Matériel de Chemin de Fer), established in 1899 to counter the railway companies' purchasing policy; the Shipbuilders' Association (Chambre Syndicale des Constructeurs de Navires), founded a few months later; and the Armaments Industry Association (Chambre Syndicale des Fabricants et Constructeurs de Matériel de Guerre). All these associations, together with the Comité des Forges, shared the same secretary-general, Robert Pinot, the man who was instrumental in shaping French heavy industry into a highly organized and influential interest group.

No such network existed in British heavy industry, or indeed in any other industry.[45] This was to a great extent due to the prevalence of free trade in British politics. As we have seen, the German and French iron

[44] See M. S. Smith, *Tariff Reform in France, 1860–1900* (Ithaca, NY, 1980).
[45] There existed, to be sure, a number of trade associations in the British iron and steel industry. The Iron and Steel Institute was founded in 1869, to facilitate discussion of technical matters; while the British Iron Trade Association was formed in 1876 to collect statistics and organize collective representation of the industry in its dealings with the government. Unlike their Continental counterparts, however, they were never very effective. See D. Burn, *The Economic History of Steel Making* (Cambridge, 1940), 10, 32; A. J. Wolfe, *Commercial Organization in the United Kingdom* (Washington, 1915), 46–7.

and steel interest groups were formed and gathered strength in the last third of the nineteenth century in order to campaign for the introduction of customs duties. This theme, together with labour legislation, remained their main object of intervention until the outbreak of the war. Conditions were different in Britain. At the time of the foundation of the Comité des Forges or the VDESI, the British iron and steel industry did not wish or need any protective tariff. Two decades later, several quarters in the industry called for trade protection.[46] However, unlike their French and German competitors, they were not in the winning camp. Free trade prevailed, because much of British industry, including iron and steel, depended on exports to foreign markets and on imports of raw materials and semi-finished products; and also because the City of London acted as international entrepôt and clearing house to the rest of the world, and called the tune in international politics. Significantly, employers' associations concerned with labour relations rather than trade matters were stronger. The most powerful was the Engineering Employers' Federation, founded in 1896, which demonstrated its strength the following year in its six-month battle with the Engineers' Union over the 48-hour week.[47] Cottonmasters were also well organized (both in their response to labour and in controlling competition), though cotton-spinning, with the influential Federation of Master Cotton Spinners' Association (FMCSA), founded 1891, remained separated from cotton-weaving.[48] In addition, chambers of commerce, which were not, as in France and Germany, state institutions, played a more important role as representatives of business interests, though not necessarily those of big business.

Interest groups played a more significant role in Germany than in Britain, where personal intervention and consultation was more efficient, or in France, where the regular transfer of senior civil servants to the private sector strengthened the personal relationships between the business, political, and administrative élites. Interestingly, in all three countries bankers were little involved in trade associations. On the other hand, the development of interest groups in Germany should not be exaggerated. Before 1914 the only ones to have grown into political forces to be seriously reckoned with were those representing heavy industry. From this standpoint, the main difference between the three countries can be seen as lying in the level of organization of their heavy industry and in the balance of power existing within the business community.

By the late nineteenth century a group of businessmen had established

[46] See U. Wengenroth, *Enterprise and Technology: The German and British Steel Industries, 1865–1895* (Cambridge, 1992).

[47] See E. Wigham, *The Power to Manage: A History of the Engineering Employers' Federation* (London, 1973).

[48] See A. McIvor, 'Cotton Employers' Organisations and Labour Relations, 1890–1939', in J. A. Jowitt and A. J. McIvor, *Employers and Labour in the English Textile Industries, 1850–1939* (London, 1988), 1–27.

itself in a predominant position in each of the three countries: City bankers in Britain, Ruhr industrialists in Germany, the Parisian business élite in France. This position was attained through a combination of economic power, social prestige, and political influence. Britain and France were both centralized states, and it seems natural that the two countries' foremost businessmen should be based in the capital. In Britain, however, the capital was more closely associated with financial activities, with the bulk of manufacturing industry located in the north of the country. Bankers' economic power derived from the City of London's key role in the British economy, but it was enhanced by strong integration into the upper classes and close relations with political power. In Germany, the rise of Berlin as a major financial and industrial centre was not enough to displace the Ruhr magnates, whose assets were primarily of an economic and political nature. The French business élite was a wider and more homogeneous group than in both Britain and Germany: it included representatives from both finance and industry as well as from the state administration, and its networks of influence stretched over the entire country. Each of these groups had interests of its own and sought to influence policy in this direction. There is no doubt that the particular configuration of big business in Britain, France, and Germany permeated each country's sociopolitical fabric and that specific business interests—especially the City in Britain and heavy industry in Germany—influenced policy-making, as has been debated in numerous studies. Comparing their long-term economic effects would require another, much longer volume.

9

Business Élites in Contemporary Europe

Discussing the socio-political position of the business élites after 1918 is both simpler and more complicated than for the pre-war generation. It is simpler because it can plausibly be argued that, whether in Britain, France, or Germany, business leaders have since then been at the top of the social hierarchy. It is more complicated because this overall success, as well as the convergence between the three countries, calls for a more subtle analysis. For one thing, wealth, or at least great wealth, was no longer the primary source of the business leaders' status and power. Though belonging to the upper middle classes who no longer had to defer to the aristocracy, business élites were none the less one élite group among others; relationships at the top could be conflictual, and lead to temporary set-backs. Above all, business leaders have been confronted with a much higher level of state intervention, which has heavily affected their own political involvement. Convergence, moreover, has been an uneven process, which only gathered pace after the Second World War; and even then, it failed to eradicate national singularities. This final chapter will consider how business élites have fared in upheaval and prosperity.

WEALTH AND THE CORPORATE ÉLITE

Estimates of business leaders' fortunes are much more difficult to gauge after the First World War. No documents are available for either France or Germany, while probate valuations become less reliable for Britain, especially after 1945, because of higher death duties. It is usually assumed that the number of millionaires heading large corporations has steadily declined this century, as a result of increased separation between ownership and management; that inherited wealth has deserted the boardrooms of the largest companies; and that family-owned, usually medium-sized enterprises have become the main vehicle of private wealth. Such assumptions undoubtedly make sense, but they require a number of qualifications. In the first place, the change has been gradual. Great wealth is more often than not inherited. And as we have seen the proportion of inheritors among the leaders of the major companies remained high in the inter-war years, between a quarter and a third of the sample. While it might be hasty to deduce that all of them were millionaires, there is a good chance that they were very wealthy indeed. In addition, large companies were still created, and huge fortunes still made, by entrepreneurs during their lifetime; this adds another 10 per cent or so to the proportion of the very rich among business leaders in the late 1920s. All in all then, and despite the lack of data, one can surmise that their percentage was not much smaller than for the generation at the helm before 1914.[1]

The number of very wealthy business leaders without doubt decreased significantly in the decades following the Second World War, though it is impossible to know by how much. For the very recent past, one can obtain a rough idea from the lists of the largest fortunes published annually by magazines such as the *Sunday Times* and *Le Nouvel Économiste*. Such estimates must of course be considered with great caution. They tend to overestimate 'new wealth', and very substantial fortunes will inevitably be missing from the top 200 or 400.[2] Nevertheless, they do reveal that in 1990, 14 of the 99 British companies (14 per cent) and 11 of the 69 French companies (18 per cent) with a turnover of £1.5 billion or more were headed by a very wealthy businessman, i.e. with a fortune of £50 million or more[3], roughly the equivalent of £1 million before 1914. Such percentages are far from negligible. In the last decade of the twentieth century, great wealth was still associated with leaders of very large corporations, even though these are no longer the very largest. The group was made up of a mixture of entrepreneurs (founders of large business groups and those responsible for the vast extension of existing companies) and inheritors (descendants of business dynasties still in charge of the company's affairs).

Entrepreneurs included the founders of supermarket and hypermarket chains in France: Gérard Mulliez of Auchan, Philipppe Bouriez of Cora, Paul-Louis Halley of Promodès, Jacques Fournier of Casino; and those of other service companies in Britain, such as Lord Forte, of the hotel company Forte, and Maurice Saatchi of the advertising agency Saatchi & Saatchi. Founders and entrepreneurs also headed industrial enterprises and conglomerates in both countries: Lord Weinstock at GEC, Lord Hanson at Hanson, and Sir David Alliance at Coats Viyella; and Francis Bouygues at Bouygues, Bernard Arnault at LVMH, and Jean-Luc

---

[1] In Britain, the only country for which some very rough estimates are possible, 12% of the chairmen and managing directors of the major companies in 1929 left £1,000,000 or more at their death (as against 21% for 1907); and 23% left between £500,000 and £1,000,000 (as against 34% in 1907). Given the number of businessmen active in 1929 who died after 1945, the percentages for 1929 are certainly more conservative than for 1907.

[2] The surveys are usually based on the stock market value of an individual's or a family's holding in a company (or on estimates for unlisted companies), which can fluctuate widely within the space of a few years. Estimates of the value of estates and works of art are sometimes attempted in the case of older wealth. A good discussion of the value of these rankings can be found in M. Pinçon and M. Pinçon-Charlot, *Grandes Fortunes: Dynasties familiales et formes de richesse en France* (Paris, 1996), 22–31.

[3] *Sunday Times Magazine*, 14 Apr. 1991; *Le Nouvel Économiste*, 14 Oct. 1994.

Lagardère at Matra. Inheritors included Lord Sainsbury, Sir Adrian Cadbury, Sir Antony Pilkington, Samuel Whitbread, Adrian Swire, the Earl of Inchcape, Maurice Laing, all at the head of a firm bearing their name, as well as Lord Laing of United Biscuits; and Pierre Peugeot (though he was not the number one), François Michelin, Serge Dassault, together with Jérôme Seydoux of Chargeurs. Similar lists have not appeared in Germany. However, the American magazine *Forbes* has published lists of business fortunes worth $1 *billion* or more. Five billionaires were leading major companies in Germany, invariably a mass retailing firm: Otto Beisheim of Metro; Erivan Haub, sole owner of Tengelmann; Karl and Theo Albrecht, the founders of Aldi (they stepped down in 1993); and Michael Otto of Otto Versand, the world's largest mail order company.[4]

What about the fortunes of the rest, the vast majority of European business leaders? Before 1914, over three-quarters of the leaders of the major British and German companies were worth in today's money £4 million to £5 million or more. What was the percentage at the close of the century? This is a question which it is impossible to answer. One can only be struck by the remuneration of chief executives of the largest companies, which reached new heights in the 1980s and 1990s, especially in the form of share options. The economic power of the business élites has undoubtedly increased, but at the same time it has become less dependent on business leaders' personal wealth.

SOCIAL STATUS

At the social level, reference to the landed aristocracy and to its relationship with the bourgeoisie loses much of its significance after the First World War. Not that the old order had entirely and suddenly disappeared. The trend was clearly under way from the late nineteenth century, and the whole process of amalgamation between the two classes continued in the inter-war years, with the aristocracy increasingly reduced to playing a minor part. Political rather than social factors were henceforth to affect the position of the business élites, though within the limits of their social status and economic power. The years between 1918 and 1945 were the most eventful in this respect.

There were few fundamental changes in Britain. Businessmen reinforced their position at the top of the social hierarchy. Not only did they remain the richest socio-professional group in the country, but commercial and industrial wealth gained in social prestige and political influence. The First World War accelerated the inexorable decline of the British aris-

---

[4] See *Forbes*, 18 July 1994.

tocracy which had begun a quarter of a century earlier, not least at the demographic level, as many of its members, particularly of the younger generation, were killed in action. The titled aristocracy, however, survived far better than the gentry, though the heyday of the Edwardian age had gone for ever.[5] Rather than being replaced by the upper middle classes, an essential component of which consisted of top businessmen and their families, the aristocracy merged even more into a new unified single British upper class, which struck many foreign observers. As the French sociologist Raymond Aron wrote in the 1950s:

Great Britain seems to me to be the best example of a country whose regime is Western but which still possess a ruling class: the higher echelons in the world of affairs, of the university, of the press, church and of politics find themselves in the same clubs; they often have family ties, they are aware of the community they constitute, they consist in a relatively defined way of the higher interests of England . . . These summits of different groups constitute a ruling class to the extent that the political class and the social elite overlap.[6]

The structure of the British upper class is by now fairly well documented, though more is known about the political than about the business élite.[7] The major change which started to take place in the 1920s was the gradual integration of top industrialists into the social élite. In the first place, British business became more centralized. Several large companies moved their head office to London or, especially in the new industries, settled from the start in the capital. Such major companies as BP, Courtaulds, GEC, GKN, ICI, Shell, Unilever, and Vickers have all had their head office in London since the 1920s. Top industrialists were now much closer to the country's social and political heart, including a residence in London or the Home Counties and membership of a London club. Another important factor of integration was the high proportion of public school-educated heads of industrial companies, which rose from 18 per cent in 1907 to 37 per cent in 1929, and stabilized thereafter. There is no doubt that the financial world remained more solidly entrenched in the Establishment. However, the demarcation was no longer between two monolithic blocks, finance and industry, but rather between finance (especially the 'big five' and the leading merchant banks) and a group of London-based major industrial companies on the one hand; and provincial industry together with the lower echelons of commerce and finance on the other.

The enhanced social status of British business is well reflected in the honours awarded to its members. There were more peers in the late 1920s

[5] See D. Cannadine, *The Decline and Fall of the British Aristocracy* (New Haven, 1990).
[6] R. Aron, 'Social Class, Political Class, Ruling Class', *European Journal of Sociology*, 1 (1960).
[7] See P. Stanworth and A. Giddens (eds.), *Elites and Power in British Society* (Cambridge, 1974); J. Scott, *The Upper Classes: Property and Privilege in Britain* (London, 1982). For the professional middle classes, see H. Perkin, *The Rise of Professional Society: England since 1880* (London, 1989).

and in the early 1950s than before the First World War: 31 per cent of the chairmen and managing directors of the leading companies in 1929, and 28 per cent in 1953, as against 18 per cent in 1907. Interestingly, only a small minority—five out of twenty-one in 1929—had inherited their title, including three sons of enobled businessmen (the 2nd Earl of Iveagh, chairman of Guinness, the 2nd Earl Bearsted, chairman of Shell, and the 2nd Viscount Hambleden, chairman of W. H. Smith). Members of the old aristocracy did not chair a single major industrial or financial company in 1929, though they had re-emerged in the banking world a quarter of a century later: by 1953 the 2nd Marquess of Linlithgow was chairman of the Midland Bank, the 3rd Earl of Selborne was chairman of the National Provincial Bank, and the 7th Baron Balfour of Burleigh was chairman of Lloyds Bank. As for the chairman of the Westminster Bank, Walter Durant Gibbs, partner in the old-established merchant bank Antony Gibbs & Sons, he was already the 4th Baron Aldenham.[8] Taken as a whole 70 per cent of the British business leaders active in 1929, and 76 per cent of those active in 1953, had at least a knighthood, the percentage of baronets falling dramatically from 13 to 2 per cent between 1929 and 1953.

This social advance of the British business élite took place at a time of continued British international dominance: the British empire remained, with the United States, one of the world's two great powers in the inter-war years.[9] The British business élite also shared in the huge prestige of victory in the Second World War. From an international angle, British business leaders were part of an imperial and world power's ruling élite. The same cannot be said of their French and German counterparts.

The changes which took place in France were of a different order. In many ways, the social complexion of the business élite was more modern in France before 1914. This was due to the early centralization of big business in Paris, to the weaker influence of the aristocracy, and paradoxically to the comparatively limited development of big business in France. The vast majority of French industrialists, and to a lesser extent bankers, belonged to the provincial middle classes. But the apex of the business community, however narrow, was more homogeneous than in Britain, with fewer regional differences and no clear divide between finance and industry; and as a whole it was more integrated into the upper classes. There was, however, much scope for a widening of the Paris-based financial and industrial *grande bourgeoisie* without altering the group's identity; this took place during the inter-war years by the addition of representatives of the new industries. The changes which occurred were thus attrib-

---

[8] Among the clearing banks, only Barclays had a practical banker as chairman: Anthony William Tuke, son of a former chairman and descendant of one of the founding families.

[9] See P. J. Cain and A. G. Hopkins, *British Imperialism: Crisis and Deconstruction 1914–1990* (London, 1993), who rightly underline the strength of Britain's position in the world between the wars.

utable to the economic and political situation rather than to any upheaval in the country's social structure. The prestige of French business, greatly enhanced by victory in the First World War and by industry's positive contribution to the war effort, was badly damaged during the depression of the 1930s. French business was held responsible for the country's alleged economic backwardness. French employers also suffered a severe blow during the first months of the Front Populaire. The strikes and factory occupations were a traumatic experience, followed by the signing of the Matignon agreements, perceived within their own ranks as a capitulation to the trade unions.[10]

Defeat and occupation were further blows, though of a different kind. The business élite remained part of the French upper classes, but for four years these were the upper classes of an occupied country. Business leaders, like all French people, had to put up with occupation, with all it entailed of dependency, oppression, and humiliation.[11] Hardship was of course unequally shared, and businessmen enjoyed privileges denied to most of their fellow-countrymen, from material comforts to being treated with some respect by the Germans. The issue of collaboration cannot be discussed here.[12] Suffice it to say that most sizeable French industrial companies did fulfil contracts for the Germans, though to a greater or lesser extent and with varying degrees of enthusiasm. Business pragmatism was the most common attitude, especially if orders were unlikely to come from any other source. Personal ambition and the prospects of high profits led some to be over-zealous; increasing doubts about the likelihood of a German victory caused many others to drag their feet after 1942, while a few businessmen joined the Resistance. The fact remains that French business was facing conditions akin to those prevailing in a colony. Some industries, especially iron and steel, were ruthlessly exploited, others managed to hold their own, taking advantage of market conditions or of a competitive edge. However, in all negotiations, German firms held the upper hand; and even when German and French businessmen could reach agreements on a practical basis, the German political authorities, in the first place the Ministry of Economics in Berlin, made sure that the defeated always knew their place.[13] The position of the French business élite reached its nadir at the Liberation, with the accusation of collaboration now added to that of economic failure. It was a vulnerability eloquently expressed in de Gaulle's (probably apocryphal) harsh words to a

---

[10] See G. Lefranc, *Histoire du Front Populaire (1934–1938)* (Paris, 1974); I. Kolboom, *La Revanche des patrons: Le Patronat français face au Front Populaire* (Paris, 1986).

[11] See P. Burrin, *La France à l'heure allemande 1940–1944* (Paris, 1995).

[12] See R. Vinen, *The Politics of French Business 1936–1945* (Cambridge, 1991); *Histoire, économie, société*, 3 (1992) (special issue on enterprises in Vichy France); R. de Rochebrune and J.-C. Hazera, *Les Patrons sous l'occupation* (Paris, 1995); Burrin, *La France à l'heure allemande*.

[13] Burrin, *La France à l'heure allemande*, 245.

delegation of senior businessmen: 'I haven't seen any of you gentlemen in London . . . Well, after all you are not in jail.'[14]

While change in Britain and France was a matter of widening the business group belonging to the social élite, in Germany it was still a tortuous process to reach full membership status. The fall of the Hohenzollern dynasty and the foundation of the Weimar Republic following defeat in the First World War undoubtedly enhanced the position of the business élite within the German upper classes. Although top businessmen belonged to the privileged classes of the old regime, they survived relatively unscathed the fall of the empire and the revolutionary threats of the early years of the Weimar Republic. Their prestige was less damaged by defeat than that of the military and the old aristocracy from which most of the higher-ranking officers were drawn. Moreover, the power base of the *Junkers* was weakened both politically and economically as a result of constitutional changes, a loss of influence on policy-making, and a decline in agricultural income compounded by a world-wide crisis of overproduction in the late 1920s. The aristocracy, to be sure, did not lose all its positions, in particular in the army and the state bureaucracy. Besides, the vast majority of big businessmen regretted the old social order, not out of political principles, but because it had guaranteed them social stability. Nevertheless, the business élite unquestionably reached the top of the social hierarchy: it was part, and considered itself to be part, of the *Obersicht*, the upper social stratum.

The Weimar Republic, however, was short-lived, and followed by a regime not naturally congenial to top businessmen. The leadership of the Nazi party was mostly composed of men drawn from the lower middle classes who had very little in common with the business élite. Hitler himself considered businessmen as 'shallow people who can't see beyond their petty affairs', and as 'rogues' and 'cold-blooded money grubbers'. And some Nazi leaders, like Goering or Goebbels, positively enjoyed establishing a new 'high society' to rival that of the traditional German upper classes.[15] The importance of a split between the social origins of the business and political élites should not be overestimated. Most often the interests and life-styles of the various élite groups converge at the top, as was for example the case during the Third Republic in France.[16] And as the Third Reich became more established, it increasingly recruited its leadership among the traditional German upper classes.[17] What matters is the

[14] Quoted in H. W. Ehrmann, *Organized Business in France* (Princeton, 1957), 104.

[15] R. Overy, *Goering: The 'Iron Man'* (London, 1984) , 34.

[16] 26% of all cabinet ministers between 1871 and 1914 came from a working-class or lower middle-class background, and 38% from the professional middle classes; J. Estèbe, *Les Ministres de la République, 1871–1914* (Paris, 1982), 20–1.

[17] See M. Kater, *The Nazi Party: A Social Profile of Members and Leaders, 1919–1945* (Oxford, 1983).

regime's ideological and political stance. Only revolutionary regimes endeavour to alter the established social structure. The Nazi regime was not anti-capitalist and never questioned the right to private property; large companies, such as the Vereinigte Stahlwerke and the big banks, were even returned to the private sector. However, its attacks on big business should not be entirely dismissed as demagogic. The Third Reich was a totalitarian regime; it had objectives of its own, independent from, and sometimes antagonistic to, big business, and it was prepared to resort to violence to implement them: the fear of concentration camps applied to business leaders.

The position of big business under the Third Reich was therefore somewhat ambiguous. Business leaders were not instrumental in Hitler's accession to power and would have preferred a more traditional form of authoritarian regime ruled by the bourgeois parties.[18] Yet they were among the regime's main beneficiaries, especially through the re-establishment of social order and economic revival brought about by rearmament. Social status is also a matter of political influence: most business leaders preserved their socio-economic privileges, but with the introduction of the Four Year Plan in 1936 (which accelerated rearmament and intensified autarchic policy), and even more so with the outbreak of war, they increasingly submitted to the Nazi apparatus and were reduced to political ineffectiveness.[19] In the end they could only follow the regime into its final catastrophe. A word must be added about Jewish businessmen. Nearly 20 per cent of German business leaders were Jewish (compared with less than 5 per cent in Britain).[20] Jews had always been strongly represented in the world of trade and finance, particularly in Berlin and Silesia, as well as in Frankfurt. They prospered during the golden age of the private firm and became full members of the German corporate élite, especially though by no means exclusively in the great universal banks. Jewish businessmen thus formed an integral part of the German business leadership, and their fate must be seen as part of the social history of the German business élite.

German business leaders ended the war in an even weaker position than their French counterparts. They had to endure the humiliation of defeat, including dismissals, mass incarcerations, and trials by the Allies. However, the beginning of the Cold War, the requirements of economic reconstruction, and networks of solidarity within the German business world ensured that, taken as a whole, the German business élite was

---

[18] See H. A. Turner, *German Big Business and the Rise of Hitler* (Oxford, 1985).

[19] This was in particular the case of the leaders of Germany's most powerful company during the Nazi era, IG Farben. See P. Hayes, *Industry and Ideology: IG Farben in the Nazi Era* (Cambridge, 1987).

[20] See W. Mosse, *Jews in the German Economy: The German-Jewish Economic Elite 1820–1935* (Oxford, 1987).

hardly affected by denazification.[21] Private property was respected: there was no long-term confiscation of shareholdings by the Allies. Even Alfried Krupp, sentenced to eight years' imprisonement by the Nuremberg trial in 1948, recovered all his property and regained control of his company after his early release in 1951. Continuity also prevailed in management. Hervé Joly has calculated that in 1949 more than a third of the executive board members of ten leading industrial companies held the same—or an equally senior—position as at the end of the war. They were more than half, however, if one takes into account natural factors of leadership renewal, such as death or retirement age; only a minority were excluded from senior managerial positions (though they were compensated by seats on supervisory boards) or had to settle for a less prominent role.[22]

However dramatic in the short term, political upheavals in France and Germany were only temporary set-backs in the long-term converging trends in the social status of the British, French, and German business élites. Since the 1950s they have stood more firmly at the very core of their country's respective upper classes. And with the loss of great power status by Great Britain and the recovery of Germany's position in the world, the 'international pecking order' of the three countries' ruling élites has become very close. National characteristics have persisted: the pre-eminence of the City establishment in Britain, the key position of senior state officials in the Paris-centred business community in France, and the federal provincialism of the leaders of large German corporations, with Düsseldorf becoming the main residential area by the early 1970s. But in the three countries the dominant position enjoyed, as a group, by the leaders of the largest corporations has prevailed over other possible internal cleavages.

BUSINESSMEN AND POLITICS

Not surprisingly, top businessmen's personal involvement in parliamentary politics waned with the advance of the twentieth century. The increased professional demands of business life, combined with the decline of Parliament as a decisive instrument of policy-making, accelerated a trend well under way before 1914. Parliament's attractions faded more slowly in Britain, where by the late 1920s a fifth of the chairmen and managing directors of the major companies were, or had been at some

---

[21] See V. Berghahn, *The Americanisation of West German Industry, 1945–1973* (Leamington Spa, 1986).

[22] H. Joly, 'L'Élite industrielle allemande: Métier, pouvoir et politiques 1933–1989', unpub. Ph.D. thesis (École des Hautes Études en Sciences Sociales, Paris, 1993), 341–7. The companies concerned were: AEG, Bosch, Daimler-Benz, GHH, IG Farben, Krupp, Mannesmann, RWE, Siemens, and Vereinigte Stahlwerke.

stage, members of Parliament. However, this impressive proportion hides the fact that most of them had their parliamentary career behind them. For some, such as William Frederick Danvers Smith, later Lord Hambleden, the chairman of W. H. Smith, or Alan Sykes, the chairman of the Bleachers' Association, it dated back to the Edwardian days. For several others, it ended in the early 1920s. The most prominent among them— Herbert Austin; Eric Geddes, chairman of Dunlop; Thomas Royden, chairman of Cunard; Alfred Mond, chairman of ICI; G. A. H. Wills, chairman of Imperial Tobacco; Owen Cosby Philipps, chairman of the Royal Mail Group—all left Parliament between 1922 and 1924. The reasons for these departures were diverse and included personal political failure and disenchantment. But it is significant that only 6 per cent of top businessmen were actually sitting in Parliament in the late 1920s, as against 16 per cent two decades earlier. They included a few *notables*, such as the brewing magnate John Gretton, chairman of Bass and Conservative MP for almost fifty years, from 1895 to 1943; he became Lord Gretton the following year. Another brewing magnate, Rupert Guinness, left Parliament in 1927, on succeeding his father as 2nd Earl of Iveagh. Isidore Salmon, chairman of J. Lyons & Co., the food manufacturers and caterers, and Walter Preston, chairman of Platt Brothers, the textile machinery-makers, were also MPs throughout the 1920s and 1930s. On the other hand, very few senior politicians moved to a leading position in the business world. The two major exceptions occurred in the financial sector with two chancellors of the exchequer, Reginald McKenna, who succeeded Edward Holden as chairman of the Midland Bank, and Robert Horne, chairman of the Commercial Union Assurance Company as well as, from 1934, the Great Western Railway Company.

The disaffection for Parliament was even stronger in France, where the only weighty presence was that of François de Wendel, the steel magnate, who was a deputy from 1914 to 1933 and then a senator until 1940. No senior politician moved to a top business position, although this was somewhat compensated by the *pantouflage* of the senior civil servants. In Germany, by contrast, there was a small increase in the presence of top businessmen in Parliament. The numbers are too small to bear any real significance. However, two industrialists of the very first rank, Carl-Friedrich von Siemens, chairman of Siemens & Halske and of Siemens Schuckertwerke, and Albert Vögler, managing director of Deutsch-Luxemburg and later of the Vereinigte Stahlwerke, sat in Parliament between 1920 and 1924. The banker Jacob Riesser, chairman of the Danat Bank supervisory board, and the lesser figure of Albert Zapf, his counterpart at Süddeutsche Zucker, were deputies throughout the 1920s. The occurrence of senior politicians moving to a top business position was as rare as in Britain and France. The opposite, however, happened when Wilhelm Cuno, managing director of the HAPAG shipping company, briefly became Reich Chancellor in 1922–3—as head of a 'government of experts'—before reverting to his business occupations: very few European business leaders ever reached such high office.

The following decades saw the final demise, even in Britain, of the business leader as member of Parliament. By the early 1950s not a single top French businessman was a deputy at the National Assembly; Ernest Carnot, chairman of the Viscose Française and well into his eighties, had held a parliamentary mandate in the closing years of the previous century. In Britain, Lords Iveagh, Rothermere, and Selborne, respectively chairmen of Guinness, Associated Newspapers, and the National Provincial Bank, had sat in the House of Commons in the 1920s and 1930s, before inheriting their peerage. Only one chairman of a major company was still involved in parliamentary politics after the Second World War. This was Oliver Lyttleton, chairman of Associated Electrical Industries (AEI) from 1945 to 1951, and again, this time as Lord Chandos, from 1954 to 1962, having been in between secretary of state for the colonies. Lyttleton, interestingly, does not fit into either the category of the businessman engaged in politics, or that of the politician turned businessman, being rather a mixture of the two. He did start his professional life in business, with Brown Shipley, the merchant bankers, moving shortly afterwards to the British Metal Corporation, where he was in regular contact with Whitehall. He held various important ministerial posts during the war, including president of the Board of Trade in 1940–1, minister of state in the Middle East in 1941–2, and minister of production between 1942 and 1945, the last two with a seat in the war cabinet. His ambivalence is well reflected by the fact that he accepted the post of secretary of state for the colonies in 1951 out of personal loyalty to Churchill and only for a limited period, before returning three years later to the business world.[23]

Ironically, by the early 1950s there were more leading businessmen in Parliament in Germany than in Britain or France. Moreover, they perfectly conformed to the ideal of the *notable* of the *belle époque*. One was Robert Pferdmenges, senior partner in the Cologne private bank Sal. Oppenheim Jr. & Cie, supervisory board chairman of Thyssen, Demag, and Concordia, the insurance company, and supervisory board member of a number of major companies, including AEG, Harpener, and Klöckner; he was a founder-member of the CDU in the Rhineland, an adviser and friend of Conrad Adenauer, and deputy at the Bundestag from 1949 to 1962. Another was Gunther Henle, Peter Klöckner's son-in-law, who started his career in the diplomatic service before becoming a partner in Klöckner & Co. and later supervisory board chairman of Klöckner-Humboldt-Deutz, the engineering group. Politicians kept away from top business positions.

[23] See R. P. T. Davenport-Hines, 'Lyttelton, Oliver, 1st Viscount Chandos (1893–1972), Metal Dealer and Electrical Manufacturer', in D. Jeremy (ed.), *Dictionary of Business Biography*, 5 vols. (London, 1984–6), vol. iii.

As a result of the co-determination in the coal and steel industries instituted in 1951, trade union leaders, some of them SPD members of the Reichstag, sat on these companies' supervisory boards, though they did not chair them. One exception was Heinrich Deist, a lawyer and former civil servant who left in 1933 and worked as an independent accountant. An acknowledged expert in the iron and steel industries, he was a member of the Steel Trusteeship which was in charge of the demerger of the huge concerns formed in the 1920s, most importantly the Vereinigte Stahlwerke. Deist was supervisory board chairman of the Bochumer Verein and SPD member of the Reichstag.

The First World War strengthened business interest groups, especially peak associations, as businessmen worked more closely with governments to face the imperatives of the war economy. This produced a striking parallelism between the three countries. In Germany the two existing rival associations, the Central Verband Deutscher Industrieller (CVDI), dominated by heavy industry, and the Bund Deutscher Industrieller (BDI), dominated by light industry, merged in 1919 to form the Reichsverband der Deutschen Industrie (RDI).[24] Elsewhere, such a peak organization had yet to be created. In Britain the initiative came from a group of industrialists led by Dudley Docker, chairman of the Metropolitan Carriage Wagon & Finance Co.: they founded in 1916 the Federation of British Industries (FBI) to express the views of the industrial business community.[25] In France the initiative came from the state: in 1919 the minister for commerce, Étienne Clémentel, encouraged the formation of the Confédération Générale de la Production Française (CGPF) in an attempt to maintain the degree of organization of French industry established during the war.[26]

The changes, however, were more apparent than real, and many of the pre-war features persisted into the 1920s, especially as far as the balance of power within the business world was concerned. In Germany there was a division of labour between questions of trade and economic policy, handled by the RDI, and questions of labour and social policy, which were the domain of another peak organization, the VDA (Vereinigung der Deutschen Arbeitgeberverbände, or Confederation of German Employers' Associations); this division, however, was of less moment than in Britain, and much overlap existed between the two organizations. More

[24] See F. Zunkel, 'Die Gewichtung der Industriegruppen bei der Etablierung des Reichsverbandes der Deutschen Industrie', in H. Mommsen, D. Petzina, and B. Weisbrod (eds.), *Industrielles System und politische Entwicklung in der Weimarer Republik* (Düsseldorf, 1974).

[25] See J. Turner, 'The Politics of "Organized Business" in the First World War', in J. Turner (ed.), *Businessmen and Politics* (London, 1984); R. P. T. Davenport-Hines, *Dudley Docker: The Life and Times of a Trade Warrior* (Cambridge, 1984).

[26] See G. Lefranc, *Les Organisations patronales en France* (Paris, 1976); R. Kuisel, *Capitalism and the State in Modern France* (Cambridge, 1981).

importantly, heavy industry was able to maintain much of its dominance over German business, despite the merger of the CVDI and the BDI and despite its diminished contribution to German industrial output. Heavy industrialists were even in a minority in the RDI, and the election of Carl Duisberg, IG Farben's supervisory board chairman, as president in 1925 has often been seen as reflecting a shift of balance within German industry. However, the division between heavy and light industry was to a large extent a division between large and small and medium-sized companies, and Duisberg was the chairman of Germany's largest company; moreover, he was succeeded by Gustav Krupp von Bohlen in 1931. In any case, heavy industry was able to use fully its own interest groups which could, if necessary, counterbalance the influence of the RDI.[27] The Langnamverein in particular, where its dominance was unquestioned, became a regional stronghold from which the newly formed central organization could be challenged; and the network of associations established in the last quarter of the nineteenth century (the VDESI, especially its northwestern branch, the Mining Association, etc.)[28] continued to operate efficiently. Furthermore, the Ruhr industrialists had the advantage of leading giant firms and of enjoying personal prestige and direct access to political power.

Heavy industry also remained strongly organized and highly influential in France, both outside and within the newly formed CGPF. The CGPF's first president was Henry Darcy, chairman of the iron and steel concern Châtillon-Commentry & Neuves-Maisons; and as in the RDI in Germany, he was succeeded in 1929 by a chemist, René Duchemin, vice-chairman of the Établissements Kuhlmann. However, the CGPF was a weak organization, mostly dependent for both its finance and functioning on outside business interest groups, above all the UIMM (Union des Industries Métallurgiques et Minières), the employers' organization for the mining, metal, machinery, electrical, and other industries, and its powerful subsidiary for the Paris region, the GIMMCP. Although it had to accommodate representatives of the rising new industries, the UIMM remained closely linked to the Comité des Forges, the ironmasters' pressure group, with which it shared its headquarters and senior officials. The CGPF was in fact controlled by the Paris-based grand patronat, and, though recognized by the authorities as the representative of French business, it was not perceived as such by the French business community at large, especially by the small and medium-sized provincial companies, and thus suffered from a lack of legitimacy. Following the signature of the Matignon accords in 1936, and the accusation of betrayal against big busi-

[27] See B. Weisbrod, 'Economic Power and Political Stability: Heavy Industry in Weimar Germany', Social History, 4 (1979), and id. Schwerindustrie in der Weimarer Republik (Wuppertal, 1978).
[28] See above, Ch. 8.

ness,[29] the CGPF underwent a number of reforms designed to extend the representation of small business, though it remained firmly controlled by big business. Its name was changed to Confédération Générale du *Patronat* (instead of *Production*) Français; this did not require it to change its acronym, which remained CGPF.

In Britain the roots of the slower development of trade— though not of employers'—organizations before 1914 (absence of an all-dominant heavy industry and prevalence of free trade) were not removed by the initiatives taken during and immediately after the First World War. The FBI, like its German and French counterparts, was in the hands of big business, but it suffered from two weaknesses which prevented it from playing a major role in British politics.[30] The first was the division of its membership over the tariff reform issue. Despite the commitment of its founders to tariff protection, and more generally to a regeneration of British industry,[31] any initiative on this matter carried the risk of splitting the organization, and thus paralysed its action until the issue ceased to be controversial in 1931. The second weakness was the existence of another, and in many respects more powerful, central organization: the National Confederation of Employers' Organizations (NCEO), which later changed its name to British Employers' Confederation (BEC). The NCEO was founded in 1919 under the aegis of the Engineering Employers' Federation and its leader Allan Smith, mostly out of a power struggle with the FBI's leaders. However, it was able to deny the FBI any role in matters of labour relations and social policy, thus further restricting the latter's area of activities.

With the advent of Nazism, the RDI had to dissolve itself in 1933 and was merged with the VDA into the Reichstand der Deutschen Industrie, an organization more in accordance with the goals of the Third Reich. The reformed and renamed CGPF was short-lived. It was dissolved, together with the Comité des Forges and the Comité des Houillères, by the Vichy government, and integrated into the 'comités d'organisation', intended to be a first step towards a corporatist reform of the economy; in fact they reproduced the old associations and were used as instruments for organizing the rationing of raw material and collaboration with Germany. New peak organizations were created after the war: the Conseil National du Patronat Français (CNPF) in France, and the Bundesverband der Deutschen Industrie (BDI) in Germany. The FBI, unlike its counterparts in Germany and France, did not have to be rebuilt after the war; on the

---

[29] The employers' delegates, all representatives of the *grand patronat*, had accepted collective contracts, union recognition, and wage increases. See Kolboom, *La Revanche des patrons*; Vinen, *The Politics of French Business*.

[30] See S. Blank, *Industry and Government in Britain: The Federation of British Industries in Politics, 1945–1965* (Lexington, Mass., 1973).

[31] See Davenport-Hines, *Dudley Docker*.

contrary, it grew in stature through its involvment in the war effort. In 1965 it merged with the CBE and the less important NUM (National Union of Manufacturers), and changed its name to CBI (Confederation of British Industry). Despite differences in organization, the FBI/CBI, CNPF, and BDI have been much closer than their pre-war predecessors, whether in their governing structure (with policy being made by the president and his official advisers, the professional staff and the committees), or in their relationship with the state (with much closer collaboration and integration of interest groups to the decision-making process).[32] All three groups have represented the business community as a whole (including small and medium-sized companies), though big business inevitably held a commanding position. Moreover, in all three countries, big business has become more homogeneous, with the leaders of the largest companies, rather than those of a particular industry, representing the dominant force: the weakened position of the heavy industries in Germany and France obviously contributed to this outcome.

The growth of pressure groups led to, and was made possible by, a high level of professionalization, and more precisely by the increased power held by senior officials acting on behalf of businessmen. In Germany, as early as the 1890s, the CVDI's *Geschäftsbüro* (the administrative office) became increasingly independent from the other organs of the association (its council and board of directors). In particular the secretary-general became solely responsible for the appointment of salaried employees, whose number rose from five to twenty-two between 1891 and 1922; the administrative office also became financially independent, including in its use of the Association's press and electoral funds.[33] Senior officials grew in importance. Robert Pinot's strong personality, coupled with his position as arbiter between rival French ironmasters, reinforced his ascendancy over the Comité des Forges, and he tended to perceive himself as its embodiment. Pinot's background was outside the business world. The son of an artillery officer and *polytechnicien*, he himself failed the entrance examination for the École Polytechnique; he was admitted to the École des Mines, but had to leave following his father's death, and continued to study law with a part-time job.[34] In Britain the central figure in the employers' movement from the First World War to the 1930s was Allan

[32] See Blank, *Industry and Government in Britain*; G. Brauenthal, *The Federation of German Industry in Politics* (Ithaca, NY, 1965); B. Brizay, *Le Patronat: Histoire, structure et stratégie du CNPF* (Paris, 1975); H. Weber, *Le Parti des patrons: Le CNPF (1946–1986)* (Paris, 1986); S. Berger, *Organizing Interests in Western Europe: Pluralism, Corporatism and the Transformation of Politics* (Cambridge, 1981).

[33] See H. Kaelble, *Industrielle Interessenpolitik in der wilhelminischen Gesellschaft* (Berlin, 1967), 9–21.

[34] See M. Rust, 'Business and Politics in the Third Republic: The Comité des Forges and the French Steel Industry, 1896–1914', unpub. Ph.D. thesis (Princeton University, 1973).

Smith. He started his career as a solicitor before becoming secretary of the Engineering Employers' Federation, and in 1916 chairman of its management committee, with executive responsibility for almost every aspect of the Federation's activities. He also played a leading role in the foundation of the NCEO, and was its first chairman between 1919 and 1922, and then an ex-officio member of its executive council.[35] The general managers of the RDI always came from the civil service. Hermann Bücher, who held the position between 1910 and 1925, had been in the administration of Cameroon until 1914; from 1915 to 1918 he was the German representative at the Turkish trade ministry, and after the Revolution he went back to the Auswärtiges Amt.[36] His successor, Ludwig Kastl, had been in the colonial administration of German South West Africa, and in 1921 was appointed to a post as Ministerialrat in the Reich Finance Ministry. The first director of the FBI from 1916 to 1932, Roland Nugent, was head of the Foreign Office's Foreign Trade Department when he was recruited for the post by Dudley Docker.

What was then the role of business leaders themselves? They obviously had to delegate the technical side of defending their interests to professional 'agents', and there has not been much difference in this respect between the three countries. How much of the 'political' side was delegated is more difficult to assess, but leading businessmen have on the whole remained in charge of their own affairs. The FBI's presidents devoted about half their working time to the job. And though influenced by the professional staff, in particular the director-general, they were not often led by the staff.[37] Friction could nevertheless arise, as for example between François de Wendel, the president of the Comité des Forges, and Robert Pinot, its secretary-general. Pinot was highly appreciated by his employers, especially for his commitment and his efficiency, though de Wendel was critical of his habit of always pushing himself forward and acting as if he had done everything. When Pinot expressed the wish to become vice-president in 1921, de Wendel was at first reluctant; he then agreed without much enthusiasm, making it clear that he would only be fifth vice-president and that in no way could he ever become president.[38] The need to discuss between themselves the major economic and political issues affecting them was felt by the leading Ruhr industrialists. On the initiative of Paul Reusch, managing director of the Gutehoffnungsshütte, they set up in 1927 the Ruhrlade, a secret organization which held monthly meetings attended by only twelve personally appointed members. Given their prominence, the really imporant political decisions

[35] See E. Wigham, *The Power to Manage: A History of the Engineering Employers' Federation* (London, 1973).

[36] H. James, *The German Slump: Politics and Economics 1924–1936* (Oxford, 1986), 175.

[37] Blank, *Industry and Government in Britain*, 53–4.

[38] J.-N. Jeanneney, *François de Wendel en République* (Paris, 1976), 137–40.

concerning the industry were taken by this 'secret cabinet', and were then passed to the official associations.[39]

The personal factor has remained an essential link in the relationship between business and politics. The chairmen of the largest companies have enjoyed increasing personal influence—through their dominating position in the peak associations, the consultative committees on which they are regularly invited to sit, and their sometimes direct access to political power. Interestingly, throughout the century British, French, and German business leaders have presented a very similar political profile. Notwithstanding pragmatism and adaptabililty, which have always been the hallmark of businessmen's political attitudes, their views have been broadly convergent in matters of party politics, state intervention, industrial relations, social policies, and others; while divergences have split each country's business community along parallel lines. A relationship, however, is a two-way process: the attitude of the state towards big business and the long-term effects of state intervention await their comparative historian.

[39] See H. A. Turner, 'The *Ruhrlade*, Secret Cabinet of Heavy Industry in the Weimar Republic', *Central European History*, 3 (1970).

Conclusion

Comparing countries often means ranking them in an implicit or explicit pecking order. Comparative economic and business history has been prone to using this approach, as exemplified by the work of two of its leading practitioners, David Landes and Alfred Chandler,[1] and carried on down the line in systematic or casual comparisons. According to conventional wisdom, Germany has been the hero of European business since the late nineteenth century, Britain the villain. Large, integrated plants using state-of-the-art technology have been contrasted with an atomistic industrial structure and outdated methods of production; professionally trained managers with 'practical men' and gentlemanly amateurs; long-term industrial finance with speculative manias; and so on. Such clichés might appear caricatures, but they hardly exaggerate the stigma of entrepreneurial failure attached to British businessmen. Dissenting views have remained the exception. Until the 1960s France was portrayed as the most backward of the three, but this view has been rejected by the revisionist school. Since then, France has often been left out of international comparisons, losing with her backwardness some of her appeal to foreign, especially American, business historians and analysts.[2]

The picture emerging from this book is different. It reflects a clear British advance well into the 1950s, and European convergence thereafter. Consider first the large companies. Far from being the laggard, Britain has been in the forefront of their development, not merely since 1945 as is usually assumed, but since the very beginning of the century. The margin separating Britain from France and Germany was sometimes substantial, especially from the 1920s to the 1950s, as becomes apparent when directly comparing the leading firms in each industry. Big business was also more diversified in Britain; from an early stage, it had spread to all sectors and branches while still remaining overwhelmingly dominated by banking and heavy industry in France and Germany. A higher level of industrial concentration and foreign direct investment played a part in the rise of big business in Britain, though this should not be exaggerated. Available

---

[1] D. Landes, *The Unbound Prometheus: Technological Change and Industrial Development in Western Europe from 1750 to the Present* (Cambridge, 1969); A. Chandler, *Scale and Scope: The Dynamics of Industrial Capitalism* (Cambridge, Mass., 1990).

[2] France has unfortunately been left out of the two most influential recent comparative analyses of the relationships between business organization and economic performance: Chandler, *Scale and Scope*, and M. Porter, *The Competitive Advantage of Nations* (London, 1990).

figures are surrounded by a high degree of uncertainty. Aggregate figures of business concentration conceal significant sectoral differences. The same is true of foreign direct investment, and multinational expansion was a characteristic of large firms in all three countries. The position of France also has to be revised, though less radically: French firms tended to be smaller than their British and German counterparts, but on the whole French big business has been closer to the German model than is often assumed. What set Germany apart was the early existence of a handful of giant industrial companies, far larger than any British or French firm; but they were the exception, not the rule. Finally, a clear convergence between the three countries has taken place in the last third of this century, as far as both the number of large firms and their sectoral distribution are concerned, though Britain has remained unusual in having an above-average number of large firms.

Of course, big business is only a part—and in our definition a small part—of the business world. Nor has it necessarily been representative of the industries in which a country has enjoyed a competitive advantage. Few of the firms contributing to the City of London's pre-eminent international role or to the strength of Gemany's machine-tools industry would qualify for big business status. Small and medium-sized enterprises have recently been rehabilitated and their contribution to economic development rediscovered. Germany's economic strength has often been seen as resting on her *Mittelstand*, her medium-sized family firms excelling in occupying niches in high-quality products; while many have noticed that Britain's comparatively poor economic performance in the 1970s coincided with the country's highest level of industrial concentration. To relativize the importance of large companies, however, is not to deny their importance. The strong development of British big business is an unmistakable sign of managerial success. Alfred Sloan, the legendary head of General Motors in the inter-war years, asserted that 'the size of a competitive enterprise is the outcome of its competitive performance'.[3] And in the Chandlerian approach, the size of a company is used as a proxy for the depth of its managerial hierarchy. Size, however, is no guarantee of success. The huge conglomerates produced by the merger frenzy of the last three decades have often proved disappointing in terms of both performance and innovative capacity, especially when compared to more flexible small and medium-sized firms. Countless large companies have declined, or even disappeared—victims of a slump, a declining sector, poor management, or falling prey to an ambitious and more enterprising competitor.

Other measures, however, confirm the strong performance of British big

---

[3] A. P. Sloan, *My Years with General Motors* (New York, 1963), p. xxvi.

business. British companies have consistently generated higher profits than their French and German counterparts, and they have achieved higher rates of return on their shareholders' equity—though huge differences between sectors and individual companies are obviously concealed by these general trends. One of the reasons for the overall higher profitability of British big business was its diversity, the fact that expanding sectors could compensate for declining ones. However, high profits have not been achieved at the expense of long-term development. By and large, the leading British companies survived longer and in greater numbers than their French and German competitors. They also grew faster until the 1950s, before being caught up in the following decades. The major weaknesses in the performance of British big business have been a slower growth rate in a few sectors and, especially, a few spectacular failures with no real equivalent in the other two countries. The motor car industry is the most striking case, embodying as it were British industrial decline. French companies have tended to be more profitable than their German counterparts, with the exception of the pre-1914 years and the early 1970s. They also performed better in terms of longevity, though the lower rate of survival of German companies was to a great extent the result of defeat in two world wars.

Britain's lead was also perceptible at the socio-political level. Integration into the upper classes has sometimes been interpreted as a sign of entrepreneurial decline: buying an estate, marrying into the aristocracy, moving into high society have all been seen as a diversion from business purposes. Yet there is no evidence that this dampened energies and led to complacency in the business class as a whole where a sufficient pool of talent was available to replace individual defections. Social status should rather be seen as an undeniable mark of success, a social recognition of business values. Britain scored highly in this respect; and so did France, with her modern, unified business élite. Despite all the talk about 'feudalization', German businessmen were in fact less integrated into the upper classes than their British and French counterparts before 1914. In the first half of the century, top British businessmen also enjoyed the prestige of belonging to the élite of a world power. 'Gentlemanly capitalists' were a highly successful business group throughout the century, not some outmoded survival of a pre-industrial ethos. Whether they have been more or less efficient in implementing their objectives than big business leaders in France and Germany is hard to tell. The intricacies of domestic policy do not easily lend themselves to international comparisons. There is no doubt that in all three countries, despite occasional set-backs and necessary compromises, big business has managed to get its way. The fact remains that the British business élite was spared many of the upsets suffered by its French and German counterparts in the

1930s and 1940s. Here again, convergence has been the dominant feature since the 1950s: in all three countries, business leaders have become the dominant force at the top of the social hierarchy.

From a European perspective, British success, rather than British failure, thus requires explanation. But should this success appear so surprising? Until the 1960s, Britain was a larger economy than France and Germany, with a higher per capita income. It was an older industrial nation, with more firmly established business traditions and wider opportunities for big business operations, deriving from the possession of an immense colonial empire and the international role of the City of London. The faster growth of the German economy and of some sectors of German industry in the three decades preceding the First World War were not enough to fill the gap—a gap which was to widen again in the following three decades marked by two world wars and the most severe depression of the twentieth century.

The success of British big business is more difficult to conciliate with Britain's economic performance after the Second World War, with growth rates much lower than in France and Germany until the 1980s, before they levelled off in all three countries. The relationship between business performance and economic performance is hard to establish. In a European comparative perspective, British large firms have performed better than the British economy as a whole, and this might well have been due to their multinational expansion which enabled them to take advantage of producing in faster-growing economies.[4] Another explanation, however, is that the notion of British decline has been vastly exaggerated. Britain's disappointing—in comparison to her Western European neighbours—economic performance after the Second World War is best explained by theories of economic growth emphasizing the effects of catching up with the leader, and the convergence between industrialized countries, rather than by all the shortcomings which have successively or simultaneously been invoked. Britain was overtaken by France and Germany in the 1960s, and has in turn benefited from the catching-up effects since the 1980s.[5] Differences, however, have been minimal. On the basis of a simple indicator giving an overall measure of economic performance (GDP per head), West Germany ranked seventh in the world in 1989, France ninth, and Britain twelfth, with a difference of 3.9 per cent between the seventh and the twelfth.[6] It is true that by the 1980s productivity in British manufac-

---

[4] See G. Jones, 'British Multinationals and British "Management Failure": Some Long-Run Perspectives', University of Reading, Discussion Papers in International and Investment and Business Studies, Series B, vol. vi, No. 175.

[5] See in particular C. Feinstein, 'Success and Failure: British Economic Growth since 1948', and B. Supple, 'British Economic Decline since 1945', both in R. Floud and D. McCloskey (eds.), *The Economic History of Britain since 1700*, 3 vols. (2nd edn. Cambridge, 1994), iii. 95–122 and 318–46.

[6] Calculated from A. Maddison, *Dynamic Forces in Capitalist Development* (Oxford, 1991), 6–7.

turing industry had fallen behind French and German levels by a margin of 30 to 40 per cent before starting to catch up; but this was compensated by higher productivity in services, which explains the narrow differences in the economy as a whole.[7] The convergence observable in European big business since the 1960s thus reflects the overall convergence which has taken place at the macro-economic level.

The object of this book is not to offer a new European business ranking headed by Britain rather than by Germany (which would be far-fetched and of limited historical interest) or even to rehabilitate British big business in the twentieth century. A European comparison raises the broader issue of the impact of national characteristics of business leadership. The three countries displayed both strong similarities and sharp contrasts. The differences, however, had but little effect on each country's overall business performance. The persistence of 'family capitalism' within the large corporation was a common feature of European big business well into the century. Interestingly, French rather than German large companies had the lowest percentage of inheritors among their chairmen and chief executives before the Second World War. In any case, it has by now been firmly established that the survival of family ownership and control had little impact on business performance. French top businessmen have also consistently received the highest level of education, though the type of education they received has often been derided as being too abstract and ill-adapted to the business world. Such arguments are appealing in theory but unfounded in practice. The German educational system was not better suited to the demands of managerial careers, with its churning out of pure science and law degrees. Not surprisingly, the percentage of university-educated British top businessmen was lower than in France and Germany, especially in the first half of the century, though this does not seem to have affected their companies' performance. On the other hand, a business-oriented type of education has featured more commonly among British businessmen (above all through accountancy training) in the last three decades. The link between the formal education of top businessmen and the performance of their companies is extremely difficult to establish. General rather than specific education has tended to be favoured at the highest level, including in Germany. This is not surprising if one considers the education of top businessmen in the context of the education of their respective country's élites.

Modern career patterns, consisting of a series of rungs leading to the very top, have appeared earlier in Germany. This does not mean, however, that top German businessmen were more 'professional' than their British or French counterparts. In the first part of the century, the two-tier board facilitated access to the board of directors for full-time salaried executives,

[7] See N. Crafts, *Can Deindustrialisation Seriously Damage your Wealth* (London, 1993); S. Broadberry, 'Manufacturing and the Convergence Hypothesis: What the Long-Run Data Show', *Journal of Economic History*, 53/4 (1993).

who would have had to be content with a senior managerial (though non-directorial) position in France and Britain. At the very top, however, things were not so different: in all three countries the chairmen and managing directors of the largest companies came from a broadly similar socio-professional background and were equally committed to their jobs. Despite convergence since the 1950s, France has remained the odd one out with its high proportion of top businessmen recruited from the senior civil service, though this should not be seen as the all-embracing explanation of the *mal français*. The structure of the firm also displayed strong similarities in the three countries, and in this respect Germany was closer to Britain and France than to the USA. The multidivisional structure—adopted by the leading sectors of American big business from the 1920s—remained exceptional in Europe before the Second World War. There is no empirical evidence that managerial hierarchies were more extensive in German companies. And although the proportion of vertically integrated firms was higher in Germany before 1914, most of them were in coal, iron, and steel. As for the relationships between finance and industry, often considered as a key difference between Britain and Germany (with France in between), their effect on business performance has been limited: the provision of funds to industry has been adequate in all three countries, especially for large companies, while the entrepreneurial leadership, let alone the control, attributed to German banks has proved vastly exaggerated in the twentieth century. If anything, finance has always weighed more heavily in the British than in the French or German economy.

Rather than uncovering the superiority of one model of business organization, the historical perspective reveals that each country had areas and periods of strengths and weaknesses, that the order of ranking occasionally changed, but that convergence has been the dominant feature. How far convergence has proceeded, however, cannot be determined on the simple basis of accumulated evidence. Comparative historians will always be torn between the conflicting temptations of lumping or splitting. There is a strong case for lumping. Convergence has taken place in most aspects of big business: in the number and sectoral distribution of large companies; in the educational levels of business leaders and the professionalization of business careers; in the social integration of business élites and the form and content of their political intervention. Some have even talked of a European 'model', in contrast to the American or Japanese ones, emphasizing the smaller size of the European firms compared to their American counterparts, the persistence of family ownership, the strength of the trade unions, the size of the state-owned sector.[8] And Europe as a whole has recently been seized with worries about loss of competitiveness and the rise of newly industrialized countries. Conver-

---

[8] See H. Kaelble, *A Social History of Western Europe, 1880–1980* (Dublin, 1989).

gence, however, does not mean uniformity. Each country has retained distinctive features inherited from its own historical experience—from a different legal and institutional framework to the prominence of specific business groups. Furthermore, comparisons with non-European countries have led to splitting as much as to lumping. The rise of German big business in the late nineteenth and early twentieth centuries has been described as more akin to the American model of 'managerial' capitalism than to the more 'personal' form of capitalism prevailing in Britain and France;[9] while more recently, attention has been exercised by the contrast between the 'Anglo-Saxon' and the 'Rhine-Alpine' models of capitalism, with Britain this time much closer to America, Germany to Japan, and France once again in between.[10]

National comparisons have their limitations. They cannot take full account of other, equally important dimensions of business activity, such as the regional where, as shown by Michael Porter, competitive industries tend to be clustered; or the international where multinational companies can transcend national constraints. Above all, they risk overlooking the basic determinants of business performance, which lie within the firm itself and ultimately are unique to each successful company. On the other hand, national institutional environments do matter. Competition between nations has increasingly been taking place at the economic and business levels, which are seen as playing a decisive part in a country's 'success' or 'failure'. Striking the right balance between the nation and the firm is not simple. This book has not provided new answers to the question of how big business has contributed to the economic development of Britain, France, and Germany in the twentieth century, nor has it offered new keys to understanding the long-term performance of the most successful European companies and the failure of others. But if its comparative approach has illuminated the national historical context in which such questions are and will continue to be investigated, it will help to ensure that the wrong questions are no longer addressed.

[9] Chandler, *Scale and Scope*; J. Kocka, 'The Rise of the Modern Industrial Enterprise in Germany', in A. D. Chandler and H. Daems (eds.), *Managerial Hierarchies* (Cambridge, Mass., 1980).
[10] See M. Albert, *Capitalisme contre capitalisme* (Paris, 1991).

APPENDIX

List of Companies Included in the Samples: 1907, 1929, and 1953

This appendix provides a list of the companies included in the samples established for the analysis of business performance and business leadership for the years 1907 (1910 for France),[1] 1929, and 1953. Companies marked with an asterisk have not been included in the analysis of profits. The tables which follow do not pretend to be new lists of the 50 or 100 largest British, French, and German companies. Such rankings, based on a variety of criteria, are available in several other studies (see introduction to Part I). Combining the criteria of share capital and workforce, the samples have been established in order to ensure, first, that all top companies were included; secondly, that all sectors were represented; and thirdly that the specific composition of each country's big business was reflected. In order to make comparisons easier, figures related to share capital and total assets are given in pounds sterling for all three countries. Two levels of classification have been adopted: the first distinguishes between industry (including extractive industries), finance, and services; and the second between broadly defined industries within each of these three sectors. The bulk of the data has been collected in the *Stock Exchange Yearbook* for Britain, the *Cote Desfossé* for France, and the *Handbuch der deutschen Aktiengesellschaften* for Germany. Company monographs and existing lists of each country's largest companies have also been useful for estimates of workforce—especially David Jeremy's 'The Hundred Largest Employers in the United Kingdom, in Manufacturing and Non-manufacturing Industries, in 1907, 1935, and 1955' (*Business History*, 33 (1991)), which has been systematically used for the workforce of Britain's major companies. The main objective of this appendix is to bring together, in a readily comparable format, data scattered in numerous publications of three different countries. Such data are readily available in the business magazine *Fortune* for the years 1972 and 1989 and do not need to be reproduced here.[2]

---

[1] Profits and profitability of the companies included in the 1907 sample have been calculated for the years 1911–13 in order to include French companies, for which systematic data are only available from 1910–11 onwards.

[2] See *Fortune*, Sept. 1973 and 30 July 1990. For the purpose of this study, the performances of all companies with a turnover of $400 million or more, and the leaders of the 35 top British and the 30 top French and German companies, have been considered for 1972. The performances of all companies with a turnover of $2.5 billion or more, and the leaders of the 33 top British, French, and German companies, have been considered for 1989.

A1. Great Britain, 1907

	Share capital	Total assets	Workforce	Chairman
I. Industry				
Heavy industry				
Vickers, Sons & Maxim	5,200	8,881	22,500	T. E. Vickers
Bolckow Vaughan	3,963	5,027	18,000	E. W. Richards
Sir W. G. Armstrong Whitworth & Co.	3,594	7,994	25,000	Sir A. Noble
Guest, Keen & Nettlefolds	2,685	6,218	21,710	A. Keen
John Brown & Co.	2,640	3,940	16,205	Sir C. B. McLaren
Wigan Coal & Iron	2,193	2,144	10,000	Earl of Crawford
United Collieries	1,800	3,562	16,000	H. Mungall
Stewarts & Lloyds	1,400	2,422	10,600	J. C. Stewart
Dorman Long & Co.	1,260	2,213	9,500	A. J. Dorman
Palmers Shipbuilding	699	1,261	7,500	Sir C. B. McLaren
*Fife Coal Co.	831		12,947	C. Carlow
*Harland & Wolff			8,500	Lord Pirrie
Textile				
Coats (J. & P.)	10,000	19,085	12,700	A. Coats
Calico Printers' Association	5,027	12,291	20,495	R. P. Hewitt
Bleachers' Association	4,570	7,816	11,280	H. S. Cross
Fine Cotton Spinners & Doublers' Association	4,500	9,191	30,000	Sir W. H. Houldsworth
Rylands & Sons	1,500	4,287	8,000	W. Carnelley
Food, drink, tobacco				
Imperial Tobacco	15,495	21,297	6,000	Lord Winterstoke
Watney, Combe, Reid	6,322	12,679		H. C. O. Bonsor
Arthur Guinness, Son & Co.	4,500	8,845	3,550	Lord Iveagh

A1. Continued

	Share capital	Total assets	Workforce	Chairman
Bass, Ratcliff & Gretton	2,720	6,543	4,000	Lord Burton
*Fry, J. S. & Sons	800		4,600	J. S. Fry
Chemicals				
United Alkali	5,819	9,981	12,000	J. Brock
Lever Brothers	3,400	5,141	4,700	W. H. Lever
Brunner Mond & Co.	2,299	4,260	4,000	Sir J. T. Brunner
*Reckitt & Sons	1,640			F. Reckitt
Kynoch	1,000	1,621	8,000	A. Chamberlain
Electrical engineering				
British Westinghouse	3,250		5,000	G. Westinghouse
General Electric Co.	596	1,189	6,000	G. Byng
Mechanical engineering				
Metropolitan Amalgamated	1,433	1,729	13,368	F. D. Docker
Howard & Bullough	1,000	1,712	5,000	Sir G. Bullough
Oil				
Shell Transport & Trading	3,000	4,257		Sir M. Samuel
Burmah Oil	1,850	3,363		J. T. Cargill
Rubber				
Dunlop Pneumatic Tyres	2,120	2,901	4,000	H. Du Cros
II. *Finance*				
Banking				
Lloyds Bank	3,852	76,132	2,880	J. S. Phillips
London City and Midland Bank	3,143	63,985	5,000[a]	A. Keen

Company				
Barclay & Co.	3,100	50,515		F. A. Bevan
National Provincial Bank of England	3,000	60,975		H. Goschen
London & County Banking Co.	2,000	53,998		G. J. Goschen
Insurance				
*Prudential Assurance	1,000	63,887		Sir H. Harben
*Royal Insurance Co.	392	14,647		W. Watson
*Commercial Union Assurance Co.	250	12,659		J. Trotter
III. *Services*				
Shipping				
Peninsular & Oriental	3,200	6,905		Sir T. Sutherland
Cunard Steam-Ship Co.	2,000	5,395	4,420	W. Watson
*British India Steam Navigation Co.	1,657			D. Mackinnon
*Ellerman Lines	1,400	2,441		Sir J. R. Ellerman
Foreign and colonial				
De Beers Consolidated Mines	4,500	12,340		A. Beit
Rio Tinto Co.	3,500	5,717		C. W. Fielding
Consolidated Gold Fields of South Africa	3,250	7,194		Lord Harris
Distribution				
Lipton	2,000	3,084		Sir T. J. Lipton
Home & Colonial Stores	1,200	1,680		W. C. Slaughter
Whiteley (William)	900	2,155	6,000	W. Whiteley
Harrods Stores	641	2,226	5,000	Sir A. J. Newton
Press				
Amalgamated Press	1,050	1,545		Lord Northcliffe

a 1914.

A2. France, 1910

	Share capital	Total assets	Workforce	Chairman
I. *Industry*				
Heavy industry				
Marine-Homécourt	1,120	4,109	13,200	L. Molinos
Schneider	1,080	4,036	15,000[a]	E. Schneider
Nord-Est	1,000	2,246		G. Griolet
Longwy	960	2,977	7,000[b]	G. Rolland
Châtillon-Commentry, Neuves-Maisons	740	3,155	11,000	H. Darcy
*De Wendel et Cie			9,000[c]	F. de Wendel
*Mines de Béthune	120		11,317[d]	E. de Marcère
*Mines de Lens	36		16,319[e]	A. Descamps
*Mines d'Aniche			10,567[f]	E. Dejardin
*Mines d'Anzin			16,393[g]	Cuvinot
Textile				
Revillon Frères	1,200	2,275		L. Revillon
Food, drink, tobacco				
Raffinerie et Sucrerie Say	1,530	3,066		J. Peytel
Chemicals				
Saint-Gobain	2,400	5,562	11,540	Marquis de Vogüé
Electrical engineering				
Thomson-Houston	2,400	5,231	4,000[h]	F. Guillain
Compagnie Générale d'Électricité	720	2,778	6,000[i]	E. Rodier

Company				Director
Mechanical engineering				
Alsacienne de Constructions Mécaniques	720	2,809	10,500	
Rubber				
*Michelin			10,000[j]	A. J. Michelin
II. Finance				
Banking				
Crédit Lyonnais	10,000	99,558	16,000[k]	E. Béthenot
Société Générale	8,000	85,214		Baron Hély d'Oissel
Comptoir National d'Escompte	6,000	66,400		A. Rostand
Paribas	3,000	24,258		M. Renouard
Banque de l'Union Parisienne	2,400	12,346		L. Villars
Banque de l'Indochine	1,440	13,178		Hély d'Oissel
Insurance				
*Assurances Générales[l]	280	38,898		Baron de Neuflize
*La Nationale[m]	1,000	28,702		Comte Pillet-Will
III. Services				
Shipping				
Messageries Maritimes	1,800	11,472		A. Lebon
Générale Transatlantique	1,560	6,710		J. Charles-Roux
Foreign and colonial				
Phosphates et Chemin de Fer de Gafsa	720	1,988		L. Molinos
Distribution				
Galeries Lafayette	900	2,667		T. Bader

A2. *Continued*

	Share capital	Total assets	Workforce	Chairman
Utilities				
Parisienne Distribution Électricité	4,000	6,241		Richemond
Générale des Eaux	1,600	6,669		Baron Hottinguer
Énergie Électrique du Littoral Méditerranéen	1,520	3,177		Féraud
Press and communication				
Société du Petit Journal	1,200	1,554		C. Prevet
*Société du Petit Parisien				J. Dupuy

[a] In Le Creusot only. Schneider's total workforce probably exceeded 25,000.
[b] 1913.
[c] In French Lorraine only. De Wendel's total workforce in France and Germany has been estimated at 28,000.
[d] 1914.
[e] 1914.
[f] 1914.
[g] 1914.
[h] 1913.
[i] 1914.
[j] 1914.
[k] 1914.
[l] Life, fire, and marine insurance combined.
[m] Life and fire insurance combined.

A3. Germany, 1907

	Share capital	Total assets	Workforce	Chairman[a]
I. Industry				
Heavy industry				
Friedrich Krupp AG	9,000	21,726	64,354	E. Haux
Gelsenkirchener Bergwerks	6,500	13,607	31,252	E. Kirdorf
'Phoenix'	5,000	9,836	31,000	H. Kamp
Harpener Bergbau	4,000	8,039	26,000	R. Müser
Hibernia	3,000	5,997	19,212	H. Lindner
Oberschlesische Eisenbahnbedarfs	2,400	3,986	11,500	O. Niedt
Deutscher Kaiser	2,338	7,712	18,931	A. Thyssen
'Union'	2,100	4,002	11,605	Mathies
Hohenlohe Werke	2,100	5,079	12,367	F. Lob
Vereinigte Königs- und Laurahütte	1,800	3,483	23,224	E. Hilger
Rheinische Stahlwerke	1,750	2,689	10,000	E. Goecke
Rombacher Hüttenwerk	1,650	5,084	7,000	R. Hinsberg
Eschweiler Bergwerksverein	1,600	2,953	9,268	H. Schornstein
Kattowitzer	1,500	2,700	10,968	G. Williger
Oberschlesische Eisen-Industrie	1,400	2,639	9,500	V. Zuckerkandl
Bochumer Verein	1,260	2,407	10,867	F. Baare

A3. *Continued*

	Share capital	Total assets	Workforce	Chairman[a]
Deutsch-Luxemburg	1,200	4,000	10,000	C. Knupe
Gutehoffnungshütte	1,200	4,266	21,657	P. Reusch
Textiles				
Nordwolle	1,125	3,245	8,000	C. Lahusen
Kammgarnspinnerei Stöhr	500	1,673	3,000	E. Stöhr
Food, drink, tobacco				
Gebrüder Stollwerck	800	1,303	2,500	L. Stollwerck
Schultheiss Brauerei	700	775		R. Funke
Chemicals				
Bayer	1,800	3,247	7,811	C. Duisberg
BASF		4,100	8,877	H. von Brunck
Hoechst	1,800	3,898	6,000	G. von Brüning
Electrical engineering				
Allgemeine Elektricitäts-Gesellschaft (AEG)	5,000	11,500	30,667	E. Rathenau
Siemens Schuckertwerke	4,500	7,418		A. Berliner
Siemens & Halske	3,150	6,279	42,866[b]	A. Berliner
Felten & Guilleaume-Lahmeyer	2,750	5,602	11,760	B. Salomon
Mechanical engineering				
Stettiner Maschinenbau 'Vulcan'	500	2,890	6,450	R. Zimmermann

II. Finance

Banking

Deutsche Bank	10,000	93,600	8,475[c]	A. Gwinner
Dresdner Bank	9,000	50,600		E. Gutmann
Disconto-Gesellschaft	8,500	42,500		A. Schöller
Darmstädter Bank	7,700	30,650		M. von Klitzing

Insurance

Concordia	300	7,167	P. Hensel
Victoria zu Berlin	150	32,258	O. Gerstenberg

III. Services

Shipping

Hamburg-Amerikanische Packetfahrt (HAPAG)	6,250	11,953	A. Ballin
Norddeutscher Lloyd	6,250	13,466	H. Wiegand

Utilities

Berliner Elektrizitäts-Werke	3,205	5,602	E. Rathenau

[a] Executive board chairman.
[b] Workforces of Siemens & Halske and Siemens Schuckertwerke combined.
[c] 1914.

B1. Great Britain, 1929

	Share capital	Total assets	Workforce[a]	Chairman
I. *Industry*				
Heavy industry				
Guest, Keen & Nettlefolds	12,590	18,340	50,000	Sir J. F. Beale
Vickers	12,469	21,884	44,162	Sir H. A. Lawrence
Dorman Long	11,248	15,498	27,452	Sir A. J. Dorman
Harland & Wolff	10,205	16,508	30,000	Viscountess Pirrie
United Steel	9,324	15,883	19,229	W. B. Jones
Stewarts & Lloyds	5,514	9,238	14,000	A. C. Macdiarmid
*Manchester Collieries	5,478		14,199	J. Ramsden
Powell Duffryn Steam Coal Co.	3,924	9,757	13,512	E. L. Hann
*Lambton, Hetton & Joicey Collieries	2,100		13,636	Lord Joicey
*Metal Box	1,319		12,813	F. N. Hepworth
Textile				
Courtaulds	32,000	46,705	22,506	S. Courtauld
Coats (J. & P.)	20,250	32,526[b]	10,000	J. O. M. Clark
British Celanese	8,461	14,578		H. Dreyfus
Fine Cotton Spinners & Doublers' Association	8,350	15,543	30,000	H. W. Lee
Bleachers' Association	6,206	12,250	8,500	Sir A. J. Sykes
Montague Burton	4,000		11,000	M. Burton

Company				
Food, drink, tobacco				
Imperial Tobacco Co.	50,858	76,544	30,000	Lord Dulverton
Distillers	12,891	21,723		W. H. Ross
Arthur Guinness, Son & Co.	9,500	16,664		Lord Iveagh
Lyons (J.) & Co.	8,376	14,492	30,000	I. Salmon
Watney, Combe, Reid	8,056	18,820	5,000	Sir R. Garton
United Dairies	5,474	6,959		J. H. Maggs
Tate & Lyle	4,412	11,366	7,000	Sir L. Lyle
Bass, Ratcliff & Gretton	3,596	10,776	4,000	J. Gretton
Cadbury Brothers	3,224		11,685	B. Cadbury
Bovril	3,000	6,195		Lord Luke of Pavenham
Chemicals				
Imperial Chemical Industries	76,355	125,180	49,706	Sir H. D. McGowan
Lever Brothers	56,628	68,712	60,000	F. D'Arcy Cooper
*Reckitt & Sons	5,060		8,100	P. B. Reckitt
Boots Pure Drug Co.	2,900	5,474	7,129	J. C. Boot
Electrical engineering				
General Electric Co.	5,854	12,970	24,000	Sir H. Hirst
Associated Electrical Industries	4,732	8,601	30,000	Sir F. J. C. Poole
Gramophone Co.	3,340	5,296	10,000c	A. Clark
British Insulated Cables	2,667	5,815	8,200	Sir A. Roger
Callenders Cable & Construction Co.	1,916	4,009d	14,000	Sir J. F. Flannery
Lucas (Joseph)	1,191	2,540	20,000	H. J. Sayer
Mechanical engineering				
Babcock & Wilcox	4,579	7,811	8,700	Sir J. Dewrance
Platt Brothers	3,710	5,972		Sir W. R. Preston

B1. *Continued*

	Share capital	Total assets	Workforce[a]	Chairman
Motor cars				
*Ford Motor Co.	7,000		7,128[e]	Sir P. Perry
Morris Motors	5,000	8,856	10,200	Sir W. R. Morris
Austin Motor Co.	2,150	4,709	19,000	Sir H. Austin
Oil				
Shell Transport & Trading	31,121	38,860[f]	9,396	Lord Bearsted
Anglo-Persian Oil	23,925	44,345	7,274	J. Cadman
Rubber				
Dunlop Rubber Co.	12,251	26,438	28,000	Sir E. Geddes
II. *Finance*				
Banks				
Barclays Bank	15,858	385,539	12,977	F. C. Goodenough
Lloyds Bank	15,810	431,183	12,993	J. W. B. Pease
Midland Bank	13,433	408,315	13,070	R. McKenna
National Provincial Bank	9,479	306,695		Sir H. Goschen
Westminster Bank	9,320	332,592		R. F. Beckett
Other finance				
*Commercial Union Assurance	3,540	51,452		Sir R. Horne
*Royal Insurance	2,800	47,565		A. A. Paton
*Prudential Assurance	1,249	228,567	17,318	Sir E. Horne

III. Services

Shipping				
Royal Mail Steam Packet	8,800	20,315[g]		Lord Kylsant
Elder Dempster	8,485	13,633		Lord Kylsant
Cunard Steam Ship	8,070	18,457	13,000	Sir T. Royden
Peninsular & Oriental	7,633	29,244		Earl of Inchcape
Foreign and colonial				
British American Tobacco	28,074	34,911		Sir H. Cunliffe-Owen
De Beers Consolidated	6,362	16,157		Sir E. Oppenheimer
Rio Tinto Co.	3,750	8,230		Sir A. G. Geddes
Distribution				
Home & Colonial Stores	2,981	6,760	15,000	W. May
Marks & Spencer	1,010	2,108	11,555	S. Marks
Press and communication				
Allied Newspapers	6,750	9,125[h]		Lord Camrose
Gaumont-British Picture Corporation	3,750	7,174		I. Ostrer
Associated Newspapers	3,350	5,886		Viscount Rothermere
*Smith, W. H.	322	13,452[i]		Viscount Hambleden

[a] 1935 unless otherwise stated.
[b] 1928.
[c] 1929.
[d] 1928.
[e] 1929.
[f] 1928.
[g] 1928.
[h] 1928.
[i] 1929.

B2. France, 1929

	Share capital	Total assets	Workforce	Chairman
I. *Industry*				
Heavy industry				
Mines de Lens	1,780	11,852	19,537	E. Bollaërt
Mines d'Anzin	1,780	6,891	25,665	G. Teissier
Mines de Marles	1,664	2,959	17,943	A. Bénac
Mines de Vicoigne-Nœuds & Drocourt	1,440	9,149	17,390	L. Dupont
Marine-Homécourt	1,440	5,661[a]		T. Laurent
Mines d'Aniche	1,312	3,441	18,484	
Nord-Est	1,096	7,945[b]		E. Cuvelette
*De Wendel	937		33,000	F. de Wendel
Longwy	840	7,459	9,724	A. Dreux
Schneider & Cie	800	5,973		E. Schneider
Houillère de Sarre et Moselle	800	3,527	11,165	H. de Peyerimhoff
Textile				
Saint-Frères	2,400	5,585	9,000	A. Saint
Dollfus-Mieg	608	2,549		E. Thierry-Mieg
Agache Fils	400	1,831		D. Agache
Food, drink, tobacco				
Say (Raffinerie et Sucrerie)	611	2,392		
Grands Moulins de Paris	800	2,378		F. de Lavit
Chemicals				
Kuhlmann	2,500	7,847	7,000	D. Agache
Alais, Froges et Camargue (Pechiney)	2,100	8,463	9,000	G. Cordier
Saint-Gobain	1,800	10,717	15,000	A. Gérard

Electrical engineering				
Thomson-Houston	2,640	5,218	10,000[c]	C. Laurent
Compagnie Générale d'Électricité	1,040	6,857	15,000	P. Azaria
Jeumont	640	2,938	3,500	V. Rault
Mechanical engineering				
Alsacienne de Constructions Mécaniques	918	4,606	16,000	L. Dardel
Fives-Lille	600	3,660[d]		Denfert-Rochereau
Motor car				
Citroën	3,200	14,146[e]	31,200	A. Citroën
Peugeot	1,520	5,750	20,000	J. P. Peugeot
*Renault	960		25,500	L. Renault
Oil				
Huiles de Pétroles	1,920	4,408		E. Mercier
*Compagnie Française des Pétroles	800	1,204		
Rubber				
Michelin	1,200	8,846		E. Michelin
II. *Finance*				
Banks				
Société Générale	5,000	108,431		A. Homberg
Crédit Lyonnais	3,264	111,531		Baron Brincard
Comptoir d'Escompte	3,200	82,243		P. Boyer
Banque de Paris et des Pays-Bas	2,400	36,410		G. Griolet
Banque de l'Indochine	576	27,151		S. Simon
Insurance				
*La Nationale[f]	360	13,722		Baron Davillier
*L'Union[g]	320	12,288		F. Vernes
*Assurances Générales[h]	280	10,721		E. Mallet

B2. *Continued*

	Share capital	Total assets	Workforce	Chairman
III. *Services*				
Shipping				
Compagnie Générale Transatlantique	1,672	11,332		J. Dal Piaz
Chargeurs Réunis	800	6,157		C. Chaumet
Messageries Maritimes	640	3,652		A. Lebon
Foreign and colonial				
SCOA (Société Commerciale de l'Ouest Africain)	1,260	2,293		F. François-Marsal
Peñarroya	1,250	5,182		—
Distribution				
Galeries Lafayette	1,600	6,550		T. Bader
Au Bon Marché	800	3,928[i]		—
Press and communication				
Agence Havas	640	1,782		L. Remier
Hachette	584	2,784		E. Fouret
Utilities				
Énergie Électrique du Littoral Méditerranéen	2,640	7,325		G. Cordier
Union d'Électricité	2,200	7,102		A. Petsche
Compagnie Générale des Eaux	410	3,862		—

[a] June 1930.
[b] June 1930.
[c] More than 10,000 employees in 1922.
[d] June 1930.
[e] June 1930.
[f] Life, fire, general, and reinsurance combined.
[g] Life, fire, and general combined.
[h] Life and fire combined.

B3. Germany, 1929

	Share capital	Total assets	Workforce	Chairman[a]
I. Industry				
Heavy industry				
Vereinigte Stahlwerke	40,000	107,290	182,591	A. Vögler
Mannesmannröhren Werke	9,263	12,550	23,323	H. Bierweis
Friedrich Krupp AG	8,000	23,639	76,750	W. Buschfeld
Harpener Bergbau	5,015	11,225	25,584	E. Fickler
Klöckner-Werke	5,500	11,691	27,924	A. Haarmann
Gutehoffnungshütte	4,000	7,990	11,139	P. Reusch
Hoesch	3,568	8,949	20,962	F. Springorum
Rheinbraun	3,360	5,772		G. Brecht
Ilseder Hütte	3,225	6,436	8,000	G. Meyer
Köln-Neuessener Bergwerksverein	2,771	5,494	7,300	F. Winkhaus
Mitteldeutsche Stahlwerke	2,500	5,046	11,212	O. Sempell
Textile				
Vereinigte Glanzstoff-Fabriken	3,825	11,563	13,400	F. Blüthgen
Nordwolle	3,750	11,991	24,500	C. Lahusen
Bemberg	2,000	3,548	5,700	
*Dierig	1,500	3,233	7,000	C. Dierig
Food, drink, tobacco				
Schultheiss-Patzenhofer Brauerei	2,550	6,082	7,100	W. Sobernheim
Ostwerke	2,275	3,920		L. Katzenellenbogen

B3. *Continued*

	Share capital	Total assets	Workforce	Chairman[a]
Süddeutsche Zucker	1,500	2,986		B. Seeliger
Gebrüder Stollwerck	823	1,322	3,300	J. Stollwerck
Chemicals				
IG Farben	55,000	104,511	114,185	C. Bosch
Wintershall	10,000	20,655	7,375	A. Rosterg
Burbach-Kaliwerke	6,250	11,767		K. Hartwig
Electrical engineering				
Allgemeine Elektricitäts-Gesellschaft (AEG)	9,313	27,422	65,000	F. Deutsch
Siemens Schuckertwerke	6,000	21,037		C. Köttgen
Siemens & Halske	5,355	20,325	116,000[b]	A. Franke
Bergmann Elektrizitäts-Werke	2,200	4,836	12,000	S. Bergmann
Robert Bosch	1,500	4,150	10,000	R. Bosch
Mechanical engineering				—
Knorr Bremse	2,500	4,261		
*Linke-Hoffmann-Busch	1,500	3,552	9,696	O. Österlen
Deutsche Schiff und Maschinenbau	1,250	3,177	12,000	—
Blohm & Voss	700	4,825	9,000	R. Rosenstiel
Motor car				
Opel	3,000	4,960	17,300	F. von Opel
Daimler-Benz	2,518	5,828		W. Kissel
Oil				
Deutsche Erdöl	5,020	7,104	16,390	E. Middendorf
Rubber				
Continental	2,005	5,102	18,135	W. Tischbein

II. Finance

Banks

Deutsche Bank[c]	7,500	145,965	14,800[d]	O. Wassermann
Disconto-Gesellschaft	6,750	85,183		E. Mosler
Dresdner Bank	5,000	125,631	9,484[e]	W. Frisch
Commerz- und Privat Bank	3,750	93,826		C. Harter
Darmstädter- und National (Danat) Bank	3,000	131,101	7,500[f]	J. Goldschmidt

Insurance

*Frankfurter Allgemeine Versicherung	1,000	4,408[g]		—
*Victoria zu Berlin	300	19,245		—

III. Services

Shipping

Hamburg-Amerikanische Packetfahrt (HAPAG)	8,069	18,973		W. Cuno
Norddeutscher Lloyd	6,445	21,497		C. Stimming

Distribution

Rudolph Karstadt	4,000	16,847		R. Karstadt

[a] Executive board chairman.
[b] Siemens & Halske and Siemens Schuckertwerke.
[c] 1929. The Deutsche Bank and Disconto-Gesellschaft merged in 1929; the capital and total assets of the new bank were respectively £14.3 million and £276.7 million.
[d] 1926.
[e] 1925.
[f] 1926.
[g] 1928.

C1. Great Britain, 1953

	Share capital	Total assets	Workforce[a]	Chairman
I. Industry				
Heavy industry				
Vickers	20,679	141,790	70,000	Sir R. Weeks
Guest, Keen & Nettlefolds	19,216	77,245	62,000	J. H. Jolly
Steel Co. of Wales	16,936	97,870	20,750	E. H. Lever
United Steel	15,291	70,364	34,785	Sir W. B. Jones
Tube Investments	12,726	57,583	32,000	I. A. R. Stedeford
Stewarts & Lloyds	11,786	73,815	42,000	A. C. Stewart
*Richard Thomas & Baldwins	10,829		25,500	E. H. Lever
Dorman Long[b]	7,515	45,284	31,000	Sir E. Hunter
Metal Box	7,270	30,271	24,818	Sir R. Barlow
Harland & Wolff	6,996	22,773	32,000	Sir F. E. Rebbeck
Textile				
Courtaulds	56,000	123,797	25,381	J. C. Hanbury-Williams
Coats (J. & P.)	20,050	77,819		R. Laidlaw
British Celanese	11,509	31,710	13,212	G. H. Whigham
Food, drink, tobacco				
Imperial Tobacco	72,959	221,397	25,000	Sir R. J. Sinclair
BAT	46,073	271,593		D. M. Oppenheim
Distillers	25,576	118,555	20,000	H. J. Ross
Guinness	14,500	31,430		Earl of Iveagh
British Cocoa & Chocolate	12,483	48,534	20,000	L. J. Cadbury
Lyons (J.) & Co.	10,892	33,460	35,000	M. Gluckstein
Tate & Lyle	8,144	24,656		G. V. Tate

Chemicals

Imperial Chemical Industries	94,729	439,170	115,306	J. Rogers
Unilever	73,511	304,827	50,287	Sir G. Heyworth
Boots Pure Drug	6,520	30,086	35,938	Lord Trent
*Reckitt & Colman	6,000	27,100		J. B. Upton
Beecham Group	5,350	25,719		Lord Dovercourt

Electrical engineering

Associated Electrical Industries	20,741	84,105	87,000	Sir G. E. Bailey
General Electric Co.	17,355	70,473	60,000	Sir H. Railing
British Insulated Callenders Cables	14,329	62,397	39,000	Sir A. Roger
English Electric	13,252	69,948	39,000	Sir G. H. Nelson
Lucas (Joseph)	7,133	36,746	45,000	A. B. Waring

Motor car

British Motor Corporation^c	34,970	91,650	23,000	L. P. Lord
*Ford Motor Co.	11,943	60,220	24,773	Sir R. Smith

Aeronautics

De Haviland Aircraft	10,771	39,710	25,990	F. T. Hearle
Hawker Siddeley	7,882	62,758	75,000	T. O. M. Sopwith
Rolls-Royce	4,000	25,109	37,500	Lord Hives

Oil

Shell Transport and Trading	66,515	110,315	25,712	Sir F. Godber
Anglo-Iranian Oil (BP)	32,844	363,335	22,212	Sir W. Fraser
Burmah Oil	24,605	54,298		Sir K. B. Harper

Rubber

Dunlop Rubber Co.	17,254	110,424	100,000	Lord Baillieu

II. *Finance*

Banks

Barclays Bank	22,915	1,474,146	20,205	A. W. Tuke
Lloyds Bank	15,818	1,332,702	18,315	Lord Balfour of Burleigh

C1. Continued

	Share capital	Total assets	Workforce[a]	Chairman
Midland Bank	15,159	1,517,322	17,000	Marquess of Linlithgow
National Provincial Bank	9,479	922,275	11,000	Earl of Selborne
Westminster Bank	9,320	939,988	12,000	Lord Aldenham
Insurance				
*Royal Insurance	5,600	122,027		A. C. Tod
*Commercial Union Assurance	3,540	138,255		J. Leslie
*Prudential Assurance	1,450	664,874	19,922	Sir G. L. Barstow
III. Services				
Shipping				
Cunard Steam-Ship Co.	10,298	74,407	15,000	F. A. Bates
Peninsular & Oriental	9,929	171,041		Sir W. C. Currie
Distribution				
Woolworths	20,000	63,453	60,000	S. V. Swash
Great Universal Stores	6,332	80,324	60,000	I. Wolfson
Marks & Spencer	5,873	30,941	28,405	Sir S. Marks
Press and communication				
Ranks[d]	11,130	45,089	26,000	J. A. Rank
Kemsley Newspapers	9,250	21,998		Viscount Kemsley
Amalgamated Press	6,900	26,515	10,500	Viscount Camrose

[a] 1955.
[b] 1954.
[c] 1954.
[d] 1954.

C2. France, 1953

	Share capital	Total assets	Workforce	Chairman
I. Industry				
Heavy industry				
Sidelor	15,306	70,454	18,647	J. Laurent
Usinor	12,245	71,902	19,000	F. Balthasar
Forges et Ateliers du Creusot	7,342	62,032	17,326	C. Schneider
Tréfileries et Laminoirs du Havre	4,617	23,539	7,500	L. Jaudeau
Nord-Est	3,889	16,537		F. Balthasar
Vallourec	3,061	16,409	5,393	M. Silhol
Pont-à-Mousson	3,061	17,257[a]		A. Grandpierre
Compagnie Française des Métaux	2,538	12,663	4,000	H. Thélier
Société Métallurgique de Normandie	2,148	22,175	4,461	F. Walckenaer
Longwy	1,329	29,262	13,607	J. Raty
*De Wendel & Cie		47,424	20,482	H. de Wendel
Textile				
Celtex	5,168	14,843		L. Chatin
*Viscose Française	2,857	11,437[b]		E. Carnot
Givet-Izieux	2,679	12,926		C. Gillet
Saint-Frères	1,855	9,800	7,000	R. Saint
Food, drink, tobacco				
Astra	5,203	12,518		H. Dehollain
Raffinerie et Sucrerie Say	2,768	12,120		T. Robert
Georges Lesieur et ses fils	1,428	6,984		P. Lesieur

C2. Continued

	Share capital	Total assets	Workforce	Chairman
Chemicals				
Pechiney	9,429	54,830		R. Piaton
Rhône-Poulenc	6,444	27,526	9,706	F. Albert-Buisson
Kuhlmann	6,224	22,792	15,000[c]	E. Périlhou
Ugine	6,122	36,655	8,600	E. Mathieu
Saint-Gobain	5,047	55,429	35,000	P. Hély d'Oissel
L'Air Liquide	2,527	17,883	4,500	J. Delorme
Electrical engineering				
Compagnie Générale d'Electricité	6,122	35,534	18,000	J. Jourdain
Alsthom	3,362	47,820		P. Le Bourhis
Thomson-Houston	2,369	25,910	6,000	E. de Lassus
Jeumont	2,156	23,414	6,800	G. de la Rochette
Mechanical engineering				
Alsacienne de Constructions Mécaniques	2,449	21,898	12,000	A. Bommelaer
Motor car				
Citroën	6,540	39,939	17,400	R. Puiseux
Peugeot	4,592	23,306	16,000	J. P. Peugeot
Renault		60,351	28,000	P. Lefaucheux
Aeronautics				
SNECMA	5,601	34,554	12,485	H. Desbruères
Oil				
Compagnie Française des Pétroles	17,762	73,446		V. de Metz
Esso Standard	11,397	56,076		S. Scheer
Huiles de Pétrole (BP)	8,032	41,404[d]	4,959	J. de Rohan

Rubber				
Michelin	6,122	19,633	13,000	R. Puiseux
II. *Finance*				
Banking				
Paribas	2,812	90,411		E. Monick
Banque de l'Indochine	1,750	93,436		E. Minost
Crédit Lyonnais	1,020	442,512		E. Escarra
Société Générale	765	379,958		P. de Moüy
Comptoir d'Escompte	408	228,264		G. Gaussel
III. *Services*				
Shipping				
Messageries Maritimes	4,082	67,757[e]		G. Anduze-Faris
Chargeurs Réunis	2,551	14,224		F. C. Fabre
Distribution				
Au Printemps	734	10,487	3,000	P. Laguionie
Press and communication				
Hachette	1,148	13,799		R. Meunier de Houssoy

[a] 1952.
[b] 1952.
[c] 1956.
[d] 1952.
[e] 1954.

C3. Germany, 1953

	Share capital	Total assets	Workforce	Chairman[a]
I. *Industry*				
Heavy industry				
Gelsenkirchener Bergwerks	31,453	144,821		O. Springorum
Mannesmann	20,513	93,264	18,000	W. Zangen
Rheinstahl	20,533	34,024	22,019	H. Reckmann
Klöckner-Werke	17,949	55,729		W. Dubusc
*Dortmund-Hörder Hüttenunion	15,726	64,420	19,764	F. Elshoff
*Phoenix	9,829	64,526	10,095	F. A. Goergen
Thyssen	9,829	54,408[b]	6,050	H. G. Sohl
*Hüttenwerk Oberhausen	8,888	35,032	13,519	G. Bruns
Ilseder Hütte	8,738	21,251	12,692	P. Möllenberg
Rheinpreussen AG	8,547	21,158	18,436	—
*Rheinische Röhrenwerke	7,863	35,194	13,042	—
Gutehoffnungshütte	7,111	9,115	54,058	H. Reusch
*Hüttenwerk Rheinhausen	5,983	36,938[c]	11,900	
Gusstahlwerk Bochumer Verein	5,897	37,167	14,361	W. Geldmacher
Textile				
Vereinigte Glanzstoff-Fabriken	7,821	18,700	10,840	E. H. Vits
Christian Dierig	4,017	8,382	3,178	A. Flaitz
Food, drink, tobacco				
*Margarine-Union	8,547	29,885		K. Blessing
Süddeutsche Zucker	5,128	13,011	5,503	C. Quensell

Chemicals				
Bayer	33,137	92,891	33,168	U. Haberland
BASF	29,068	71,371	27,208	C. Wurster
Hoechst	24,424	59,886	14,572	K. Winnacker
*Chemische Werke Hüls	10,256	24,192	7,745	P. Baumann
Wintershall	8,974	25,386	4,729	W. Zentgraf
Degussa	6,538	17,418	6,939	H. Schlosser
Electrical engineering				
Siemens & Halske	20,513	63,236	96,400[d]	E. von Siemens
Siemens Schuckertwerke	17,094	69,872		F. Bauer
AEG	7,521	56,241	35,100	F. Spennrath
Felten & Guilleaume Carlswerk	6,615	14,486	4,848	J. Horatz
Accumulatoren-Fabrik	5,994	13,245		G. Quandt
Robert Bosch	4,103	25,848	22,884	H. Waltz
Mechanical engineering				
Klöckner-Humboldt-Deutz	5,556	22,410	16,853	H. Jakopp
Demag	3,624	26,256		H. Reuter
MAN	3,419	35,448	20,311	O. Meyer
Motor car				
Daimler-Benz	6,167	29,075	35,000	F. Könecke
Oil				
*Deutsche Shell	10,256	36,625	5,647	—
*Esso AG	10,000	38,316		G. Geyer
Deutsche Erdöl	8,547	24,501	16,401	E. Grages

C3. *Continued*

	Share capital	Total assets	Workforce	Chairman[a]
Rubber				
Continental	7,556	19,473	13,657	W. Garbe
II. Finance				
Banking				
*Deutsche Bank	13,675			H. Abs
*Dresdner Bank	12,821			A. Hoelling
*Commerzbank	8,547			H. Erkelenz
Insurance				
Allianz Versicherung	3,009	32,954	3,547	H. Goudefroy
*Münchner Rückversicherung	1,282	27,843		A. Alzheimer
III. Services				
Shipping				
HAPAG	3,963	20,584		W. Traber
Distribution				
Karstadt	5,128	16,372		H. Loenen

[a] Executive board chairman.
[b] 1954.
[c] 1952.
[d] Siemens & Halske and Siemens Schuckertwerke.

INDEX